Pfeiffer

An Imprint of Jossey-Bass Inc., Publishers

THE 1997 ANNUAL: Volume 1 Training

(The Twenty-Eighth Annual)

Pfeiffer

An Imprint of Jossey-Bass Inc., Publishers

Copyright © 1997 by Pfeiffer, An Imprint of Jossey-Bass Inc., Publishers

Published by

An Imprint of Jossey-Bass Inc., Publishers
350 Sansome Street, 5th Floor
San Francisco, California 94104-1342
(415) 433-1740, FAX (415) 433-0499
(800) 274-4434; FAX (800) 569-0443

Pfeiffer

Printed in the United States of America

Looseleaf ISBN: 0-88390-489-6
Paperbound ISBN: 0-88390-491-8
ISSN: 1046-333X

Library of Congress Catalog Card Number 86-643030

Visit our website at: http://www.pfeiffer.com

Outside of the United States, Pfeiffer products can be purchased from the following Simon & Schuster International Offices:

Prentice Hall Canada
PTR Division
1870 Birchmount Road
Scarborough, Ontario M1P 2J7
Canada
(800) 567-3800; Fax (800) 263-7733

Prentice Hall
Campus 400
Maylands Avenue
Hemel Hempstead
Hertfordshire HP2 7EZ
United Kingdom
44(0) 1442 881891; Fax 44(0) 1442 882288

Prentice Hall Professional
Locked Bag 531
Frenchs Forest PO NSW 2068
Australia
61 2 9907 5693; Fax 61 2 9905 7934

Prentice Hall/Pfeiffer
P.O. Box 1636
Randburg 2125
South Africa
27 11 781 0780; Fax 27 11 781 0781

Simon & Schuster (Asia) Pte Ltd
317 Alexandra Road
#04-01 IKEA Building
Singapore 159965
Asia
65 476 4688; Fax 65 378 0370

PREFACE

The 1997 editions of the *Annual* series introduce another significant milestone in the history of Pfeiffer & Company. In May of 1996, Pfeiffer became an imprint of Jossey-Bass Inc., Publishers, of San Francisco, California. We at Jossey-Bass, and our Pfeiffer team, are committed to upholding the quality and usefulness of content that the *Annuals* have offered since their inception in 1972.

One key to the success of the *Annual* series has been how well it meets the needs of human resource development (HRD) practitioners—be they trainers, consultants, performance-improvement technologists, facilitators, or educators. The contents of each *Annual* focus on increasing the reader's professional competence by providing materials of immediate, practical use.

In 1995, Pfeiffer & Company began to publish two *Annuals* each year. Volume 1 is focused on training, and Volume 2 is focused on consulting. For the purposes of the *Annuals,* we consider training to be that which has an impact on individuals and consulting to be that which has an impact on organizations. Obviously, it is difficult in some cases to place materials strictly in one category or another, so there is some overlap in what the two volumes cover. Our readers have let us know that they welcome and use both volumes. We are delighted to have the opportunity to showcase twice as much of the finest materials available in the HRD field.

The 1997 Annual: Volume 1, Training reflects our intention to continue to publish materials that help our readers to stay on the cutting edge of the field. In keeping with this objective, users may duplicate and modify materials from the *Annuals* for educational and training purposes, as long as each copy includes the credit statement that is printed on the copyright page of the particular volume. However, reproducing Jossey-Bass/Pfeiffer materials in publications for sale or for large-scale distribution (more than one hundred copies in twelve months) requires *prior written permission.* Reproduction of material that is copyrighted by another source (as indicated in a footnote) requires written permission from the designated copyright holder. Also, reproduction on computer disk or by any other electronic means requires prior written permission.

For the *Annual* series, we actively seek materials from our readers as practicing professionals in the field. We are interested in receiving presentation and discussion resources (articles that include theory along with practical application); inventories, questionnaires, and surveys (paper-and-pencil inventories, rating scales, and other response tools); and experiential learning activities (group learning designs based on the five stages of the experiential learning cycle: experiencing, publishing, processing, generalizing, and applying). Contact the Pfeiffer Editorial Department at the Jossey-Bass offices for copies of our guidelines for contributors, and send submissions to the *Annual* editor at the same address.

As always, our appreciation is extended to the dedicated people who produced this volume. We are grateful to Dr. Beverly Byrum-Robinson, who once again has reviewed all the experiential learning activities and contributed her perspective as a facilitator. Her insightful recommendations are irreplaceable in ensuring the quality of these activities. We applaud the efforts and accomplishments of our Pfeiffer editorial staff, who worked under sometimes difficult circumstances during the transition period: senior development editor (and overall editor for this year's *Annuals*) Arlette C. Ballew; senior development editor Carol Nolde; former Pfeiffer managing editor Marion Mettler; assistant editor Susan Rachmeler; production editor Dawn Kilgore; graphic designer and page compositor, Judy Whalen; and cover designer, Lee Ann Hubbard.

We also want to acknowledge the efforts of Dr. Beverly L. Kaye, who encouraged many of her colleagues to contribute to this year's *Annuals*. Finally, as always, we are grateful to our authors for their generosity in sharing their professional ideas, techniques, and materials so that other HRD practitioners may benefit.

ABOUT PFEIFFER

Pfeiffer is actively engaged in publishing insightful human resource development (HRD) materials. The organization has earned an international reputation as the leading source of practical resources that are immediately useful to today's consultants, trainers, facilitators, and managers in a variety of industries. All materials are designed by practicing professionals who are continually experimenting with new techniques. Thus, readers and users benefit from the fresh and thoughtful approach that underlies Pfeiffer's experientially-based materials, books, workbooks, instruments, and other learning resources and programs. This broad range of products is designed to help human resource practitioners increase individual, group, and organizational effectiveness and provide a variety of training and intervention technologies as well as background in the field.

Pfeiffer is an imprint of Jossey-Bass Inc., Publishers.

CONTENTS

---

*See Experiential Learning Activities Categories, p. 5, for an explanation of the numbering system.

GENERAL INTRODUCTION
TO THE 1997 ANNUAL

The 1997 Annual: Volume 1, Training is the twenty-eighth volume in the *Annual* series. Each *Annual* has three main sections: twelve *experiential learning activities;* three *inventories, questionnaires, and surveys;* and a series of *presentation and discussion resources.* Each of the pieces is classified in one of the following categories: Individual Development, Communication, Problem Solving, Groups, Teams, Consulting, Facilitating, and Leadership. Within each category, pieces are further classified into logical subcategories, which are explained in the introductions to the three sections.

The *Annual* series is a collection of practical and useful materials for professionals in the broad area described as human resource development (HRD). These materials are written by and for professionals, including trainers, organization-development/effectiveness consultants, performance-improvement technologists, educators, instructional designers, and others. As such, the series continues to provide a publication outlet for HRD professionals who wish to share their experiences, their viewpoints, and their procedures with their colleagues. To that end, Pfeiffer/Jossey-Bass publishes guidelines for potential authors. These guidelines, revised in 1996, are available from the Pfeiffer Editorial Department at Jossey-Bass Inc., Publishers, in San Francisco, California.

Materials are selected for the *Annuals* based on the quality of the ideas, applicability to real-world concerns, relevance to current HRD issues, clarity of presentation, and ability to enhance our readers' professional development. In addition, we choose experiential learning activities that will create a high degree of enthusiasm among the participants and add enjoyment to the learning process. As in the past several years, the contents of each *Annual* span a range of subject matter, reflecting the range of interests of our readers.

A list of contributors to the *Annual* can be found at the end of the volume, including their names, affiliations, addresses, telephone numbers, facsimile numbers, and e-mail addresses (if available). Readers will find this list of contributors useful if they wish to locate the authors of specific pieces for feedback, comments, or questions. Further information is presented in a brief biographical sketch of each contributor that appears at the conclusion of his or her article. These elements are intended to contribute to the "networking" function that is so valuable in the field of human resource development.

1

The editorial staff continues to be pleased with the high quality of materials submitted for publication. Nevertheless, just as we cannot publish every manuscript we receive, readers may find that not all the works included in a particular *Annual* are equally useful to them. We invite ideas, materials, and suggestions that will help us to make subsequent *Annuals* as useful as possible to our readers.

Introduction
to the Experiential Learning Activities Section

Experiential learning activities are extremely varied. They should be selected according to the needs of the participants and the abilities of the facilitator. Many different activities might accomplish similar goals. However, if the activity is to address the participants' unique needs, the facilitator must be able to assist the participants in processing the data from that experience.

Each experiential learning activity in this *Annual* includes a description of the goals of the activity, the size of the group and/or subgroups that can be accommodated, the time required to do and process[1] the activity, a list of the materials and handouts required, the physical setting, step-by-step instructions for facilitating the experiential-task and discussion phases of the activity, and variations of the design that the facilitator might find useful. All of these activities are complete; the content of all handouts is provided.

The 1997 Annual: Volume 1, Training includes twelve activities, in the following categories:

Individual Development: Diversity

569. Adoption: Examining Personal Values and Group Consensus, by Morley Segal and Cynthia Franklin

570. Globalization: Understanding and Managing Interdependence, by Bonnie Jameson

571. Generational Pyramids: Communicating by Assumption, by Heidi Ann Campbell and Heather J. Campbell

---

[1] It would be redundant to print here a caveat for the use of experiential learning activities, but HRD professionals who are not experienced in the use of this training technology are strongly urged to read the "Introduction" to the *Reference Guide to Handbooks and Annuals* (1997 Edition). This article presents the theory behind the experiential-learning cycle and explains the necessity of adequately completing each phase of the cycle to allow effective learning to occur.

Individual Development: Life/Career Planning

572. Collaborating for Success: Accomplishing Goals Through Networking, by Robert Hargrove

573. High Jump: Illustrating the Impact of Expectations, by Steven B. Hollwarth

Communication: Conflict

574. Thumbs Up, Thumbs Down: A Conflict-Management Icebreaker, by Roger Gaetani

Communication: Styles

575. Go Left, Go Right: Identifying Work-Style Preferences, by Cher Holton

Problem Solving: Generating Alternatives

576. Broken Triangles: Experimenting with Group Problem Solving, by Janet Mills

Groups: How Groups Work

577. Rope Trick: Experiencing How Groups Function, by Meredith Cash

578. Lincoln Decision Committee: Learning About Group Skills, by Robert K. Conyne and Lynn S. Rapin

Facilitating: Skills

579. Eight Training Competencies: Enhancing Trainer Skills, by Bonnie Jameson

Leadership: Ethics

580. Living Ethics: Meeting Challenges in Decision Making, by Gilbert Joseph Duran, Erna E. Gomar, Marianne Stiles, Christina A. Vele, and Judith F. Vogt

Other activities that address certain goals can be located by using the "Experiential Learning Activities Categories" chart that follows, or by using our comprehensive *Reference Guide to Handbooks and Annuals*. The *Reference Guide,* which is updated regularly, indexes the contents of all *Annuals* and *Handbooks of Structured Experiences* that we have published to date. With each revision, the *Reference Guide* becomes a complete, up-to-date, and easy-to-use resource for selecting appropriate materials from *all* of the *Annuals* and *Handbooks.*

EXPERIENTAL LEARNING ACTIVITIES CATEGORIES

569. Adoption: Examining Personal Values and Group Consensus

Goals

- To provide participants with a chance to work toward consensus.

- To offer participants an opportunity to examine how their personal values affect their decisions.

- To offer participants an opportunity to experience the effects of individual values on group decision making.

Group Size

Two to six subgroups of five to seven members each.

Time Required

Approximately one and one-half hours.

Materials

- A copy of the Adoption Task Sheet for each participant.

- A pencil for each participant.

Physical Setting

A room large enough so that each subgroup can work without disturbing the others. Movable chairs should be provided for the participants. Portable writing surfaces are helpful but not essential.

Process

1. The facilitator explains the goals of the activity.

2. Each participant is given a copy of the Adoption Task Sheet and a pencil and is asked to read the first section of the handout, entitled "Instructions." After the participants have read this section, the facilitator elicits and answers questions about the task. (Five minutes.)

3. Each participant is instructed to work alone to rank order the prospective parents and to write his or her selections in the portion of the task sheet labeled "Personal Choices." (Fifteen minutes.)

4. The facilitator asks the participants to form subgroups. The members of each subgroup are instructed to discuss the rank ordering of the prospective parents, to work toward consensus, and to write the subgroup's selections in the portion of the task sheet labeled "Subgroup Choices." The facilitator emphasizes that *consensus* does not mean that every member agrees with the order, but that all members *consent* to the order and no member objects to it. (Forty-five minutes.)

5. After forty-five minutes the facilitator reconvenes the total group and asks the following questions:

   ■ Who was your subgroup's first choice? What was your rationale for that choice?

   ■ Which person or people turned out to be the least desirable? On what basis did your subgroup make that choice?

   ■ How did your subgroup reach consensus? What was easy about reaching consensus? What was difficult about it?

   ■ How do you feel about the outcome?

   ■ What did you learn about how your personal values affect your personal decisions? What did you learn about how individual values affect group decision making?

   ■ When you return to your organizational environment, how can you use what you learned?

   (Twenty minutes.)

Variations

■ If the participants have learned a particular method for reaching consensus, they may practice that method by using this case study. Then they may review how helpful or successful the method was.

■ If the facilitator is leading a discussion about certain group values, this activity may be used as a springboard to the discussion. The case study may be adjusted to the issues that the facilitator is raising.

- The case study may be adapted to highlight cross-cultural differences by creating subgroups along cultural lines. For example, if the total group includes citizens of both the U.S. and Japan, one subgroup may consist of only citizens of the U.S.; one subgroup, only citizens of Japan; and another subgroup, citizens of both. A discussion could then ensue about different cultural values and the challenges and benefits of cross-cultural team membership.

Submitted by Morley Segal and Cynthia Franklin.

Morley Segal is a professor of public administration at American University. He is co-founder of the American University-NTL Master's Program in Organizational Development. Professor Segal is the author of Points of Influence: A Guide to Using Personality Theory at Work, *to be published by Jossey-Bass in 1997.*

Cynthia Franklin is an adjunct professor of public administration at American University. She is a principal of CAF Associates, a consulting company specializing in leadership development and results-based organizational change.

ADOPTION TASK SHEET

INSTRUCTIONS

Assume that there are not nearly as many infants available for adoption as there are people trying to adopt them. Therefore, decisions must be made regarding which of the prospective parents will adopt an infant. You are a member of a committee that will choose from those applying to adopt a Caucasian male infant. All applicants live in the same large city.

Your first task is to read the descriptions under the heading "The Choices" on this handout. Without consulting anyone, rank order the prospective parent(s) from 1 (the most desirable) to 7 (the least desirable) and write the appropriate numbers in the blanks provided under "Personal Choices." Use your own value system for making your decisions.

After all participants complete the first task, your facilitator will announce that it is time to assemble into subgroups. Your second task takes place in your subgroup, where you and your fellow subgroup members will be asked to discuss and eventually reach consensus on the rank ordering of prospective parents. You are not expected to abandon your own values and priorities, but be open to reason and argument if other members show you that your values can be served with another choice.

Reaching a subgroup decision by *consensus* does not mean that every member agrees with the rank order, but that all members *consent* to that order and no member objects to it. Do not use majority rule or "horse trading." When you have reached consensus, write the appropriate numbers in the blanks provided under "Subgroup Choices."

If no consensus can be reached, there will be a six-month delay before another decision can be made. During that time, the child would remain in the orphanage.

THE CHOICES

Read the following descriptions of prospective parents. Then rank order your personal choices, on a scale from 1 to 7 (1 = most desirable, 7 = least desirable), by writing numbers in the blanks in the left column. When you are working with your fellow subgroup members, write the subgroup choices in the blanks in the right column.

Personal Choices	Subgroup Choices
_____Ralph and Joanne	_____Ralph and Joanne
_____Laura and Josh	_____Laura and Josh
_____Jonathan and Elaine	_____Jonathan and Elaine
_____Charley	_____Charley
_____Jeffrey and Allison	_____Jeffrey and Allison
_____Cynthia and Frank	_____Cynthia and Frank
_____Helen and Glenda	_____Helen and Glenda

Ralph and Joanne

Age and Occupation: Ralph, age twenty-four, is a foreman on an assembly line in a local manufacturing plant. He spent two years at a community college and is considering a training program for computer programmers. Joanne, age twenty-three, is a high-school graduate. She also received training as a beautician and is a hairdresser at a large beauty salon.

Stability of Family and Marriage: Ralph and Joanne were high-school sweethearts and their marriage is stable. They maintain close relations with both sets of parents, who already have a number of grandchildren and are eager for more.

Health: Both are in good health, although Ralph is slightly overweight. He was a high-school football star, and he still participates with some of his former teammates in informal games on Saturday afternoons. Joanne does not have a regular form of exercise, but she recently bought an exercise videotape and plans to follow it.

Commitment to Childcare: Joanne intends to stay home with the child until he enters kindergarten. Then she will take a part-time job, which she believes will be easy to find in her field.

Educational Opportunities: The child would attend a public school, where the average class size is twenty-six. Ralph and Joanne live in a declining neighborhood, and the school in this district has had increasing incidents of violence. They plan to move to a more prosperous neighborhood before the child enters school, but at present they cannot afford to. They plan to save for the child's higher education, which would be his choice of college, trade school, or another type of training.

Racial Background and Additional Information: Both are Caucasian. During their four years of marriage, Joanne has been unable to become pregnant.

Laura and Josh

Age and Occupation: Both are college graduates and work in social-change jobs. Josh, age thirty-eight, is a community organizer. Laura, age thirty-seven, works with Salvadoran refugees. In these occupations, both are able to express their liberal political beliefs.

Stability of Family and Marriage: Josh and Laura are not married but participated in a commitment ceremony and signed a legal agreement to protect the rights of any children whom they might adopt. They are committed to each other but made the choice not to marry out of a sense of solidarity with gay and lesbian couples, who are denied legal marriage. Both sets of parents are divorced and are excited at the prospect of having another grandchild.

Health: Both are in good health and jog almost daily.

Commitment to Childcare: Both plan to work part-time until the child is old enough for preschool, so that they can share parenting responsibilities. Their employers have agreed to a reduction in hours if they adopt the child.

Educational Opportunities: The child would attend a public school with an average class size of twenty-six. After his high-school graduation, they plan for their child to join them in social work for a year before entering the state university.

Racial Background and Additional Information: Josh and Laura, both Caucasian, have already adopted two children. Both the Vietnamese boy and the Salvadoran girl, who has a disfigured hand, were six years old when they were adopted. Now the boy is twelve; the girl, ten. Josh and Laura are looking forward to parenting an infant.

Jonathan and Elaine

Age and Occupation: Jonathan, age fifty-seven, is the CEO of a fast-growing film distributorship. Most of these movies are off-beat comedies, but some are classified as "soft porn." Elaine, age thirty-two, is a consultant with an international accounting firm. Already, despite her relative youth, she is a junior partner in the business. Both are earning excellent salaries.

Stability of Family and Marriage: The marriage is stable. Their parents live in other states and visit the couple once or twice a year.

Health: Both seem to be in good health. Elaine quit smoking three years ago. Jonathan is still a heavy smoker. He has tried many times to quit and once was successful for a year. He has promised Elaine to quit permanently when they adopt a child.

Commitment to Childcare: The couple plans for a young woman from France to live in their house and help care for the child. Elaine and Jonathan plan to continue with their full-time careers.

Educational Opportunities: The child will ride a school bus across town to a Lutheran school, where the average class size is fourteen. Graduates from this school tend to be accepted by the top colleges in the nation.

Racial Background and Additional Information: Jonathan is Caucasian; Elaine was born in the United States of a Caucasian father and an Asian mother. Elaine and Jonathan do not have any children. Elaine believes that many of the problems she encountered as a child were related to her mixed race. She is unwilling to make her child face those problems and wants to adopt a Caucasian.

Charley

Age and Occupation: Charley is the CEO of a large corporation, which he founded. His personal assets are worth several million dollars. He spends long hours on the job. He is fifty-two years old.

Stability of Family and Marriage: After twenty-one years of marriage Charley's wife and his only child, a son, were killed in an automobile crash. He has no heir to his fortune.

Health: Charley manages his high-blood pressure through medication. He plays golf on rare occasions, uses the treadmill in his office for a few minutes about twice a week, and goes to his athletic club for a workout and massage every month or so. He has a thorough physical examination every year, when his doctor reminds him to lose twenty pounds before his weight becomes a problem.

Commitment to Childcare: Charley is determined to give an adopted child every advantage possible. Although Charley has little leisure time, his outings with his son would be "quality" time. He would make sure that the people he hired to care for the child would train and discipline the child with love. He wants a well-behaved son who will enjoy and appreciate the extravagance of an indulgent father.

Educational Opportunities: In addition to attending a private school, the child would have tutors for academic subjects and private teachers and coaches for extracurricular activities, such as music and sports. When business would require Charley to go out of the country, he would not hesitate to take his son out of school to accompany him on the trip. A tutor and maid would also travel with them. Charley plans for his son to attend an Ivy League college and take over his business.

Racial Background and Additional Information: Charley has a dark-olive complexion, black hair, and dark-brown eyes. He claims to be Caucasian but was adopted at birth and has no record of his biological parents. Charley's entire fortune would be inherited by his son.

Jeffrey and Allison

Age and Occupation: Jeffrey, age thirty-five, is a lawyer in a large firm and expects to be made a partner soon. Allison, age thirty-nine, has a master's degree in broadcasting and is a successful producer of television commercials.

Stability of Family and Marriage: Two years ago Jeffrey and Allison separated briefly and are now seeing a marriage counselor, who believes they are working hard on their relationship. Both Jeffrey and Allison have friendly relationships with their working-class parents but never include the parents in social activities with their friends.

Health: Both appear to be in excellent health. They ski and play tennis, and Jeffrey windsurfs. Conventional medical records are not available, because both are actively involved in programs of alternative medicine and natural healing.

Commitment to Childcare: Allison plans to work as a part-time, freelance consultant from her home after they adopt a child. The couple will hire a full-time housekeeper, but Allison will be the primary caretaker of the child.

Educational Opportunities: They have already made inquiries about enrolling the child in a private school that has an average class size of twelve. They plan for the child to attend a top-rated private college and will encourage him to study for an advanced degree.

Racial Background and Additional Information: Both Jeffrey and Allison are Caucasian. They have been unsuccessful in having a child of their own.

Cynthia and Frank

Age and Occupation: Thirty-year-old Cynthia has a Ph.D. in clinical psychology with a specialization in the treatment of alcohol abuse. She works thirty-five hours per week. Frank, age twenty-eight, is a first-year medical resident and works sixty or more hours per week. He plans to specialize in chest surgery and seems to have a promising future.

Stability of Family and Marriage: Their three-year marriage is stable. Contact with both sets of parents is limited, however, because of their ongoing opposition to the marriage. Cynthia's father has advanced liver disease as a result of lifelong alcohol abuse.

Health: Their health is good. Exercise is generally limited to their half-hour-a-day, aerobic-exercise program, which they rigorously follow. Cynthia is a self-admitted alcoholic (from age eighteen to twenty-six), but she faithfully attends AA meetings and has been sober for four years.

Commitment to Childcare: Cynthia states she will put her career on hold, stay home with the child for the first five years, and then return to a part-time job.

Educational Opportunities: The child would attend public school with an average class size of twenty-six. Although Cynthia and Frank would want their child to go to college, they have not thought through any specifics.

Racial Background and Additional Information: Frank is African-American and Cynthia is Caucasian. They have no children but are eager to have several. Cynthia has had two miscarriages, and her doctor has advised her not to become pregnant again.

Helen and Glenda

Age and Occupation: Helen, age thirty-six, is a sixth-grade teacher. Glenda, age twenty-seven, is an accountant.

Stability of Family and Marriage: Helen was married for two years. She wanted children very much, and her husband refused to father a child. This disagreement was only one of many problems before the divorce. The laws of their state did not permit Helen and Glenda to marry each other, but they participated in a commitment ceremony and signed a legal agreement to protect the rights of any child they might adopt. Glenda's parents have accepted the relationship and are looking forward to a grandchild. Helen's parents have not accepted the relationship, but Helen is sure they will be delighted with a grandchild.

Health: Both are in excellent health. They are avid hikers and campers. Helen was a competitive swimmer and still swims regularly. Glenda plays tennis. Both stress how they will expose the child to outdoor life.

Commitment to Childcare: Glenda has a small trust that would allow both women to hold part-time jobs and share parenting.

Educational Opportunities: The child would attend a small, progressive, alternative school with an average class size of twelve. They hope they will be able to send him to a private college.

Racial Background and Additional Information: Both are Caucasian. They want to adopt both a boy and a girl. They prefer that the boy be the older child.

570. GLOBALIZATION: UNDERSTANDING AND MANAGING INTERDEPENDENCE[1]

Goals

- To increase participants' understanding of the paradigm of globalization and the potential ramifications of this paradigm.

- To offer participants an opportunity to reflect on and discuss (1) the five major facets of life that are affected by globalization and (2) how those facets interact.

- To assist participants in determining (1) ideas for creating new perspectives based on globalization, (2) values represented in those ideas, and (3) behaviors based on the ideas and values that will benefit themselves as well as others with diverse backgrounds.

Group Size

Five groups of five members each. One or more groups may have six members if necessary.

Time Required

Two hours and thirty-five to forty-five minutes.

Materials

- A copy of the Globalization Background Sheet for each participant.

---

[1] Before conducting this activity, the facilitator is strongly advised to read *Managing Globalization in the Age of Interdependence* by G.C. Lodge, 1995, San Francisco, CA: Jossey-Bass. This book, which is part of the Warren Bennis Executive Briefing Series, is designed to be read in two hours.

- A different Globalization Work Sheet for the members of each group: sheet A for the Cultural/Societal Group, B for the Economic Group, C for the Political Group, D for the Technological Group, and E for the Environmental Group.
- A copy of the Globalization Presentation Sheet for each participant.
- A copy of the Globalization Perspective Sheet for each participant.
- A newsprint sheet prepared in advance with the following information:

Facets of Life Affected by Globalization

1. Cultural/Societal

2. Economic

3. Political

4. Technological

5. Environmental

- Name tags for all participants: a tag marked "Cultural/Societal" for each member of the Cultural/Societal Group, a tag marked "Economic" for each member of the Economic Group, and so on.
- Several sheets of blank paper and a pencil for each participant.
- A clipboard or other portable writing surface for each participant.
- A newsprint flip chart and a felt-tipped marker for each group.
- Masking tape for each group and for the facilitator.

Physical Setting

A room large enough for the groups to work without disturbing one another. Movable chairs should be provided, and plenty of wall space must be available for posting newsprint.

Process

1. The facilitator introduces the activity by announcing its goals.
2. The facilitator distributes copies of the Globalization Background Sheet and asks the participants to read it. (Five minutes.)

3. After the participants have finished reading, the facilitator leads a discussion about the handout, highlighting main points and answering questions. (Ten minutes.)

4. The facilitator posts the newsprint sheet that was prepared in advance and explains that a separate group will work with each of the five facets of life affected by globalization. Then the participants are assembled into five groups: "Cultural/Societal," "Economic," "Political," "Technological," and "Environmental." Name tags matching these group names are distributed. Each group is sent to a separate area of the room, with as much space between groups as possible. (Five minutes.)

5. Copies of Globalization Work Sheet A are given to the Cultural/Societal Group, B to the Economic Group, C to the Political Group, D to the Technological Group, and E to the Environmental Group. The facilitator also distributes paper, pencils, and clipboards or other portable writing surfaces and gives each group a newsprint flip chart and a felt-tipped marker. The members of each group are asked to brainstorm responses for each column on their work sheet. They are also asked to choose a leader and a recorder. The leader's job is to keep the group on track and to monitor time. The recorder's job is to write the members' responses on newsprint, reproducing the three-column structure from the work sheet; after each newsprint sheet is filled, it is posted in the group's assigned area. (Thirty minutes.)

6. The facilitator distributes copies of the Globalization Presentation Sheet and asks each group to follow the instructions on the handout to prepare a three-minute presentation on the information generated during brainstorming. While the groups are working on their presentations, the facilitator remains available to answer questions. (Twenty minutes.)

7. The total group is reconvened. The facilitator asks the presenters to take turns giving their presentations. Each group's newsprint list is posted and is kept in view until Step 11. (Fifteen minutes.)

8. The facilitator instructs the participants to form different groups of five members each, with each member representing a different facet of life affected by globalization (one member with a "Cultural/Societal" name tag, one with an "Economic" name tag, one with a "Political" name tag, and so on). *Note:* If some of the previous groups had six members, then some of the new groups may also have six members, with two people representing one of the facets.

9. The facilitator distributes copies of the Globalization Perspective Sheet and reviews the instructions with the participants, ensuring that they understand the task. Then they are told to begin. (Ten minutes.)

10. The facilitator explains that in each group the members are to take turns sharing their ideas, values, and behaviors; after each member has reported, the group is to discuss the content briefly. The facilitator asks each group to choose a leader and a recorder for this step. The leader's responsibilities are to keep the group on track, to monitor time, and to deliver a three-minute presentation on the content of the sharing and discussion to the total group. The recorder's responsibility is to write the members' ideas, values, and behaviors on newsprint, which the leader will use in his or her presentation. (Twenty to thirty minutes.)

11. The facilitator reconvenes the total group and removes the accumulated newsprint sheets from the walls. The individual leaders are instructed to take turns posting the newsprint information from the previous step and presenting information. If there is enough wall space, all newsprint from all groups remains posted. (Twenty minutes.)

12. The facilitator leads a concluding discussion based on these questions:

- How did you feel about globalization before you participated in this activity? How do you feel about it now?

- What did you learn about the interaction of the five facets of life that are affected by globalization?

- What did you learn about the potential ramifications of globalization? What conflicts have arisen or might arise as a result of globalization?

- What would happen if you began to behave in a manner consistent with a new perspective based on globalization? What would happen if others did the same?

- How can you adopt some of the suggested ideas, values, and behaviors at work? In your own home? In your community? What support could you depend on? What barriers might you face? How could you strengthen the support and overcome the barriers? What is the first step you will take?

- How might your efforts at work and in your community benefit people in other areas? What could be done to spread that benefit?

(Twenty minutes.)

Variation

- Another phase may be added by having the total group brainstorm the characteristics of a system (for example, an organization) based on the perspective, values, and behaviors associated with globalization.

Submitted by Bonnie Jameson.

Bonnie Jameson is a consultant and trainer in human resource development and organization development. She works with corporate, nonprofit, and educational organizations and designs and facilitates management programs and other workshops and courses. She currently teaches strategic planning and building effective organizations in the extension program at California State University, Hayward. Ms. Jameson's specialties include training for trainers and the Myers/Briggs Type Indicator.™ Pfeiffer published her training package, Inspiring Fabled Service, *in 1996.*

GLOBALIZATION BACKGROUND SHEET[1]

Globalization is the process whereby the world's people are becoming increasingly interconnected in all facets of their lives—cultural, economic, political, technological, and environmental. A major contributor to globalization is the ever-increasing flow of information, money, and goods through multinational corporations. Other contributors are exploding consumer desires, especially in the rapidly growing countries of Asia, and ingenious corporate managers, who are driven by a variety of urges—to serve their communities or their shareholders, to gain wealth and power, or simply to exercise their skills and talents.

Although this activity has positive results for many, for others it brings a world of unwelcome surprises. For example, globalization threatens the world's fragile ecosystem and adds to the confusion brought about by the political disintegration following the end of the Cold War. Globalization is also upsetting old ways of life and challenging cultures, religions, and systems of belief.

In addition, globalization is accentuating diversity. Imagine the world to be a global village of 1,000 inhabitants. Today, 564 of them would be Asian, 210 Europeans, 86 Africans, 80 South Americans, and 60 North Americans. By the year 2020, Africans will outnumber Europeans 185 to 107, and Asians, with 577 people, will continue to be the clear majority.

The people in the global village will represent a multitude of ways of thinking about ultimate reality and the community. Many religions will be represented: Christianity, Hinduism, Buddhism, Animism, Judaism, and others. Fortune will discriminate among people, leaving only 60 in control of half of the income, while 500 are hungry.[2]

There is no consensus about the purposes that globalization serves and the direction it should take. It proceeds, therefore, in limbo; as it intensifies, it highlights conflicts about its effects and priorities. These conflicts arise from different systems for interpreting values. The dilemma is to determine whether there is some overarching value system within which a consensus seems possible.

Whether globalization is ultimately a positive force in the world will depend on how it is controlled. We must learn to manage the tensions that it creates.

---

[1] From *Managing Globalization in the Age of Interdependence* (pp. xi-xv) by G.C. Lodge, 1995, San Francisco, CA: Jossey-Bass.

[2] Figures assembled by Professor James L. Case, Harvard Business School, using World Development Forum Data.

Globalization Work Sheet A: Cultural/Societal Group

Forces	Assumptions	Choices
What are some positive and negative cultural/societal forces?	What assumptions lead us to one-way thinking about cultural/societal forces?	What new cultural/societal choices might benefit people with diverse backgrounds?

Globalization Work Sheet B: Economic Group

Forces	Assumptions	Choices
What are some positive and negative economic forces?	What assumptions lead us to one-way thinking about economic forces?	What new economic choices might benefit people with diverse backgrounds?

Globalization Work Sheet C: Political Group

Forces	Assumptions	Choices
What are some positive and negative political forces?	What assumptions lead us to one-way thinking about political forces?	What new political choices might benefit people with diverse backgrounds?

Globalization Work Sheet D: Technological Group

Forces	Assumptions	Choices
What are some positive and negative technological forces?	What assumptions lead us to one-way thinking about technological forces?	What new technological choices might benefit people with diverse backgrounds?

Globalization Work Sheet E: Environmental Group

Forces	Assumptions	Choices
What are some positive and negative environmental forces?	What assumptions lead us to one-way thinking about environmental forces?	What new environmental choices might benefit people with diverse backgrounds?

GLOBALIZATION PRESENTATION SHEET

Instructions: Using the data generated in your group, develop a three-minute presentation that explains the main idea behind the data. (If you discover that you have more than one main idea, choose one to be the focus of the presentation.) Select one member to be the presenter.

STRUCTURE OF PRESENTATION

The suggested structure for your presentation is as follows:

1. *Opening:* Tell the participants your main idea.
2. *Body:* Present three to five points in support of your main idea.
3. *Conclusion:* Summarize your presentation and briefly rephrase your main idea.

GLOBALIZATION PERSPECTIVE SHEET

Instructions: In the spaces that follow, write down (1) *one idea* about how you could form a new perspective for yourself based on globalization, (2) *one or two values* represented in that idea, and (3) *two behaviors* consistent with the idea and value(s). The idea, value(s), and behaviors should be:

- Ones that are based on your *first* group's newsprint list;

- Ones that you are able and willing to adopt; and

- Ones that will benefit yourself as well as others with diverse backgrounds.

IDEA

VALUE(S)

BEHAVIORS

571. GENERATIONAL PYRAMIDS: COMMUNICATING BY ASSUMPTION

Goals

- To offer participants an opportunity to examine how perceived differences in values affect the ways in which people work and communicate with one another.

- To encourage participants to explore how their assumptions about people from different generational groups affect their interactions with those people.

Group Size

Three to six subgroups of four or five participants each.

Time Required

Approximately one and one-half to two hours.

Materials

- Two computer labels or stick-on name tags for each participant: One label bears the name of the participant's assigned generational group (Baby Boomers, Generation Xers, or the Nintendo Generation); the other label bears an assumption that people are to make about the participant. Using the Generational Pyramids Assumption and Belief Sheet, the facilitator prepares these labels ahead of time.

- A 3" x 5" index card for each participant, listing a specific belief associated with the participant's assigned generational group. Using the Generational Pyramids Assumption and Belief Sheet, the facilitator prepares the cards in advance.

- A bag containing ten to fifteen different objects for each group. Examples of objects are a compact disc, a Pop-Tart® box, a Pepsi®can, a computer disk, a can of Play-Doh®, a small stuffed animal, a small bible, play money, a rock, a small bandage, a surgical mask and/or gloves, political bumper stickers, a peace symbol, and a balloon.

- A newsprint flip chart and several felt-tipped markers in different colors for each group.

- Masking tape for each group.

- One copy of the Generational Pyramids Theory Sheet (used by the facilitator to prepare a lecturette).

Physical Setting

A room with a table and chairs for each group. The tables should be separated with as much space as possible so that the groups do not disturb one another.

Process

1. The facilitator explains the goals of the activity and then delivers a lecturette based on the Generational Pyramids Theory Sheet. (Ten to fifteen minutes.)

2. The participants are divided into three groups. The first group is assigned to be "Baby Boomers"; the second group, "Generation Xers"; and the third, "the Nintendo Generation." Each participant is given one label, bearing the assigned group name, and is asked to place it on his or her front; at the same time, the facilitator places a second label, bearing an assumption that people are to make about the participant (based on the group designation), on his or her back. The facilitator explains that while working on the upcoming task, each group's members should treat one another according to the labels worn on the back. (Five minutes.)

3. Within each group, each member is given a 3" x 5" index card denoting a specific belief held by the assigned generational group. The facilitator explains that during the upcoming task, each member is to play the role of the assigned generational group and to act according to the belief, but not to reveal that belief. Several minutes are allowed for the members of each group to read the labels on one another's backs and to acquaint themselves with the assumptions they should make about one another. (Five minutes.)

4. The facilitator gives each group a bag of items, a newsprint flip chart, several felt-tipped markers in different colors, and masking tape. The

facilitator explains that each group will have thirty minutes to do the following:

- By group consensus, select eight items from those in the bag;

- By group consensus, rank the items from one to eight, according to value; and

- Using any or all of the items and materials, construct a "pyramid of values."

The groups are told that they are free to define what their pyramids look like and that later each group will be choosing a spokesperson to explain the pyramid to the total group. (Five minutes.)

5. Before beginning the group task, the facilitator reminds the participants of the important points to keep in mind:

- They are to treat others as though the assumptions on the others' backs are true; and

- They are to act out the beliefs on their own index cards.

Then the groups are told to begin. Periodically the facilitator informs them of the remaining time. (Thirty minutes.)

6. After thirty minutes the facilitator stops the task work and announces that the groups have five minutes in which to select their spokespersons and to reach agreement on the explanations of their pyramids. (Five minutes.)

7. The spokespersons are invited to take turns explaining their groups' pyramids. (Ten to fifteen minutes.)

8. The participants are told to look at the assumptions on the labels on their backs. Within each group the members spend ten minutes sharing their perceptions of how they were treated, the beliefs they acted out (from their 3" x 5" cards), and any personal feelings concerning the stereotypes that people have about *their own* (not their assigned) generational groups. (Ten minutes.)

9. The entire group is reassembled, and the facilitator leads a concluding discussion based on questions such as these:

- How do you think your assigned assumption affected the way others treated you?

- How did you feel about the belief you were given? How did you act out that belief? How did your behavior in connection with that belief affect your interactions with others?

- How would you describe the way in which the members of your group worked together to complete the task?

- How was this activity true to life? What have you learned about generational stereotypes? Which of these stereotypes have you experienced?

- What other generational stereotypes can you think of? How do these stereotypes affect the way you treat people?

- What can you do to improve communication between generations?

(Fifteen to twenty minutes.)

Variations

- Rather than age groupings, the basis of the activity may be work groups, with the emphasis on building understanding within an organization. Assumptions about different work roles and realistic beliefs about jobs may be assigned.

- The activity may be based on ethnic groupings and used to teach diversity awareness.

- Other generational groups may be incorporated into the activity, according to the ages of the participants.

- The activity may be changed by using construction materials that represent or relate to the participants' specific values.

- The facilitator may preassign values to specific objects (for example, a globe signifies environmental concerns or a bandage signifies healthcare issues).

Submitted by Heidi Ann Campbell and Heather J. Campbell.

Heidi Ann Campbell is an experiential educator at Eagle Village, an adventure-based facility in Hersey, Michigan. As a team-building facilitator, she has done research into values acquisition and its relation to generational issues. Her work has appeared in various publications, such as Personnel Journal *and* Christianity Today *magazine. She has presented her research on values and youth at several conferences, including those of the Association for Experiential Education International and the Michigan Academy of Arts, Letters and Sciences.*

Heather J. Campbell is an instructor and counselor with the Battle Creek, Michigan, Public Schools, at their Outdoor Education Center. She teaches environmental-education classes and works as a challenge-education facilitator with fifth- and sixth-grade students. Recently, she assisted in conducting a study of youth values and presented the findings at several conferences, including that of the Association for Experiential Education International. She also works in the area of curriculum development.

GENERATIONAL PYRAMIDS
ASSUMPTION AND BELIEF SHEET

ASSIGNED GENERATIONAL GROUP (label on front)	ASSUMPTIONS (label on back)	BELIEFS (3" x 5" card)
Baby Boomers	Ex-hippie	If I don't like something, I boycott it; social action is important.
	War protester turned right-wing conservative	People under 30 can't be trusted.
	Doesn't trust anyone under 30	I should be put on a pedestal; that's where I've always been.
	Thinks society revolves around him/her	I am tolerant of diversity and comfortable with change.
	DINK: Double income, no kids (out for self)	The world was better in the 60s.
Generation Xers	Lazy/Slacker	People see me as a child, and I resent it.
	MTV junkie	I have to deal with a confusing world that I didn't create.
	Avoids responsibility and commitment	I feel indifferent to things that seem to matter to others.
	Decisions are shaped by media/pop culture	I like to have a variety of experiences without responsibility.
	Ambivalent, confused	I rebel against the molds that society pushes me into.
Nintendo Generation	No attention span	If it's not fun, it's not worth doing.
	Techno-Wizard	Only I know what's good for me.
	Undisciplined; comes from broken home	Technology is what makes the world better.
	Little respect for authority; self-centered	I can state my opinion at the expense of anyone.
	Beavis & Butthead are role models	The world is violent, and it scares me.

GENERATIONAL PYRAMIDS
THEORY SHEET

We all see the world from different perspectives—through different filters. These filters are the result of many variables, such as upbringing, experiences, genes, culture, gender, and the history of our time. They help us to make sense of our world, evaluate situations, and attach meaning to things.

Another important factor that shapes people's perspectives is the influences that their social histories—their "generations"—have on them. Table 1 defines today's generations (Howe & Strauss, 1993).

Table 1. Definitions of Today's Generations

Generation's Name	Years of Birth	Age in 1997
G.I. Generation	1901-1924	73-96
Silent Generation	1925-1942	55-72
Baby Boomers	1943-1960	37-54
Generation X/13th Generation	1961-1981	16-36
Nintendo/Millennial Generation	1982-2002	15 and younger

Members of the same generation share a social history and define themselves in relation to one another through cultural values, beliefs, and symbols that become a distinctive "historical-social" consciousness. This occurs in late adolescence and early adulthood—the formative years for the shaping of a distinct outlook (Mannheim, 1952).

Defining people in terms of generations began in the Twentieth Century. In the United States in the 1920s, an interest arose in identifying specific values by time span. From the 1920s on, there was a rise in "generational tribalism":

1. First came an awareness of accelerated change and a sense of "progress" brought on by the end of World War I.

2. Next came an awareness of nostalgia and a desire to retrieve lost innocence.

3. Then came a fascination with decades, for example, the Roaring Twenties or the Fabulous Forties.

4. Finally there arose the concept of "generational wars," in which each generation tends to view the world from its own perspective, thus setting itself off from those ahead and those following (Guiness, 1994).

Defining oneself by generation creates a solidarity of identity, but it can also build barriers between generations. The following paragraphs present some of the descriptions of the three youngest generational groups that exist today.

BABY BOOMERS: BIRTH YEARS 1943-1960

Baby Boomers (also known as the Pepsi®, Rock, Love, Now, or Me Generation) grew up in an era characterized by the affluence following World War II and by the threat posed by the Cold War. The term "teenager" was coined in the 1950s, and the Boomers were the first group of teens to be exploited and idolized by the media. Landon Jones (cited in Roof, 1993), author of a landmark book on Baby Boomers, points out:

> They were the first generation of children to be isolated by Madison Avenue as an identifiable market. That is the appropriate word: isolated. Marketing and especially television isolated their needs and wants from those of their parents.... The dictatorship of the new...was integral to the baby boom experience. (p. 4)

Society put the Baby Boomers on a pedestal, and Boomers are still fighting to stay there. With more than 76 million members (one-third of the present U.S. population), they are the largest generation in the history of the U.S.

The Boomers were influenced by various social and political events. The Vietnam War and Watergate contributed to their diminished trust in leaders. They found their voice through protest; they became activists both against the war and in support of issues such as civil rights and the Equal Rights Amendment. The music of the Beatles, Bob Dylan, and Woodstock affected much of their sentiment. Many of the events and changes that Boomers helped to usher in were blatant, even violent.

However, the silent revolution that took place in values was also significant and contributed to what many feel is the shift in values expressed in following generations. Political scientist Ronald Inglehart (1971) states that during times of prosperity, values tend to shift in the direction of greater concern for individuality, the quality of life, and intellectual and spiritual development. Accordingly, trends in the late 1960s highlighted three core values for the Boomer generation: tolerance, a belief in self, and the belief that strength comes from within (Roof, 1993).

At the end of the 1960s, the Boomers mellowed; there was less protesting, more attraction to the materialism they once abhorred, and a strengthening of their "me-ism." This change in attitude set the stage for the next generation.

GENERATION X: BIRTH YEARS 1961-1981

Generation Xers (also known as the 13th Generation or the Baby Busters) have been described as indifferent to practically everything that is interesting, infuriating, exhilarating, or amusing (Cohen, 1993). Although some of them have bought into the idea, promulgated by the media, that a lowered attention span is normal for them, others are repulsed by the media's "juvenilization" of them and are resisting or even fighting this image.

The depiction of Generation Xers is often gloomy. In a report entitled "The Ethics of America's Youth," the Josephson Institute for the Advancement of Ethics (cited in Howe & Strauss, 1993) wrote, "An unprecedented proportion of today's youth lack commitment to core moral values like honesty, personal responsibility, respect for others and civic duty."

Whether the Xers have sold out to the belief that idealism is dead or are fighting the hopelessness they see as being foisted on them, their voices are punctuated by confusion and frustration. In the book *Twentysomething*, Steven Gibb (1991) writes, "We were sired by tradition, nursed on experimentation and raised by ambiguity. Ambivalence is second nature to the twentysomething generation." Donatell Arpaia, a student from Fairfield University, says, "Who are we to look to? Every generation is supposed to have role models. Where are ours? Madonna? Michael Jackson? People wonder why we are so confused, wouldn't you be?" (Howe & Strauss, 1993).

Several other factors (cited in Howe & Strauss, 1993) have influenced the Xers as well:

1. From 1960 to 1986, parental time spent with children dropped by ten to twelve hours per week, representing a change of about 40 percent.[1]

---

[1] Information from David Eggebeen, Peter Kohlenberg, and Victor Fuchs, demographers.

2. In 1990, 76 percent of mothers of six- to seventeen-year-olds worked outside the home.[2]

3. In 1988, only 50.9 percent of children lived with both of their birth parents.[3]

In comparison to their predecessors, Generation Xers have been referred to as "the postponed generation." Statistics indicate that they are finishing college later, marrying later, having children later, and entering the job market later than their parents. As Nancy Smith, art director for the *Washington Post,* says, "They are growing up yet still children, seeking experience without responsibility" (Anderson, 1995).

THE NINTENDO GENERATION: BIRTH YEARS 1982-2002

The Nintendo Generation (also called the Millennial Generation or the Ritalin Generation) was born into a world of microwaves and VCRs. Technology has shaped the children in this generation and will continue to do so. Some observers believe that technology may be shaping them for a life fixated on nothing, due to their limited attention spans.

Louv (1990) points out that the Nintendo Generation is unique:

Today's children are living a childhood of firsts. They are the first day-care generation; the first truly multicultural generation; the first generation to grow up in...an environment defined by computers and new forms of television; the first post-sexual-revolution generation; the first generation for which nature is more abstraction than reality; the first generation to grow up in new kinds of dispersed, deconcentrated cities—not quite urban, rural, or suburban. (p. 4)

The members of this generation face snowballing trends that will affect their perspective:

1. By 2020, 20 percent of the U.S. population will be non-English speaking (Carlson & Goldman, 1991).

2. By 2000, the multiproblem child (e.g., language barrier, no father in the home, working mother, drug habit on the part of child or parent, and criminal activity) will require society's attention and efforts. These problems, rather than physical barriers, will define the new handicapped child (Carlson & Goldman, 1991).

---

[2] Information from the U.S. Bureau of Labor Statistics.
[3] Information from the U.S. Public Health Service.

3. According to the National Academy of Sciences, Institute of Medicine, 12 to 22 percent of children suffer from mental or emotional disorders such as depression, hyperactivity, chronic drug use, and anorexia (Louv, 1990).

The change in the traditional family is having a significant impact on the Nintendo Generation. A junior high school student is quoted as saying:

> I think the family still exists as more of an—outline. There might be two people and they might be married or live together and they might have a child and maybe they get divorced...and the unit will look about the same, but the people behave more like separate entities, especially the children.... It seems more empty—more people out for themselves mostly. (Louv, 1990)

Furthermore, cartoon characters such as Bart Simpson and Beavis & Butthead are the role models of the Nintendo Generation. The message these characters convey is that nothing is offensive; stating an opinion is the right of everyone at the expense of anyone. As Charles Young wrote in *Rolling Stone* (cited in Rushkoff, 1994) about Beavis & Butthead: "Because they are stupid, they are free. Because they are free, we will make them rich. Beavis & Butthead are America's inner teenager."

References and Suggested Readings

Anderson, L. (1995, 2nd quarter). Baby busters: Generation in the shadows. *Equipping the Saints* (magazine published by the Vineyard Christian Fellowship Association).

Carlson, R., & Goldman, B. (1991). *20/20 vision.* Stanford, CA: Stanford Alumni Association.

Cohen, M.L. (1993). *A cross-country quest for a generation: The twenty-something American dream.* New York: NAL/Dutton.

Gibb, S. (1991). *Twentysomething: A self-help guide to making it through your twenties.* Chicago: Noble.

Guiness, O. (1994). *Fit bodies fat minds.* Grand Rapids, MI: Baker.

Howe, N., & Strauss, B. (1993). *13th generation: Abort, retry, ignore, fail?* New York: Vintagebook.

Inglehart, R. (1971, December). The silent revolution in Europe: Intergenerational change in post-industrial societies. *American Political Science Review,* pp. 991-1017.

Jones, L. (1981). *Great expectations: America and the baby boom generation.* New York: Ballantine.

Louv, R. (1990). *Childhood's future.* New York: Anchor Books, Doubleday.

Mannheim, K. (1952). *Essays on the sociology of knowledge.* New York: Oxford University Press.

Roof, W. (1993). *A generation of seekers: The spiritual journeys of the baby boom generation.* San Francisco: Harper.

Rushkoff, D. (1994). *The genX reader.* New York: Ballantine.

572. COLLABORATING FOR SUCCESS: ACCOMPLISHING GOALS THROUGH NETWORKING

Goals

- To encourage participants to think of accomplishing things in their organizations in terms of a "network model" in addition to the traditional "hierarchical model."

- To assist participants in identifying (1) the people who need to be included in their networks, (2) the roles those people need to play, and (3) the roles the participants themselves need to play.

- To offer participants an opportunity to plan ways to optimize their networks.

Group Size

A maximum of thirty participants. In Step 3 the participants assemble into subgroups of three; if necessary, some subgroups may have four members each.

Time Required

Approximately one and one-half hours.

Materials

- A copy of the Collaborating for Success Theory Sheet for each participant.

- A copy of the Collaborating for Success Work Sheet for each participant.

- A pencil for each participant.

- A clipboard or other portable writing surface for each participant.

- A sheet of newsprint and a felt-tipped marker for each participant. *Note:* The markers must be the kind that do not penetrate ("bleed through") newsprint.

- A newsprint flip chart (in case the participants need extra sheets of newsprint).

- Masking tape for posting newsprint.

Physical Setting

A large room in which the participants can work without interruption. Movable chairs should be provided. Enough wall space must be available so that each participant can post a sheet of newsprint on the wall; also, the newsprint sheets should be far enough from one another so that three or four people can stand in front of each sheet and discuss its contents.

Process

1. The facilitator states that the upcoming activity has to do with using a "network model" to accomplish things in an organization instead of the more traditional "hierarchical model." The participants are given copies of the Collaborating for Success Theory Sheet and are asked to read it. After all participants have read the handout, the facilitator elicits and answers questions about the two models. (Ten minutes.)

2. Each participant receives a copy of the Collaborating for Success Work Sheet, a pencil, a clipboard or other portable writing surface, a sheet of newsprint, and a felt-tipped marker. The facilitator instructs the participants to spend forty-five minutes working independently to complete the work sheet. The facilitator also explains that for Sections 1, 4, and 5, the participants should write responses directly on the work sheet; for Sections 2 and 3, the participants should complete the task on newsprint, taping the newsprint to the wall. (Several rolls of masking tape are distributed among the participants.) While the participants are working, the facilitator remains available to answer questions and provide assistance. (Forty-five minutes.)

3. The participants are told to assemble into subgroups of three by gathering with the people nearest them. (One or more subgroups of four may be formed if necessary.) The members of each subgroup are instructed to take turns reviewing one another's network posters. The facilitator explains the procedure:

- The member whose network is being reviewed will explain the network briefly and summarize the changes needed to optimize it.

- The other subgroup members will offer feedback on (1) whether the proposed changes seem likely to enhance the network and support the goal and (2) what additional changes might be useful.

(Fifteen to twenty minutes.)

4. The facilitator reassembles the total group and asks the following questions:

- What have you learned about yourself and your own roles in your network?

- What have you learned about the members of your network and their roles?

- What have you learned about the possible benefits of networking?

- When you begin using the network model in your organization, what support will you be able to rely on? What obstacles might you face? What might you do about those obstacles?

- How can you encourage people in your network, department, or organization to use the network model?

The facilitator encourages the participants to keep their newsprint drawings and their completed work sheets, to review them from time to time, and to make whatever changes are necessary. (Twenty minutes.)

Variations

- The activity may be focused on the participants' personal networks rather than their organizational networks. In this case the facilitator should eliminate the theory sheet and rewrite the work sheet slightly.

- The participants may work in pairs for feedback and action planning.

- The newsprint drawings may be reviewed and processed for common themes.

Submitted by Robert Hargrove.

Robert Hargrove is the president and CEO of Hargrove and Partners. He is also the founder of Transformational Learning Inc., a firm based in Brookline, Massachusetts, that offers consulting and training services. He has conducted seminars throughout North America, Europe, and Asia on topics such as transformational leadership, personal transformation and learning, team learning, and collaborative consulting. He is the author of a variety of articles and of Masterful Coaching: Extraordinary Results by Transforming People and the Way They Think and Interact, *published by Pfeiffer in 1995.*

COLLABORATING FOR SUCCESS
THEORY SHEET

The hierarchical organizational chart is commonly used to describe the structure of an organization and key accountabilities. It consists of boxes representing organizational positions, with connecting lines indicating who reports to whom (Figure 1). However, a hierarchical chart does not reflect how people work together. If we see our work in terms of the hierarchical model, this viewpoint may keep us from communicating and collaborating with people who can help us to meet goals.

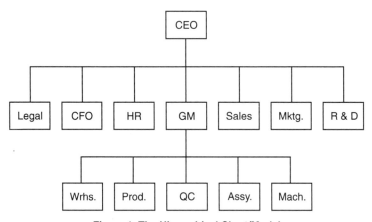

Figure 1. The Hierarchical Chart/Model

For all of us, success on-the-job is at least partially, if not largely, dependent on short interactions. Even in the age of e-mail, communication is often oral—either face-to-face or over the phone. During these conversations we create commitments intended to advance effective action in the organization's best interests. Frequently we hold these conversations with people over whom we have no authority, for example, peers, members of other departments, external suppliers, and customers. We go outside the boundaries of the hierarchy to create relationships for getting things done.

A model that more realistically illustrates this activity—and one that encourages the creation of other beneficial relationships—is the network model (Figure 2). In this model a person is shown at the hub of a wheel. Others who belong in that person's network are connected to him or her by spokes that illustrate the relationships involved.

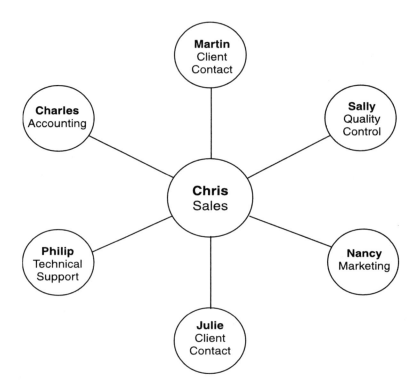

Figure 2. The Network Model

The hierarchical model is based on formal power and authority; the flow of activity is from the top down. In contrast, the network model is based on responsibility and commitment. The flow in this model is from the center outward, reaching into the organization and beyond to form partnerships and alliances.

But a network functions effectively only if each person in it accepts responsibility for his or her goals, priorities, communications, and relationships. A network requires a willingness to ask "Who requires what information, resources, and support and by when?" A network also requires each person to be open, to listen, and to participate actively. Each person must communicate with these two questions in mind: "What is possible? What will be the domain of action in which we will collaborate?" In this way a network facilitates communication that will lead to effective action.

The 1997 Annual: Volume 1, Training/© 1997 by Pfeiffer

COLLABORATING FOR SUCCESS
WORK SHEET

Instructions: Spend forty-five minutes completing this work sheet. A suggested time for each section has been provided.

SECTION 1: IDENTIFYING THE GOAL AND THE PLAYERS

Complete Section 1 on this work sheet (ten minutes).

1. What is the main goal that you want to achieve in your work? You probably have many goals, but choose the one that drives you the most.

2. Whom do you need to communicate/collaborate with to achieve this goal?

3. What does each person have at stake in achieving this goal?

Section 2: Mapping the Players

Complete Section 2 on newsprint (five minutes).

1. Tape a sheet of newsprint to the wall. Make sure there is plenty of space between your sheet and the ones on both sides of yours.

2. In the center of the sheet, write your name, your primary responsibility, and a very brief summary of the main goal that you listed in Section 1. Draw a circle around them.

3. Using a circular configuration (see the example below), write the names of people you presently communicate/collaborate with and their primary responsibilities, and draw circles around them. Leave plenty of space between circles to accommodate the information required in Section 3—and in case you want to add other people later.

Example:

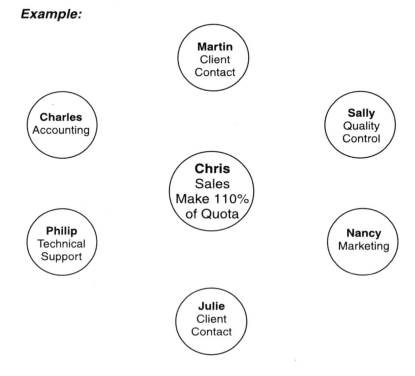

SECTION 3: CONNECTING THE PLAYERS

Complete Section 3 on the same sheet of newsprint (ten minutes).

1. To identify your relationship with each person in your network, follow this procedure:

   ■ If the relationship is frequent or is essential to meeting your main goal, draw two solid lines connecting you with that person.

   ■ If the relationship is infrequent or is not essential to meeting your main goal, draw one dashed line connecting you with that person.

   ■ If the relationship falls somewhere between these two extremes, draw one solid line connecting you with that person.

2. Near each line designate what is provided in the relationship: information, service, or support (see the example below).

3. Draw an arrow by each line indicating the flow of what is provided (to you, by you, or both).

Example:

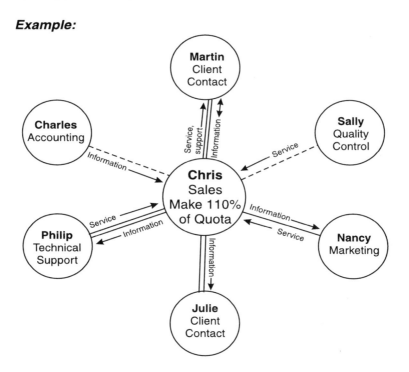

SECTION 4: OPTIMIZING YOUR NETWORK

Complete Section 4 on this work sheet (ten minutes).

1. With whom do you need to build a stronger relationship or a better alignment of responsibilities and goals?

2. With whom do you need to communicate more? Less?

3. Which communications make something positive happen?

4. Which communications do not result in effective action?

5. Who is not in your network but should be?

SECTION 5: ACTION PLANNING

Complete Section 5 on this work sheet (ten minutes).

Review the network drawing you completed in Section 3 and your answers to the questions in Section 4. Consider each relationship separately and whether you need to make any changes to help you reach your main goal: make requests, offer assistance, make commitments, increase/decrease communication, and so on. Also consider any other people that you would like to include in your network and in what capacity. Then complete an action plan. (Following is an example.)

Example:

Person in Network	Changes to Be Made	Action Steps	By When?
Julie	Establish line of communication (information) from Julie to me	Ask her to let me know (in addition to repair techs) when she has trouble with Model 690	6/18: ask Julie if she's amenable

Person in Network	Changes to Be Made	Action Steps	By When?

573. HIGH JUMP:
ILLUSTRATING THE IMPACT OF EXPECTATIONS

Goals

- To demonstrate the impact of both negative and positive expectations on performance.

- To encourage participants to consider how expectations affect the extent to which they reach their goals.

Group Size

Two to five subgroups of three to six members each.

Time Required

One hour to one hour and fifteen minutes.

Materials

- A copy of the High Jump Instruction Sheet A-1 for each participant.

- A copy of the High Jump Instruction Sheet A-2 for each participant.

- A copy of the High Jump Instruction Sheet B-1 for each participant.

- A copy of the High Jump Calculation Sheet for each participant.

- Two sheets of newsprint for each subgroup, posted to the wall prior to the arrival of the participants. (See Step 1.)

- A set of ankle weights for each subgroup. All sets must be identical, and each set should weigh no more than five pounds (two and one-half pounds per ankle). *Note:* Depending on the general physical condition of the participant group, the facilitator may opt for lighter ankle weights.

- A yardstick for each subgroup.

- A felt-tipped marker for each participant. No two members of a subgroup should have markers of the same color.

- A newsprint flip chart and a felt-tipped marker for the facilitator's use.
- Masking tape for posting newsprint.

Physical Setting

A room large enough for the subgroups to work without discovering that one subgroup has different instructions. The room must have a ceiling of at least eleven feet. Movable chairs should be provided for the participants.

Process

1. Prior to the arrival of the participants, the facilitator tapes two sheets of newsprint to the wall in each area where a subgroup will work: The top of the first sheet should be at least eleven feet from the floor (see the High Jump Instruction Sheet A-1, second paragraph), and the top of the second sheet should be taped to the bottom of the first. The facilitator should identify each subgroup's area by writing a number (1, 2, and so on) at the bottom of the second sheet.

2. After the participants have arrived, the facilitator introduces the activity by explaining that they will be asked to take part in two exercises but that they will not be competing against one another. The facilitator also stresses the importance of following the written instructions that will be distributed.

3. The facilitator divides the participants into subgroups, with approximately the same number of members in each. Each subgroup is asked to select an area and to congregate in that area. Each participant is given a felt-tipped marker. No two members of the same subgroup are given a marker of the same color. (Five minutes.)

4. A copy of the High Jump Instruction Sheet A-1 is given to each participant. After the participants have reviewed the instructions, the facilitator states that *any participant who is unable to do the exercise because of physical reasons need not participate.* Then the participants are told to start jumping. When all jumps have been marked, the facilitator instructs the participants to exchange markers with other members of their subgroups so that no one ends up with the color that he or she used for the first jump. (Ten minutes.)

5. Each member of *one subgroup only* receives a copy of the High Jump Instruction Sheet A-2. All other participants receive copies of the High Jump Instruction Sheet B-1. Each subgroup is given a pair of ankle weights. As the participants are reviewing their instructions, the facilita-

tor circulates and speaks to the groups. To the group with the High Jump Instruction Sheet A-2, the facilitator makes comments such as the following:

"Now that you have warmed up with the first jump, you'll be able to jump higher this time. You are asked to jump only two inches higher, so that will be easy. Even with the weights on your ankles, you'll be surprised at how high you can jump. Some of you may even jump three inches higher."

To the other groups, the facilitator makes comments such as the following:

"Don't be disappointed if you don't jump as high this time. After all, you'll be jumping with five more pounds than you did last time, and you can't imagine how heavy those five pounds will feel. Just see how close you come to your first mark."

(Ten minutes.)

6. After the facilitator has spoken to each group and after each participant has reviewed his or her instructions, the facilitator announces that it is time to put on the ankle weights and start the second round of jumping. (Five to ten minutes.)

7. After the second round of jumps, a copy of the High Jump Calculation Sheet is given to each participant. A yardstick is given to each subgroup. The facilitator asks the participants to follow the instructions on the handout and to ask questions if they have trouble calculating their scores. (Five to ten minutes.)

8. When all scores have been calculated, the facilitator reconvenes the total group and asks the members of each subgroup to call out their scores. The facilitator records these on the flip chart, saving the special subgroup's scores until last. *Note:* Ordinarily, the scores of the members of the special subgroup are significantly higher than those of the other participants. (Five minutes.)

9. The facilitator elicits observations regarding the scores and asks for speculations about why one subgroup had higher scores. (Five minutes.)

10. A copy of the High Jump Instruction Sheet B-1 is given to each member of the special subgroup, and a copy of the High Jump Instruction Sheet A-2 is given to all other participants. The participants are instructed to read their sheets. (Five minutes.)

11. The facilitator leads a discussion, asking questions such as the following:

- How would your second jump have been different if you had read the instruction sheet that you just received? Why?

- If you believe that you *cannot* do a task, what effect does that belief have on your performance? What is the impact of setting and visualizing a low goal?

- If you believe that you *can* do a task, how does that belief affect your performance? What is the impact of setting and visualizing a high goal?

- What are some examples of how your expectations of yourself affected the extent to which you reached your goals?

- How can you apply what you have learned in your personal life? In your current job? In your career?

(Fifteen minutes.)

Variation

- Activities other than jumping may be used. However, trials would be necessary to confirm that the activity was responsive to positive and negative expectations.

Submitted by Steven B. Hollwarth.

Steven B. Hollwarth is the vice president of the Service & Administrative Institute, a consulting firm in Ponte Vedra Beach, Florida, that specializes in business process improvement. He has spent the last twelve years of his career consulting and training throughout North America in all aspects of the modern quality movement. He has broad experience in both the manufacturing and service industries. One of his primary interests is designing and developing highly interactive training for team building and empowerment. This activity was designed for his leading-edge course on empowerment.

HIGH JUMP
INSTRUCTION SHEET A-1

Each member of your subgroup will take a turn jumping as high as possible. You are not competing with anyone else.

Each member will be responsible for tracking his or her own jump. As you jump from a standing position, hold your writing hand as high as possible and use your felt-tipped marker to mark the height of your jump. You may hold the marker any way you wish, and you may bend your knees before making the jump.

The first person who jumps should stand near the left side of the paper; make a mark on that part of the paper; and then initial the bottom of the paper, under the mark. The next person should move slightly to the right of that mark, so that the second mark will not be directly above or below the first person's mark. The second person should also initial the bottom of the paper, parallel with his or her mark. The third person should stand and jump slightly to the right of the second mark, and so on.

Your goal is to jump as high as you can. Use any energy, knowledge, or experience that will help you to accomplish this task.

HIGH JUMP
INSTRUCTION SHEET A-2

Your task is to jump even higher than before. Use a marker of a different color to mark the height of this jump (switch markers with someone in your subgroup). You are to follow the sequence and procedure you used for the first jump, so the first member will mark this jump directly (or almost directly) above or below his or her first mark. It is not necessary to sign the paper again.

Remember that you are not competing with anyone else. Your goal is to *jump two inches higher* than you jumped the first time.

The difference in this jump will be the weight that you attach to each ankle. The ankle weight is symbolic of the challenges that you must meet to be successful. If you formulate a clear vision of what you want to accomplish, you will find that your subconscious will tap inner strength to overcome obstacles. Your muscles will be more responsive, your coordination will be better, and your performance will be more effective.

Before jumping, look at your first mark. Visualize two inches higher on the paper. Your goal is to make a mark two inches above the one you are looking at. Remember that you are capable and you can do it.

When the facilitator gives you the signal, the first jumper should attach the ankle weights and go for the high jump!

HIGH JUMP
INSTRUCTION SHEET B-1

Your task this time is to jump with weights attached to your ankles. Use a marker of a different color to mark the height of this jump (switch markers with someone in your subgroup). You are to follow the sequence and procedure you used for the first jump, so the first member will mark this jump directly (or almost directly) above or below his or her first mark. It is not necessary to sign the paper again.

Remember that you are not competing with anyone else. Your goal is to see how high you can jump when you are encumbered with weights.

The ankle weights can have the same effect as emotional baggage (stress, anger, fear, frustration, and so on). You will be amazed at how heavy the weights feel as you try to lift your feet off the floor. Also, anything that upsets the natural movements of your body introduces inefficiency in physical activities. You may recall instances in which you started wearing a new type of shoe and kept tripping. Your body "knew" how high to lift your foot in your old shoes, but the new shoes required a different lift.

When the facilitator gives you the signal, the first jumper should attach the ankle weights and jump. Please try not to laugh at the other jumpers! Show them the same courtesy that you want them to show you.

HIGH JUMP
CALCULATION SHEET

Using the yardstick, calculate the difference in the height of your two jumps, to the nearest inch.

If your first jump was higher, your score will be the negative difference in the two jumps. For example, if your first jump was two inches higher than your second jump, your score is -2.

If your second jump was higher, your score will be the positive difference multiplied by two. For example, if your second jump was two inches higher than your first jump, your score is +4.

If your jumps were equal (or less than one-half inch apart), your score is zero. If your first jump was slightly higher, list your score as -0; if your second jump was slightly higher, list your score as +0.

Record your score on the bottom of this sheet. Calculate only your individual score, not your subgroup's score.

574. Thumbs Up, Thumbs Down: A Conflict-Management Icebreaker

Goals

- To open a session or a training event on conflict management.

- To illustrate the fact that people sometimes erroneously assume that conflict or competition is necessary to resolve a problem or situation.

Group Size

Six to fifty participants.

Time Required

Approximately fifteen minutes.

Physical Setting

A room in which the participants can sit beside or close to one another. Movable chairs are desirable but not essential.

Process

1. The facilitator starts the activity by saying, "Let's do a quick experiment. Turn to the person sitting next to you and take that person's hand like this." The facilitator approaches one of the participants and takes his or her hand in the posture shown in Figure 1. However, *the facilitator is careful not to use the term "thumb wrestling" and gives no further instructions or clues.* If the participants ask questions, the facilitator repeats, "Take your partner's hand like this."

Figure 1. Illustration of Hand Positioning for Step 1

2. Once the partners have positioned their hands properly, the facilitator announces the objective: "Each of you is to get your partner's thumb down, like this." To demonstrate, the facilitator releases the participant's hand and models the position alone by moving the thumb down from its upright position so that it rests on top of the index finger. *The facilitator must not use his or her other hand to push the thumb down.* (By this time most participants will assume that they will be thumb wrestling and that the objective can only be accomplished through that form of conflict.)

3. The facilitator asks the participants to reposition their hands as they did during Step 1 and then says, "Begin." (If there is an odd number of participants, the facilitator should work with the remaining participant and follow that person's lead.)

4. After one person from each pair has triumphed, the facilitator says, "Winners?," and pauses, waiting for a show of hands. Similarly, the facilitator says, "Losers?," and waits for a show of hands. *Note:* If both people in a partnership raise their hands, the facilitator asks them to explain how they both won. The ensuing explanation will eliminate the need for Step 5.

5. The facilitator then says, "Watch me," and goes back to the participant who had helped him or her model the posture in Step 1. They reassume the Step 1 positioning of hands, and the facilitator says to the partner, "Let's try putting both of our thumbs down together." Then each puts his or her thumb down on the forefinger so that no conflict is involved.

6. The facilitator processes the activity briefly with the following questions:

   - What did you assume that you were supposed to do in this activity? How does your assumption differ from what you just saw?

   - How did you feel when you and your partner were trying to meet the objective? How did you feel immediately after you finished?

   - What did you think or feel after you witnessed the cooperative approach to meeting the objective?

- What does this activity tell you about conflict? About your assumptions regarding conflict?

- What have you learned that will help you the next time you approach a conflict?

(Ten minutes.)

Variations

- This activity may be used when learning is blocked through the interference of other dynamics in the group. For example, it may be used as an intervention with an ongoing team when the members are experiencing interpersonal conflict or are battling one another instead of the team problem.

- The participants may be assembled into two groups, one based on competition and the other based on cooperation. The facilitator then addresses the differences in processing.

- The activity may be used as an icebreaker in a team-building session when the team members are having difficulty cooperating with one another.

Submitted by Roger Gaetani.

Roger Gaetani is the director of training at Sunrise, Inc., a producer of greeting cards and related gift items. He has worked as an instructional designer, a teacher, and a training consultant in colleges and universities in Morocco, Saudi Arabia, and the U.S. In addition, he has developed innovative programs in team building, communications, wellness, and parenting for various businesses. Currently he is creating a corporate university at Sunrise. He is also the coproducer of "Parenting Place," a series of six parenting programs that have appeared on public television.

575. Go Left, Go Right:
Identifying Work-Style Preferences

Goals

- To introduce participants to the concept of preferences in work styles.

- To help each participant to develop awareness of his or her work-style preferences.

- To identify similarities and differences among participants' work styles.

Group Size

As many as thirty participants or all members of an ongoing work group.

Time Required

Approximately one hour to one hour and fifteen minutes.

Materials

- A newsprint copy of the Go Left, Go Right Preferences List (prepared ahead of time by the facilitator).

- Masking tape for posting newsprint.

Physical Setting

A room with enough space so that the participants can form two subgroups of unequal size. As the participants switch subgroups several times, the facilitator should ensure that they can move freely from one side of the room to the other.

Process

1. The facilitator introduces the activity by referring to the concept of different preferences or styles of doing things. Examples are the different ways in which people give directions to the same place, the different ways in which people unwind after a day at work, the different types of movies that people prefer to watch, and so on. The facilitator says that people also have different preferences regarding how they work and the types of work they do. (Five minutes.)

2. The facilitator displays the prepared newsprint poster, folded up from the bottom and secured with a small piece of masking tape so that only the title is obvious. The facilitator says that he or she will display and then call out two related phrases to describe different preferences regarding work. Participants are told that they are to move to the left side of the room and stand there if they prefer the description in the left column of the poster and to the right side of the room if they prefer the description in the right column.

3. The facilitator moves the poster down to reveal only the first pair of terms: "Detail Oriented" (on the left) and "Big-Picture Oriented" (on the right). The facilitator calls out these terms and encourages participants to move quickly to signify their preferences. The participants are asked to note who is on each side of the room. If the group is an ongoing work group, the facilitator jots down names in the appropriate places on the poster. (Five minutes.)

4. The facilitator goes through the rest of the poster, calling out and displaying one pair of terms at a time, with participants indicating their preferences by moving to the left or right side of the room. Each time the participants are asked to note who is where; if an ongoing work group is involved, the facilitator records names appropriately on the poster. (Thirty to forty-five minutes.)

5. When all preferences have been indicated, the entire group is reassembled. The facilitator helps the participants to debrief the activity. The following questions may be asked:

   - How did it feel to have to decide your preferences?

   - How did it feel to display your preferences to others?

   - What were your feelings about the people whose preferences were the same as yours? What were your feelings about the people whose preferences were different?

   - What patterns did you observe in the groupings?

- What implications do you think your work preferences have for the way in which you do your job? What implications do they have for the way in which your work group does its job?

- How can you apply your insights from this activity in your real life?

(Fifteen to twenty minutes.)

Variations

- If time allows, the members of each preference grouping for each set of terms may take a few minutes to formulate a description of their "side" of the preference, and the two groups may present their sides to each other.

- With an ongoing work group, the processing may include an exploration of how the information revealed could be used to better assign work tasks, to enhance group relationships, or to increase team productivity and effectiveness.

- If only a small amount of time is available, the facilitator may shorten the list of poster terms.

- To save time the facilitator may display the entire content of the newsprint poster at one time and ask the participants to write their initials beside their preferences.

Submitted by Cher Holton.

Cher Holton, Ph.D., C.S.P., is the president of Bringing Harmony to Life, a division of The Holton Consulting Group, Inc., based in Raleigh, North Carolina. With her husband and partner, Bil, she has worked with corporations throughout the U.S. since 1984, focusing on team-relationship and service issues. She has management experience with Westinghouse Electric, the National Bureau of Standards, and the U.S. Postal Service. She is the coauthor of The Manager's Short Course, *which has been translated into three languages and was selected as one of the top thirty business books by Soundview Executive Book Summaries.*

GO LEFT, GO RIGHT
PREFERENCES LIST

Detail Oriented	Big-Picture Oriented
Face-to-Face/Phone Discussions	Memos/E-mail/Voice Mail
People Focus	Task Focus
Facts and Information	Intuition, Gut Feelings
Direct Feedback	Diplomatic Feedback
Spontaneous, Flexible	Structured, Organized
Outgoing, Talkative	Reserved, Reflective
Tactical, Short Term	Strategic, Long Range
Trust Me to Do It	Show Me That You Will Do It
Rule with Head	Rule with Heart
Afternoon Person	Morning Person
Spirit of the Law	Letter of the Law
Team Player	Individual Achiever
Focus on Results	Focus on Process
Doer	Planner
Confront Issues Directly	Handle Issues Indirectly

The 1997 Annual: Volume 1, Training/© 1997 by Pfeiffer

576. Broken Triangles: Experimenting with Group Problem Solving

Goals

- To offer participants an opportunity to experience some of the elements of cooperation in solving a group problem.

- To develop participants' awareness of behaviors that may obstruct or contribute to the solution of a group problem.

- To allow the participants to experience how the completion of a group task is affected by behavioral restrictions.

Group Size

As many as six subgroups of five participants each. If the total group is not divisible by five, one to four participants may be assigned to help the facilitator monitor the activity.

Time Required

Approximately forty-five minutes.

Materials

- One set of broken triangles for each subgroup (prepared in advance; see the Broken Triangles Preparation Sheet for the Facilitator).

- One copy of the Broken Triangles Instruction Sheet for each participant.

Physical Setting

A room large enough for the subgroups to work without being able to see the other subgroups' puzzles. Each subgroup needs a table with five chairs.

Process

1. The facilitator forms subgroups of five participants each and, if applicable, asks the remaining participants to help monitor compliance to the restrictions listed on the instruction sheet. Each subgroup selects one of its members to be captain.

2. Each participant is given a copy of the Broken Triangles Instruction Sheet. The facilitator reads the handout aloud, eliciting and answering questions and ensuring that everyone understands the instructions. (Five minutes.)

3. A set of broken triangles is given to each subgroup captain. The facilitator asks the captains to leave the bags unopened until the signal to begin work is given.

4. The facilitator asks the subgroups to begin. It is important that the facilitator and participant monitors closely observe the process during this activity. Attention should be called to anyone disobeying the rules, and the entire group should be reminded of the specific rule that was broken. (Twenty minutes.)

5. When the last subgroup has completed the task, the facilitator reconvenes the total group and leads a discussion by asking questions such as the following:

   - How focused were you on your subgroup's task, as opposed to completing your own puzzle?

   - Under what conditions were you willing to give up pieces of a finished puzzle? How did you feel about giving pieces away?

   - Which of your behaviors helped you complete the task? Which of your behaviors hindered you?

   - How did you feel about the restrictions imposed on you? How did these restrictions affect your performance? What did you do to overcome those restrictions?

   - Why did some people break the rules? What was the effect of calling attention to those who broke the rules?

- At work, what kinds of rules and restrictions hinder you and your work group in communicating, solving problems, and achieving goals? What do you do to get past those rules and restrictions?

- What did you learn during this activity about communicating and cooperating to solve a group problem when restrictions are imposed? What can you do in the future to improve your performance despite restrictions?
(Fifteen to twenty minutes.)

Variations

- Ten-person subgroups may be formed, with two duplicate sets of five triangles each distributed. Subgroups of six to nine members may also be formed; in this case, a broken-triangle set with one triangle for each person would be prepared, with as many duplications of the five triangles as necessary.

- When some subgroups have completed their puzzles and others are still working, the facilitator may convene a "consultant group" from those who have finished and ask these participants to come up with one piece of advice for those who are still working. The "consultants" then observe the effect of that advice on the working subgroups. After ten minutes, if all subgroups still have not finished, the consultants may volunteer a second piece of advice. Again, they should observe the effects.

- Extra participants may be assigned to be observers. Or the participants may be assembled into six-member subgroups so that every subgroup has an observer.

- The activity may be conducted with ongoing teams.

Submitted by Janet Mills. This activity is an adaptation of (1) "Broken Squares: Nonverbal Problem Solving" (p. 25) by Tom Isgar, 1968, in *A Handbook of Structured Experiences for Human Relations Training*, Vol. I, by John E. Jones and J. William Pfeiffer (Eds.), San Francisco, CA: Pfeiffer, an imprint of Jossey-Bass Inc., Publishers; and (2) Communication Patterns in Task-Oriented Groups" by Alex Bavelas, in *Journal of the Acoustical Society of America*, 1950, *22*, 225-230. See also "The Five Squares Problem: An Instructional Aid in Group Cooperation" by Alex Bavelas, in *Studies in Personnel Psychology*, 1973, *5*, 29-38. Adapted with permission.

Janet Mills, Ph.D., *is a professor of public administration and communication at Boise State University in Idaho. She assists public agencies with team building and organizational effectiveness and has been a faculty member of the Institutes for Organization Management (U.S. Chamber of Commerce) since 1978.*

BROKEN TRIANGLES PREPARATION SHEET
FOR THE FACILITATOR

A set of "broken triangles" is to be given to each subgroup. This set consists of five bundles of poster-board puzzle pieces. Each bundle contains three pieces of the puzzle, and these three pieces are paper clipped together. Each of the five bundles is stored in a sandwich-size, resealable plastic bag. When properly arranged, the puzzle pieces in the set will form five triangles of equal size and shape.

To prepare a set, cut out five squares of poster board, each exactly six inches square. (All five squares of the set must be from the same color of poster board.) Find the midpoint of one side of a square, and create an isosceles triangle (a triangle with two equal sides) by drawing a light line from the midpoint to each of the opposite corners of the square (see Figure 1). Repeat this process for the other four squares. Then cut out all of the triangles. Save the triangles and discard the cutaway pieces of the squares.

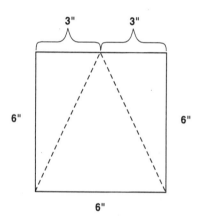

Figure 1. Making an Isosceles Triangle from a Square

Lightly draw lines on each triangle as indicated in Figure 2, and cut on those lines. (Do not reproduce the letters shown in Figure 2; these are for your information only.) The five pieces marked "A" must be exactly the same size. Similarly, the two pieces marked "B" must be exactly the same size, and the two marked "E" must be the same size. Several combinations of puzzle pieces will form one or two triangles, but only one combination will form all five triangles.

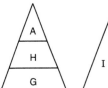

Figure 2. Creating the Final Puzzle Pieces

Repeat the entire process to make as many sets as there will be subgroups. Although all pieces of a set must be made from the same color of poster board, each set should be made from a different color. This precaution will keep pieces from the various sets from getting mixed up.

Into each sandwich-size, resealable plastic bag, place the following bundles of puzzle pieces, paper clipped together:

Bundle 1: A, A, A

Bundle 2: A, A, C

Bundle 3: B, D, E

Bundle 4: F, H, E

Bundle 5: G, B, I

BROKEN TRIANGLES INSTRUCTION SHEET

Your subgroup captain will be given a plastic bag that contains a set of puzzle pieces for forming five triangles. Your captain then will give you and each of the other subgroup members three pieces, paper-clipped together. The three pieces you receive belong to you; you alone will decide whether or not to give any of your pieces to other members of your subgroup.

When the facilitator gives the signal to begin, you and your fellow subgroup members will begin the task of forming *five triangles of equal size and shape*.

The following restrictions are imposed during this activity:

1. There is to be no *verbal* communication of any kind.

2. There is to be no nonverbal communication: no begging, pointing, staring, or emotional displays.

3. Each member must complete a puzzle of his or her own. The members may not create a central communal space for constructing puzzles together.

4. A member may pass only one puzzle piece at a time to another member.

5. Each member must keep at least one puzzle piece at all times.

577. Rope Trick:
Experiencing How Groups Function

Goals

- To offer participants an opportunity to experience how group members organize themselves to accomplish a task.

- To offer participants a chance to experience how group members communicate in planning and completing a task.

- To develop participants' awareness of the leadership styles that arise in groups as the members complete tasks.

Group Size

Three subgroups of ten to twelve members each. *Note:* Two of the members of each subgroup are observers.

Time Required

One hour and thirty to forty-five minutes.

Materials

- A copy of the Rope Trick Observer Sheet for each of the six observers.

- A pencil for each observer.

- A clipboard or other portable writing surface for each observer.

- For each participant except the observers, a kerchief (or other suitable material) to be used as a blindfold.

- A fifty-foot length of clothesline rope (available at supermarkets or hardware stores), cut into three pieces: (1) a piece twenty feet long to make a square, (2) a piece eighteen feet long to make a triangle that will fit on top of the square, and (3) a piece twelve feet long to make a circle that will fit inside the square. See Figure 1 for an illustration of the "house" structure that the participants ultimately create with these pieces of rope.

- A newsprint reproduction of Figure 1, prepared by the facilitator prior to conducting the activity.

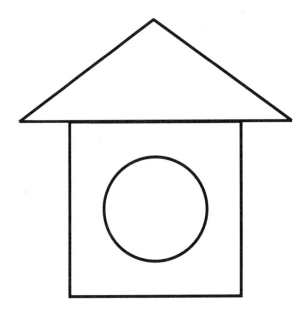

Figure 1. The Rope House

- A newsprint flip chart and felt-tipped markers.
- Masking tape for posting newsprint.

Physical Setting

An unobstructed indoor or outdoor area that is at least 40' x 50'. There must be enough room for the members of all three subgroups to move around while constructing shapes from the rope.

Process

1. The facilitator introduces the activity, divides the participants into subgroups of ten to twelve members each, and designates the subgroups as A, B, and C. Two members of each subgroup are asked to be observers. (Ten minutes.)

2. The subgroups are positioned in separate circles, and the facilitator places one of the three pieces of rope inside each circle. The participants are advised not to touch the rope prior to beginning the activity. The facilitator distributes blindfolds to all participants except the observers and instructs the participants to put on their blindfolds so that they cannot see. (Ten minutes.)

3. The participants are told that first they will be completing a practice round. The facilitator explains the process:

   ■ Each subgroup forms a geometric shape with its rope, *using the full extension of that rope:* Group A forms a square, Group B forms a circle, and Group C forms a triangle.

   ■ The members of each subgroup are to spend some time planning how they will construct the shape before they begin. The planning time ends when one of the members touches the rope.

   ■ Once a member has touched the subgroup's rope, all members must pick up the rope.

   ■ Every member must adhere to certain restrictions about handling the rope: Once the rope is picked up, the hand that picks it up must remain on the rope throughout the activity. Each member may slide his or her hand along the rope (for example, by holding his or her thumb and forefinger together and creating a "hole" for the rope to slip through), but may not release the rope with that hand.

   ■ There are no restrictions on the use of the other hand.

   ■ The observers' job is to monitor the activity; to announce the remaining time at five-minute intervals; and to help people get over or under ropes and away from obstacles. The facilitator will help with these responsibilities.

   (Five minutes.)

4. The facilitator announces that fifteen minutes are allotted for the practice round, including both planning and forming the geometric shapes, and then tells the subgroups to begin.

5. While the subgroups are working, the facilitator and the observers monitor for adherence to the rules and restrictions and for safety concerns. Also, if a subgroup's rope becomes knotted and/or the members are hopelessly entangled, the facilitator or an observer instructs one member to remove his or her blindfold for one minute to rectify the situation. (Fifteen minutes.)

6. At the end of the fifteen-minute period, the facilitator calls time, asks the participants to remove their blindfolds, and posts the newsprint reproduction of Figure 1. The facilitator explains that now that the participants have completed the practice round, they are ready for the second round: They will again be blindfolded, create the same geometric shapes, and adhere to the same rules and restrictions. However, this time the subgroups need to combine their efforts so that they can ultimately create the outline of a primitive "house," using the square for the basic structure, the triangle for the roof, and the circle for the window. The facilitator announces that the time allotted for this task is ten minutes.

7. The facilitator gives each observer a copy of the Rope Trick Observer Sheet, a clipboard or other portable writing surface, and a pencil. The facilitator explains that during the upcoming round the observers are to write answers to the questions on their observer sheets, again monitor for the participants' safety, and again help people get over or under ropes and away from obstacles. This time, however, the facilitator will assume the responsibilities of ensuring adherence to the rules and restrictions and announcing the remaining time at intervals.

8. The facilitator asks the participants to put on their blindfolds and begin the second round of the activity. (Ten minutes.)

9. When all subgroups have placed their ropes, the facilitator instructs the members to remove their blindfolds and to view their creation. (Five minutes.)

10. The total group is reassembled. The facilitator asks the observers to give brief reports on the contents of their observer sheets. (Approximately fifteen minutes.)

11. The facilitator leads a concluding discussion about the second round. The following questions may be useful:

■ How do you feel about the final product? How would you assess the quality of your functioning as you and the other subgroups worked together?

■ What would you do differently if you were to do this task again?

- How did this activity represent the ways in which work teams organize, communicate, and accomplish tasks?

- What have you learned from this activity that you will use in the future?

(Ten to fifteen minutes.)

Variations

- If the subgroups are composed of ongoing teams, the final processing may focus on how the teams actually work and how the members' interaction can be improved, based on the learnings from this activity.

- Processing may also occur after the practice round.

- Within each subgroup, half of the members may be required to wear blindfolds. The other members participate without blindfolds but are required not to speak. The subsequent dynamics are discussed during the processing.

Submitted by Meredith Cash.

Meredith Cash is a training specialist for the South Dakota Bureau of Personnel in Pierre. Her primary interests are management and supervisory training and career-enrichment training. She has worked with both the private and public sectors and currently serves as the Secretary of the National Association of Government Training and Development Directors.

ROPE TRICK OBSERVER SHEET

Instructions: During the upcoming round, jot down answers to the following questions. In addition, monitor for the participants' safety and help them get over or under ropes and away from obstacles. Do not answer any questions about how to complete the task. When the second round has been completed, you will be asked to report your observations to the total group.

1. How do the members organize themselves to accomplish the task?

2. What kind of leadership evolves? How does it occur? How does it change as the members work? How would you describe the effectiveness of leadership communication?

3. How do the subgroup members communicate with one another? How effective is their communication?

4. How does the group deal with problems?

5. What else do you notice about the group's process? What do you notice before they pick up the rope? After they pick up the rope?

6. How efficiently and effectively does the subgroup complete its task?

7. What do you see being applied from the practice session?

578. Lincoln Decision Committee: Learning About Group Skills

Goals

- To familiarize participants with six essential group skills: (1) encouraging participation, (2) clarifying and summarizing comments, (3) observing and identifying process events, (4) obtaining goal clarity, (5) implementing methods for group problem solving and decision making, and (6) managing conflict.

- To offer participants an opportunity to practice these skills or to observe others as they practice.

Group Size

Ten participants: eight role players and two observers. (As many as four extra participants may be accommodated as observers.)

Time Required

Two hours and five to ten minutes.

Materials

- A copy of the Lincoln Decision Committee Theory Sheet for each participant.

- A copy of the Lincoln Decision Committee Background Sheet for each participant.

- A set of Lincoln Decision Committee Role Sheets for the role players. (Each player receives a different one of the eight sheets.)

- A name tag for each role player. Prior to conducting the activity, the facilitator writes a separate role designation on each of the eight tags, leaving enough space below the designation for the participant to write his or her first name.

- A felt-tipped marker for each role player.

- A copy of the Lincoln Decision Committee Observer Sheet A for one of the observers.

- A copy of the Lincoln Decision Committee Observer Sheet B for the other observer.

- A pencil for each observer.

- A clipboard or other portable writing surface for each observer.

- A newsprint flip chart.

- Masking tape for posting newsprint.

Physical Setting

A room large enough to accommodate a table for the role players as well as two (or more) observers seated around the role players. The table should be large enough to seat eight people. Movable chairs should be provided for all participants.

Process

1. The facilitator delivers a brief lecturette based on the Lincoln Decision Committee Theory Sheet, identifying and describing six essential group skills. The facilitator explains that there are other important skills as well, but that the activity will concentrate on the six identified. After the lecturette the facilitator elicits and answers questions and then distributes copies of the theory sheet, explaining that the participants may need to refer to the content later. (Ten minutes.)

2. The facilitator asks for eight volunteers to participate in a role play that will illustrate the group skills described in the theory sheet. After the eight have been chosen, the facilitator asks them to be seated around the table. The remaining participants are instructed to serve as observers and are asked to be seated close to the table, positioned so that they will be able to see and hear what happens but not intrude on the role play. (Five minutes.)

3. The facilitator distributes copies of the Lincoln Decision Committee Background Sheet and asks the participants to read this handout. (Ten minutes.)

4. Each role player is given a different role sheet, a name tag to match, and a felt-tipped marker. The role players are asked to write their first names on the tags under their role designations and to put on their name tags. The facilitator asks them to read their role sheets and study the theory sheet and background sheet as necessary to prepare for their roles. (Five minutes).

5. While the role players are preparing for their roles, the facilitator meets with the observers in a separate part of the room. One observer is given a copy of the Lincoln Decision Committee Observer Sheet A, and the other observer is given a copy of the Lincoln Decision Committee Observer Sheet B. Both observers are given pencils and clipboards or other portable writing surfaces. The facilitator explains that each observer is responsible for observing only three of the six skills, as indicated on the sheet; for recording observations on the sheet; and for sharing observations and offering recommendations to the role players later. (Five minutes.)

6. Once all materials have been read, the observers are asked to resume their positions close to the table. The role players are provided with newsprint and masking tape, so that they can make and post notes during their meeting. The facilitator reminds the role players to incorporate the six behaviors as much as possible and then asks them to begin the role play. (Thirty minutes.)

7. After thirty minutes the facilitator stops the meeting and asks the observers to give feedback from Part 1 of their observer sheets. The facilitator leads a discussion, highlighting the use (or lack of use) of the group skills, as noted by the observers. The observers then are asked to act as "consultants," offering recommendations for improving the effectiveness of the group of role players. (Fifteen minutes.)

8. The facilitator instructs the role players to pick up where they left off and continue their meeting, again using the six group skills whenever possible. (Twenty-five minutes.)

9. The facilitator stops the meeting and asks the observers to provide feedback, based on their notes from Part 2 of their observer sheets. (Five to ten minutes.)

10. The facilitator leads a concluding discussion, asking questions such as the following:

   - What other instances of the six group skills did you notice?

   - What were the differences between the first part of the meeting and the second part? What can you conclude from those differences?

   - What have you learned about the six group skills?

- How can you apply these skills when you are working with your own group, a project team, or a task force?

(Fifteen minutes.)

Variations

- Other group skills may be highlighted (for example, giving information, modeling effective behavior, giving and receiving feedback, and confronting members about their behavior). Two good sources of information on group skills are *Professional Standards for Training of Group Workers*, 1990, Alexandria, Virginia: Association for Specialists in Group Work; and R. Conyne and L. Rapin, January 1994, *Task Group Workshop*, presented at the ASGW National Group Work Conference, St. Petersburg, Florida.

- To shorten the activity, the facilitator may omit the second part of the role play.

- Additional role-play groups may be formed, depending on the number of participants, available facilitators, and space.

- Role sheets may be created for an organization rather than a school committee.

Submitted by Robert K. Conyne and Lynn S. Rapin.

Robert K. Conyne, Ph.D., is a professor of counseling and program coordinator in the counseling program at the University of Cincinnati, where he has also served as a department head and associate vice provost for student life. He also has been a staff psychologist and professor of counselor education at Illinois State University. Dr. Conyne was president of the Association for Specialists in Group Work (1995-96) and is a fellow of the American Psychological Association, American Psychological Society, and ASGW; a past editor of the Journal for Specialists in Group Work; *the author of six books and numerous articles; and a frequent presenter at national conferences.*

Lynn S. Rapin, Ph.D., is a counseling psychologist in private practice and an adjunct associate professor of counseling at the University of Cincinnati. Much of her private practice is devoted to organization development and to consultation interventions with management and troubled teams. She is the current cochair and past chair of the Ethics Committee of the Association for Specialists in Group Work and has served on the association's editorial board. She has written chapters for three books and has presented or published numerous papers in the areas of consultation, program development, and group work.

LINCOLN DECISION COMMITTEE
THEORY SHEET

A task group must accomplish two objectives: (1) complete pieces of work (tasks) that meet the specific goals of the organization and (2) maintain effective dynamics and interactions within the group. There are a number of skills associated with these two objectives, but this theory sheet describes six that are especially important:

- Encouraging participation;

- Clarifying and summarizing comments;

- Observing and identifying process events;

- Obtaining goal clarity;

- Implementing group methods for problem solving and decision making; and

- Managing conflict.

SIX IMPORTANT GROUP SKILLS

1. Encouraging Participation

The leader can aid discussion and set a collaborative tone for a meeting by providing an agenda and background materials before the group meets, by reviewing the purpose of the meeting once the members have arrived, and by arranging for the members to sit in a circle so that visual contact is maximized. Here are some other ways in which the leader and other members can encourage participation:

- State that all members' opinions are valued and desired.

- Ask for opinions, ideas, and elaboration on statements.

- Elicit different perspectives.

- Brainstorm for ideas without evaluating them.

- Link people who express similar ideas: "Ted and Sue, you both seem to be saying that the budget cuts have had a negative effect on morale."

- Ask for further comments from members who share a viewpoint different from that of the majority: "Sarah and Bill, your perspective seems different. We'd like to hear more about it from each of you so that we can understand your viewpoint."

- Thank individual members and the group as a whole for contributions.

2. Clarifying and Summarizing Comments

Clarification and summary increase the depth of a discussion, enhance understanding, and reduce defensiveness. To clarify, someone either restates his or her understanding of what has been said, or asks the member who spoke to rephrase the comment. To summarize, someone recaps the content and/or feelings that have been presented.

3. Observing and Identifying Process Events

A group's effectiveness can be increased when its members monitor and discuss the ways in which they approach their tasks. For example, the members should note high and low participators, levels of influence, group norms, and so on.

Monitoring the group's process allows the members to identify problems and take corrective action. For example, if responsibility for a discussion is not being equally shared, the leader or another member can say something like "We haven't heard from Chris or Lee. How do you see the issue?"

4. Obtaining Goal Clarity

The leader should always discuss the group's goal at the beginning of a meeting, making sure that the members agree on that goal before proceeding. The leader also can write important points on a flip chart or a whiteboard to direct the group discussion. In addition, the group should identify each member's responsibility in relation to the goal.

5. Implementing Group Methods for Problem Solving and Decision Making

Task groups generally are engaged in problem solving and decision making, which consist of the following steps:

- Defining the problem;
- Determining objectives and criteria for success;

- Generating alternative strategies for accomplishing the objectives;

- Selecting the strategy with the greatest potential for accomplishing the objectives and meeting the criteria; and

- Creating plans for implementing and evaluating the strategy.

The group members also need to establish ground rules for making decisions: "Will we use majority vote, consensus, or some other method?" In addition, they should monitor their progress against the plan: "How close are we to having a description of the problem?"

6. Managing Conflict

In order to manage their emotional responses, the group members must accept the fact that conflict is natural. However, when group members feel understood, they are less likely to attack.

The members should acknowledge conflict when it arises and make it part of the group's shared work. For example, the leader or a member might say, "Sam and Theresa, you seem to have very different points of view. Perhaps we need to hear from each of you in more detail."

If the group reaches an impasse, the members should try forming subgroup clusters and spending fifteen minutes brainstorming ideas about how to get beyond the impasse. Then the ideas are shared in the total group.

LINCOLN DECISION COMMITTEE
BACKGROUND SHEET

THE COMMITTEE

Objectives

The principal of Lincoln Elementary School has formed a group to make decisions concerning the school's (1) vision and mission, (2) goals, (3) budget, and (4) principal, should that position become vacant. This group is known as the "Lincoln Decision Committee."

The committee may act as a whole or through ad hoc subcommittees. However, any issues requiring decisions or recommendations must be brought before the entire committee.

Composition

The committee includes the following eight people:

- Two teachers;
- Two staff members (one of whom is the assistant principal, appointed by the principal);
- Two parents; and
- Two community members.

The school's teacher, staff, and parent groups elect their own representatives to the committee. The representatives, in turn, select the community members. The committee members report the committee's activities to their constituents and elicit feedback and assistance.

Chairperson

The committee chairperson must be a parent or a community member and is elected by the committee members. The chairperson at this time is a community member.

Terms

Each member (except the principal) serves a three-year term. Any member may be elected or selected to serve additional terms, provided that he or she continues to represent the same constituency.

Meetings

Nine meetings per school year are recommended. One annual meeting is required, to review the school's goals and budget and the committee's purpose. Additional meetings may be called by the chairperson or scheduled by the committee.

A quorum (two-thirds of committee membership) is necessary for all decision making. The committee may seek assistance from the school's administration if it is unable to make decisions or experiences unresolvable conflict.

CONTEXT

Lincoln Elementary is an urban school with students in kindergarten through the eighth grade. Approximately 60 percent of the students are from minority groups. The school has a good reputation in the community and has experienced a steady increase in volunteer participation during the last four years.

The decision committee has conducted three meetings this year. The members agree that they are overwhelmed with the number of important issues to be addressed. They are committed to resolving these issues, but they are all very busy. The two teachers and the two staff members (the assistant principal and the staff counselor) work an early schedule (7:45 a.m. to 3:15 p.m.), while some of the other committee members work through the dinner hour. Early-evening meetings are a problem for most members. Meetings are scheduled for one and one-half hours but generally run for two or two and one-half hours, because of the large number of issues to be discussed.

The assistant principal, who was assigned to the committee by the principal, is new to the school and is in a steep learning curve.

AGENDA FOR TODAY'S MEETING

The committee has been concentrating on identifying the school's goals for the current year. In previous meetings, the committee has addressed the goals of increasing academic achievement, improving communication at all levels, and revising the discipline plan.

The agenda for the meeting today is *the goal of improving interracial and intercultural understanding at the school.* The members will discuss the goal, identify major issues, and develop a plan for achieving the goal.

LINCOLN DECISION COMMITTEE
ROLE SHEET 1

TEACHER

You are a "traditionalist" and proud of it. You believe that the role of a school is to educate students in the basics: reading, writing, and arithmetic. The purpose of the school is to pass on knowledge and Western culture from generation to generation. You are wary of anything "new": innovation, experimentation, pilot programs, multiculturalism, and community involvement. Stability, tradition, conservatism, "tried-and-true" values, and classroom control are the cornerstones of your approach. You plan to be guarded in your participation at the committee meeting.

LINCOLN DECISION COMMITTEE
ROLE SHEET 2

TEACHER

You are a "change agent" and proud of it. You believe that the role of a school is to liberate and empower students so that they can think for themselves and work well with others. The purpose of the school is to help students realize their potential and use their developing competence to improve society. You are wary of anything "old": tradition, conservatism, "tried-and-true" values, and teacher-controlled classrooms. Innovation, experimentation, pilot programs, multiculturalism, and community involvement are the cornerstones of your approach.

LINCOLN DECISION COMMITTEE
ROLE SHEET 3

ASSISTANT PRINCIPAL

You are the new assistant principal of Lincoln Elementary School, having joined the staff a few months ago. You are just "learning the ropes," getting to know the school personnel, parents, policies and procedures, and committees (including this one). You find yourself wanting to please everyone, but the desires of different groups are not always compatible. You are also beginning to be frustrated, because when you take a position on a matter, the principal often does not support you and follow through on it.

-- - --.-- -- -- -- -- -- -- - -- -- -- -- -- -- -- -- -- -- -- -- -- -- -- -- - -

LINCOLN DECISION COMMITTEE
ROLE SHEET 4

STAFF COUNSELOR

You are the only counselor in this school of eight hundred children. You were hired the year before last as the first counselor. You are overwhelmed by the demands you face. Children at all grade levels need attention, and you have to use your time efficiently to reach as many children as possible. You have instituted some interventions at every grade level, including group activities and individual attention. You have noticed that there is interracial tension at most grade levels and that it is greater in the higher grades. You are very interested in the goal of today's meeting.

Lincoln Decision Committee
Role Sheet 5

Parent of Seventh Grader

You work in the Post Office and have been very involved in the school as a volunteer in the PTA. This is your second year on the committee. You have heard that children are often involved in fights on the bus and the playground. You wonder if these incidents are racially motivated.

Lincoln Decision Committee
Role Sheet 6

Parent of First Grader

You are a realtor and you appreciate the diversity of your community. Your first grader does not seem to be as happy at Lincoln as you expected her to be. You have talked with her teacher, who seems to be a very nice person and is as perplexed about your daughter's lack of enthusiasm as you are. You pursued a position on this committee to learn more about how the school actually works. You try to see the positive in most situations, and you will use that approach during the meeting.

LINCOLN DECISION COMMITTEE
ROLE SHEET 7

COMMUNITY REPRESENTATIVE

You are a successful and respected artist, specializing in watercolors. You are extremely concerned about discipline in the school. You have heard that black males receive more detentions and suspensions than all other groups combined. You want the school to address this inequity. You plan to be vehement in the expression of your position.

- -

LINCOLN DECISION COMMITTEE
ROLE SHEET 8

COMMITTEE CHAIRPERSON; COMMUNITY REPRESENTATIVE

You are a front-line supervisor in a large local corporation. You have your hands full in you role as chairperson of this committee. Every meeting is full of ideas and challenges. The committee has so much business to transact in the short time available that you need the full cooperation of all members to get the work done. You have set today's agenda to cover only the goal of improving interracial and intercultural understanding at the school. You will try to keep the group on track and obtain some clarity about exactly what the members want to accomplish. You anticipate that there will be some conflict, but you don't want it to stop the progress of the group.

                    The 1997 Annual: Volume 1, Training/© 1997 by Pfeiffer

LINCOLN DECISION COMMITTEE
OBSERVER SHEET A

COMMITTEE MEETING, PART 1

Use this sheet to assist you in observing and giving feedback. Answer the following questions in the spaces provided; consider the behavior of all committee members and give specific examples. Also jot down any recommendations for improving the meeting.

1. How was participation encouraged?

2. How were ideas clarified and summarized?

3. What group processes were identified by the members?

Recommendations

COMMITTEE MEETING, PART 2

1. How was participation encouraged?

2. How were ideas clarified and summarized?

3. What group processes were identified by the members?

LINCOLN DECISION COMMITTEE
OBSERVER SHEET B

COMMITTEE MEETING, PART 1

Use this sheet to assist you in observing and giving feedback. Answer the following questions in the spaces provided; consider the behavior of all committee members and give specific examples. Also jot down any recommendations for improving the meeting.

1. How was the goal clarified?

2. What procedures for group problem solving and decision making were established?

3. How did the group members manage conflicts that arose?

Recommendations

COMMITTEE MEETING, PART 2

1. How was the goal clarified?

2. What procedures for group problem solving and decision making were established?

3. How did the group members manage conflicts that arose?

579. EIGHT TRAINING COMPETENCIES: ENHANCING TRAINER SKILLS

Goals

- To acquaint participants with eight training competencies.

- To offer participants an opportunity to increase their skills in these competencies.

Group Size

Eight to forty trainers or prospective trainers, preassigned by the facilitator into eight subgroups of one to five members each.

Time Required

Approximately three and one-half hours.

Materials

- A name tag cut from colored construction paper for each participant. The following eight colors are used in equal portions, with one color for each subgroup: blue, yellow, green, orange, red, pink, purple, and brown. The facilitator fills out the name tags in advance, preassigning the participants to subgroups. (If preassignment is not possible, the participants may be assigned to subgroups when they arrive for the activity; in this case they should be asked to fill out their own name tags.)

- A straight pin for each participant's name tag.

- One copy (printed on blue paper) of the Eight Training Competencies Blue Sheet: How Adults Learn for each member of the blue subgroup.

- One copy (printed on yellow paper) of the Eight Training Competencies Yellow Sheet: Planning Instruction for each member of the yellow subgroup.

- One copy (printed on green paper) of the Eight Training Competencies Green Sheet: Managing Instruction for each member of the green subgroup.

- One copy (printed on orange paper) of the Eight Training Competencies Orange Sheet: Presentation Techniques for each member of the orange subgroup.

- One copy (printed on red paper) of the Eight Training Competencies Red Sheet: Motivation for each member of the red subgroup.

- One copy (printed on pink paper) of the Eight Training Competencies Pink Sheet: Instructional Strategies for each member of the pink subgroup.

- One copy (printed on purple paper) of the Eight Training Competencies Purple Sheet: Communication for each member of the purple subgroup.

- One copy (printed on brown paper) of the Eight Training Competencies Brown Sheet: Evaluation for each member of the brown subgroup.

- A newsprint flip chart and several felt-tipped markers for each of four subgroups.

- A newsprint flip chart and a felt-tipped marker for the facilitator's use.

- Masking tape for posting newsprint.

Physical Setting

A room large enough for the subgroups to meet without disturbing one another. Movable chairs should be provided for the participants.

Process

1. As the participants arrive, they are instructed to find their name tags and put them on with the straight pins.

2. The facilitator introduces the activity by announcing its goals.

3. The facilitator asks the participants to form eight subgroups by joining with the other participants who are wearing name tags of the same color.

4. Each member of a subgroup is given a copy of the Eight Training Competencies [Color] Sheet that matches the color of his or her subgroup's name tags.

5. The facilitator explains the following process, writing it on newsprint and posting the newsprint at the same time: All members of each subgroup will study the training competency assigned to them. They will have ten minutes to develop a method to teach the competency to another subgroup. Four of the subgroups will then have ten minutes to teach their competencies to four other subgroups, as follows:

- Blue will teach Yellow "How Adults Learn."

- Green will teach Orange "Managing Instruction."

- Red will teach Pink "Motivation."

- Purple will teach Brown "Communication."

At the end of ten minutes, time will be called, and the paired subgroups will switch roles and begin a second teaching round, as follows:

- Yellow will teach Blue "Planning Instruction."

- Orange will teach Green "Presentation Techniques."

- Pink will teach Red "Instructional Strategies."

- Brown will teach Purple "Evaluation."

(Five minutes.)

6. After the participants have reviewed their sheets, the facilitator gives each subgroup a newsprint flip chart and several felt-tipped markers and then instructs the subgroups to begin the planning session. (Ten minutes.)

7. The facilitator asks the designated subgroups to meet to share competencies, as directed by the instructions on their sheets. The facilitator reminds the participants that for the first ten minutes Blue will teach Yellow; Green will teach Orange; Red will teach Pink; and Purple will teach Brown. (Ten minutes.)

8. After ten minutes the facilitator calls time and instructs each learning subgroup to become the teaching subgroup: Yellow will now teach Blue, Orange will teach Green, and so on. (Ten minutes.)

9. The facilitator states that four subgroups have each learned two competencies. The paired subgroups will now have twenty minutes to plan their next task: a joint teaching session, which also will last twenty minutes. The facilitator says that after the planning period, the following teaching procedure will occur:

- Blue-Yellow will teach Green-Orange "How Adults Learn" and "Planning Instruction."

- Red-Pink will teach Purple-Brown "Motivation" and "Instructional Strategies."

Then the paired subgroups will switch roles, and for the next twenty minutes:

- Green-Orange will teach Blue-Yellow "Managing Instruction" and "Presentation Techniques."

- Purple-Brown will teach Red-Pink "Communication" and "Evaluation."

(Five minutes.)

10. The facilitator tells the paired subgroups to begin the planning session. (Twenty minutes.)

11. The facilitator asks the subgroups to begin the teaching session: Blue-Yellow meets with Green-Orange, and Red-Pink meets with Purple-Brown. (Twenty minutes.)

12. The facilitator calls time and instructs the paired subgroups to reverse roles: Green-Orange will teach Blue-Yellow, and Purple-Brown will teach Red-Pink. (Twenty to twenty-five minutes.)

13. The facilitator calls time and states that now everyone knows four competencies. The facilitator instructs the participants to form two subgroups: Blue-Yellow-Green-Orange and Red-Pink-Purple-Brown. The facilitator explains that each new subgroup will have thirty minutes to prepare to teach the other subgroup. Blue-Yellow-Green-Orange will have thirty minutes to teach "How Adults Learn," "Planning Instruction," "Managing Instruction," and "Presentation Techniques." Then the subgroups will reverse roles, and Red-Pink-Purple-Brown will have thirty minutes to teach "Motivation," "Instructional Strategies," "Communication," and "Evaluation." (Five minutes.)

14. The facilitator tells the two subgroups to begin the planning session. (Thirty minutes.)

15. The facilitator asks the first subgroup to make its presentation. (Thirty minutes.)

16. The second subgroup is asked to make its presentation. (Thirty minutes.)

17. The facilitator reconvenes the total group; congratulates the participants on their accomplishments; and leads a discussion of the activity, recording salient comments on newsprint. The following questions may be asked:

- What reactions do you have to the process used in this activity? What were your experiences as a teacher? As a learner?

- How does the process used in this activity vary from the standard way of teaching? What are the advantages? What are the disadvantages?
- What generalizations can you make about training adults? About the training process?
- How will you apply what you have learned when you train others?
- In what other ways can you apply this experience on-the-job?

(Fifteen minutes.)

Variations

- The activity may be shortened by (1) using only four competencies or (2) having two subgroups simply teach each other.
- The process may be used with other competencies, such as those having to do with management or with training trainers.
- The activity may be debriefed by assessing how well each competency was demonstrated.

Submitted by Bonnie Jameson.

Bonnie Jameson *is a consultant and trainer in human resource development and organization development. She works with corporate, nonprofit, and educational organizations and designs and facilitates management programs and other workshops and courses. She currently teaches strategic planning and building effective organizations in the extension program at California State University, Hayward. Ms. Jameson's specialties include training for trainers and the Myers/Briggs Type Indicator.*[TM] *Pfeiffer published her training package,* Inspiring Fabled Service, *in 1996.*

EIGHT TRAINING COMPETENCIES BLUE SHEET

Instructions: The first task of your group is to learn about the training competency ("How Adults Learn") described in this handout. Assume that the information provided is correct and do not add personal knowledge to this information.

Later you will be taught additional competencies; be an active learner in each instance. All tasks will have time limits, and the facilitator will keep you apprised of the time.

You may refer to this sheet at any time. The remaining instructions have been numbered for easy reference.

1. After you have examined the description and key points of "How Adults Learn," your group will have ten minutes to plan how to teach this information to the Yellow group. When the facilitator gives you the signal, meet with the Yellow group and teach it what you have just learned. This teaching session will last ten minutes. The Yellow group will then have ten minutes to teach you its competence ("Planning Instruction").

2. At this point, your group and the Yellow group will have learned two competencies. You will merge with the Yellow group, and your new group (Blue-Yellow) will spend twenty minutes designing a training program to teach both competencies ("How Adults Learn" and "Planning Instruction") to the Green-Orange group.

3. When the facilitator gives you the signal, meet with the Green-Orange group and spend twenty minutes teaching the two competencies you already have learned. Then the Green-Orange group will have twenty minutes to teach you two other competencies ("Managing Instruction" and "Presentation Techniques").

4. After that session, your new group and the Green-Orange group will have learned four competencies. Again you will combine groups, so your new group will be Blue-Yellow-Green-Orange. This larger group will spend thirty minutes designing a training program to teach the four competencies you already have learned ("How Adults Learn," "Planning Instruction," "Managing Instruction," and "Presentation Techniques").

5. Your group will then spend thirty minutes teaching your competencies to the Red-Pink-Purple-Brown group, which, in turn, will spend thirty minutes teaching you its four competencies ("Motivation," "Instructional Strategies," "Communication," and "Evaluation").

6. At this point, all participants will have learned eight training competencies. Congratulations will be in order, and the facilitator will reconvene the total group for a discussion.

DESCRIPTION OF COMPETENCY: "HOW ADULTS LEARN"

Adults like to be self-directed in learning new information, skills, and behaviors. They like to be actively involved in the learning experience. Adult learning is based on a need to know. Adults have a broad base of experience; they connect new learnings to past experiences. They need to apply their learning to the real world in order to internalize it.

Adults have different learning styles. For example, some adults take in information in a concrete, practical way, focusing on detail. Others take in information globally, forming connections and possibilities internally, and prefer the large picture rather than the detail.

Key Points

- Adult learners like to be self-directed.

- Adults want to be actively involved in the learning process.

- Adults learn when they have a need to know.

- Adults connect new learning to past experiences.

- Adults need to apply their learnings in the real world.

- Adults have different learning styles.

EIGHT TRAINING COMPETENCIES YELLOW SHEET

Instructions: The first task of your group is to learn about the training competency ("Planning Instruction") described in this handout. Assume that the information is correct and do not add personal knowledge to this information.

Later you will be taught additional competencies; be an active learner in each instance. All tasks will have time limits, and the facilitator will keep you apprised of the time.

You may refer to this sheet at any time. The remaining instructions have been numbered for easy reference.

1. After you have examined the description and key points of "Planning Instruction," your group will have ten minutes to plan how to teach this information to the Blue group. When the facilitator gives you the signal, meet with the Blue group, which will spend ten minutes teaching you another competency ("How Adults Learn"). Then you will have ten minutes to teach the Blue group your competency ("Planning Instruction").

2. At this point, your group and the Blue group will have learned two competencies. You will merge with the Blue group, and your new group (Blue-Yellow) will spend twenty minutes designing a training program to teach both competencies ("How Adults Learn" and "Planning Instruction") to the Green-Orange group.

3. When the facilitator gives you the signal, meet with the Green-Orange group and spend twenty minutes teaching the two competencies you already have learned. Then the Green-Orange group will have twenty minutes to teach you two other competencies ("Managing Instruction" and "Presentation Techniques").

4. After that session, your new group and the Green-Orange group will have learned four competencies. Again you will combine groups, so that your new group is Blue-Yellow-Green-Orange. This larger group will spend thirty minutes designing a training program to teach the four competencies you already have learned ("How Adults Learn," "Planning Instruction," "Managing Instruction," and "Presentation Techniques").

5. Your group will spend thirty minutes teaching your competencies to the Red-Pink-Purple-Brown group, which, in turn, will spend thirty minutes teaching you its four competencies ("Motivation," "Instructional Strategies," "Communication," and "Evaluation").

6. At this point, all participants will have learned eight training competencies. Congratulations will be in order, and the facilitator will reconvene the total group for a discussion.

DESCRIPTION OF COMPETENCY: "PLANNING INSTRUCTION"

The needs of participants drive any successful training program. A needs analysis allows the trainer to understand the participants' needs. After these needs are determined, the objectives of the training can be decided, and a plan can be developed to achieve the objectives.

A clear vision of needs, objectives, and desired outcomes is important. Planning also involves action steps to achieve the outcomes, scheduled time frames, and transitions. Another planning function is finding or developing the resources and the instructional strategies to implement the plan. It is necessary to delegate and clarify roles and responsibilities for tasks. Finally, a method of evaluating the success of the training is essential.

Key Points

A needs assessment is the first step in planning.

- Learning objectives are determined by the needs.

- A vision of desired outcomes is important.

- Action steps need to be created to achieve each desired outcome.

- Various resources are needed to implement the plan.

- Roles and responsibilities must be assigned and clarified.

- It is important to evaluate how well desired outcomes are achieved.

Eight Training Competencies Green Sheet

Instructions: The first task of your group is to learn about the training competency ("Managing Instruction") described in this handout. Assume that the information is correct and do not add personal knowledge to this information.

Later you will be taught additional competencies; be an active learner in each instance. All tasks will have time limits, and the facilitator will keep you apprised of the time.

You may refer to this sheet at any time. The remaining instructions have been numbered for easy reference.

1. After you have examined the description and key points of "Managing Instruction," your group will have ten minutes to plan how to teach this information to the Orange group. When the facilitator gives you the signal, meet with the Orange group and teach it what you have just learned. This teaching session will last ten minutes. The Orange group will then have ten minutes to teach you its competency ("Presentation Techniques").

2. At this point, your group and the Orange group will have learned two competencies. You will merge with the Orange group, and your new group (Green-Orange) will spend twenty minutes designing a training program to teach both competencies ("Managing Instruction" and "Presentation Techniques") to the Blue-Yellow group.

3. When the facilitator gives you the signal, meet with the Blue-Yellow group, which will spend twenty minutes teaching you two more competencies ("How Adults Learn" and "Planning Instruction"). Then you will spend twenty minutes teaching the Blue-Yellow group the two competencies you already have learned.

4. After that session, your new group and the Blue-Yellow group will have learned four competencies. Again you will combine groups, so that your new group is Blue-Yellow-Green-Orange. This larger group will spend thirty minutes designing a training program to teach the other participants the four competencies you already have learned ("How Adults Learn," "Planning Instruction," "Managing Instruction," and "Presentation Techniques").

5. Your group will spend thirty minutes teaching your competencies to the Red-Pink-Purple-Brown group, which, in turn, will spend thirty minutes teaching you its four competencies ("Motivation," "Instructional Strategies," "Communication," and "Evaluation").

6. At this point, all participants will have learned eight training competencies. Congratulations will be in order, and the facilitator will reconvene the total group for a discussion.

DESCRIPTION OF COMPETENCY: "MANAGING INSTRUCTION"

Managing instruction means providing four essential elements in any instructional event: meaning, structure, action, and caring. A trainer needs to be aware of all four elements when conducting a training session.

Meaning consists of the knowledge and wisdom that are incorporated into the curriculum to create meaningful content. It includes making the subject come alive, relating it to other things, and indicating how it can be used.

Structure includes creating a physical setting that allows training objectives to be accomplished; setting ground rules or group norms; providing time frames and transitions; and using direct, assertive behavior to develop a clear, agreed-on agenda and role definitions.

Action means designing strategies for participant involvement so that adult learning needs are met. These strategies encourage participation, motivation, creativity, risk taking, and experimentation.

Caring means creating a safe, positive learning environment so that all participants feel included and valued. Caring enhances belonging, affiliation, self-esteem, harmony, synergy, and relationships.

Key Points

The following four essential elements must be considered in managing instruction: meaning, structure, action, and caring.

- Meaning is achieved by employing a dynamic, interesting, relevant curriculum.

- Structure is established by providing appropriate procedures, physical environment, objectives, ground rules, agenda, and roles.

- Action is created by encouraging participation and involvement in a variety of activities.

- Caring is evident in the creation of a safe and positive learning environment.

Eight Training Competencies Orange Sheet

Instructions: The first task of your group is to learn about the training competency ("Presentation Techniques") described in this handout. Assume that the information is correct and do not add personal knowledge to this information.

Later you will be taught additional competencies; be an active learner in each instance. All tasks will have time limits, and the facilitator will keep you apprised of the time.

You may refer to this sheet at any time. The remaining instructions have been numbered for easy reference.

1. After you have examined the description and key points of "Presentation Techniques," your group will have ten minutes to plan how to teach this information to the Green group. When the facilitator gives you the signal, meet with the Green group, which will spend ten minutes teaching you another competency ("Managing Instruction"). Then you will have ten minutes to teach the Green group the competency you studied ("Presentation Techniques").

2. At this point, your group and the Green group will have learned two competencies. You will merge with the Green group, and your new group (Green-Orange) will spend twenty minutes designing a training program to teach both competencies ("Managing Instruction" and "Presentation Techniques") to the Blue-Yellow group.

3. When the facilitator gives you the signal, meet with the Blue-Yellow group, which will spend twenty minutes teaching you two more competencies ("How Adults Learn" and "Planning Instruction"). Then you will spend twenty minutes teaching the Blue-Yellow group the two competencies you already have learned.

4. After that session, your new group and the Blue-Yellow group will have learned four competencies. Again you will combine groups, so that your new group is Blue-Yellow-Green-Orange. This larger group will spend thirty minutes designing a training program to teach the other participants the four competencies you already have learned ("How Adults Learn," "Planning Instruction," "Managing Instruction," and "Presentation Techniques").

5. Your group will spend thirty minutes teaching your competencies to the Red-Pink-Purple-Brown group, which, in turn, will spend thirty minutes teaching you its four competencies ("Motivation," "Instructional Strategies," "Communication," and "Evaluation").

6. At this point, all participants will have learned eight training competencies. Congratulations will be in order, and the facilitator will reconvene the total group for a discussion.

DESCRIPTION OF COMPETENCY: "PRESENTATION TECHNIQUES"

The trainer has three roles: presenter, skills trainer, and facilitator. Each role requires a variety of skills and behaviors, which can be learned.

The presenter delivers information from an expert point of view. Important skills for this role include (1) the ability to organize information with an opening, a body, and a conclusion and (2) a platform style that appropriately uses gestures, vocal tone, and eye contact. Overcoming nervousness and fear of the audience is also important.

The skills trainer must be proficient in demonstrating the skills or behaviors to be learned and in giving feedback on the participants' performance.

The facilitator is a process manager. All of the learning comes from the participants—what they make of the experience. The facilitator's task is to lead group processes effectively, so that learning objectives can be met through the active involvement of the participants. The facilitator must be skilled in observing and commenting on group process. Other important skills are neutrality, nondefensiveness, and assertiveness.

Key Points

- A trainer has three roles: presenter, skills trainer, and facilitator.

- The presenter delivers content from the expert point of view.

- The skills trainer demonstrates skills or behaviors and gives feedback to participants when they practice.

- The facilitator is a process manager, ensuring that the learning comes from the participants.

EIGHT TRAINING COMPETENCIES RED SHEET

Instructions: The first task of your group is to learn about the training competency ("Motivation") described in this handout. Assume that the information is correct and do not add personal knowledge to this information.

You will be taught additional competencies; be an active learner in each instance. All tasks will have time limits, and the facilitator will keep you apprised of the time.

You may refer to this sheet at any time. The remaining instructions have been numbered for easy reference.

1. After you have examined the description and key points of "Motivation," your group will have ten minutes to plan how to teach this information to the Pink group. When the facilitator gives you the signal, meet with the Pink group and teach it what you have just learned. This teaching session will last ten minutes. The Pink group will then have ten minutes to teach you its competency ("Instructional Strategies").

2. At this point, your group and the Pink group will have learned two competencies. You will merge with the Pink group, and your new group (Red-Pink) will spend twenty minutes designing a training program to teach both competencies ("Motivation" and "Instructional Strategies") to the Purple-Brown group.

3. When the facilitator gives you the signal, meet with the Purple-Brown group and spend twenty minutes teaching the two competencies you already have learned. Then the Purple-Brown group will have twenty minutes to teach you two other competencies ("Communication" and "Evaluation").

4. After that session, your new group and the Purple-Brown group will have learned four competencies. Again you will combine groups, so that your new group is Red-Pink-Purple-Brown. This larger group will spend thirty minutes designing a training program to teach the other participants the four competencies you already have learned ("Motivation," "Instructional Strategies," "Communication," and "Evaluation").

5. The Blue-Yellow-Green-Orange group will spend thirty minutes teaching you four competencies ("How Adults Learn," "Planning Instruction," "Managing Instruction," and "Presentation Techniques"). Then you will have thirty minutes to teach that group the four competencies you already have learned.

6. At this point, all participants will have learned eight training competencies. Congratulations will be in order, and the facilitator will reconvene the total group for a discussion.

DESCRIPTION OF COMPETENCY: "MOTIVATION"

Understanding human motivation is an important trainer competence. People are motivated to learn when their basic human needs are met and when the learning is based on a personal need to know. Consideration of the participant's learning style also contributes to his or her motivation.

Survival, safety, belonging, esteem, and self-actualization needs are basic to human beings (Maslow, 1943). Every time people enter a new learning situation, lower-level needs arise and must be satisfied before self-actualization can occur. Therefore, it is important for trainers to satisfy lower-level needs first by greeting participants, making introductions, using icebreakers, and establishing group norms and agendas. Other important aspects of motivation are recognition, rewards, and praise.

Key Points

- People are motivated to learn when their basic human needs are met.

- Basic needs include survival, safety, belonging, esteem, and self-actualization.

- Trainers need to be aware of various styles of learning and to be flexible in their teaching styles in order to motivate all trainees.

- Recognition, rewards, and praise are other important parts of motivation.

Reference

Maslow, A.H. (1943). A theory of human motivation. *Psychological Review, 50*(4), 370-396.

Eight Training Competencies Pink Sheet

Instructions: The first task of your group is to learn about the training competency ("Instructional Strategies") described in this handout. Assume that the information is correct and do not add personal knowledge to this information.

Later you will be taught additional competencies; be an active learner in each instance. All tasks will have time limits, and the facilitator will keep you apprised of the time.

You may refer to this sheet at any time. The remaining instructions have been numbered for easy reference.

1. After you have examined the description and key points of "Instructional Strategies," your group will have ten minutes to plan how to teach this information to the Red group. When your facilitator gives you the signal, meet with the Red group, which will spend ten minutes teaching you another competency ("Motivation"). Then you will have ten minutes to teach the Red group the competency you studied ("Instructional Strategies").

2. At this point, your group and the Red group will have learned two competencies. You will merge with the Red group, and your new group (Red-Pink) will spend twenty minutes designing a training program to teach both competencies ("Motivation" and "Instructional Strategies") to the Purple-Brown group.

3. When the facilitator gives you the signal, meet with the Purple-Brown group and spend twenty minutes teaching the two competencies you already have learned. Then the Purple-Brown group will have twenty minutes to teach you two other competencies ("Communication" and "Evaluation").

4. After that session, your new group and the Purple-Brown group will have learned four competencies. Again you will combine groups, so that your new group is Red-Pink-Purple-Brown. This larger group will spend thirty minutes designing a training program to teach the other participants the four competencies you already have learned ("Motivation," "Instructional Strategies," "Communication," and "Evaluation").

5. The Blue-Yellow-Green-Orange group will spend thirty minutes teaching you four competencies ("How Adults Learn," "Planning Instruction," "Managing Instruction," and "Presentation Techniques"). Then you will have thirty minutes to teach that group the four competencies you already have learned.

6. At this point, all participants will have learned eight training competencies. Congratulations will be in order, and the facilitator will reconvene the total group for a discussion.

DESCRIPTION OF COMPETENCY: "INSTRUCTIONAL STRATEGIES"

Instructional strategies are the tactics, methods, and techniques used to achieve learning objectives. They range from strategies that require very passive behavior from the participants, such as reading or listening to lectures, to strategies that require very active behavior, such as engaging in role plays and other experiential activities.

Icebreakers and warmup activities are used to open training sessions and to help the participants become acquainted with one another and relax. Small groups help to involve everyone in a low-risk setting while allowing participants to learn from their peers. A number of techniques can add variety to the instructional design, for example, guided imagery; using art, movement, and music; and writing in journals.

Key Points

- Instructional strategies are the methods and techniques used to achieve learning objectives.

- Strategies range from very passive to very active.

- Using small groups is an important way to involve participants in active learning.

- Techniques such as guided imagery, art, music, movement, and writing in journals help to meet the needs of a variety of learning styles.

EIGHT TRAINING COMPETENCIES PURPLE SHEET

Instructions: The first task of your group is to learn about the training competency ("Communication") described in this handout. Assume that the information is correct and do not add personal knowledge to this information.

Later you will be taught additional competencies; be an active learner in each instance. All tasks will have time limits, and the facilitator will keep you apprised of the time.

You may refer to this sheet at any time. The remaining instructions have been numbered for easy reference.

1. After you have examined the description and key points of "Communication," your group will have ten minutes to plan how to teach this information to the Brown group. When the facilitator gives you the signal, meet with the Brown group and teach it what you have just learned. This teaching session will last ten minutes. The Brown group will then have ten minutes to teach you its competency ("Evaluation").

2. At this point, your group and the Brown group will have learned two competencies. You will merge with the Brown group, and your new group (Purple-Brown) will spend twenty minutes designing a training program to teach both competencies ("Communication" and "Evaluation") to the Red-Pink group.

3. When the facilitator gives you the signal, meet with the Red-Pink group, which will spend twenty minutes teaching you two more competencies ("Motivation" and "Instructional Strategies"). Then you will spend twenty minutes teaching the Red-Pink group the two competencies you already have learned.

4. After that session, your new group and the Red-Pink group will have learned four competencies. Again you will combine groups, so that your new group is Red-Pink-Purple-Brown. This larger group will spend thirty minutes designing a training program to teach the other participants the four competencies you already have learned ("Motivation," "Instructional Strategies," "Communication," and "Evaluation").

5. The Blue-Yellow-Green-Orange group will spend thirty minutes teaching you four competencies ("How Adults Learn," "Planning Instruction," "Managing Instruction," and "Presentation Techniques"). Then you will have thirty minutes to teach that group the four competencies you already have learned.

6. At this point, all participants will have learned eight training competencies. Congratulations will be in order, and the facilitator will reconvene the total group for a discussion.

DESCRIPTION OF COMPETENCY: "COMMUNICATION"

Effective communication requires the following interpersonal skills: listening, questioning, feedback, self-disclosure, and assertiveness. An understanding of individual and group behavior is also helpful.

Listening includes paraphrasing others' ideas to check for understanding, feelings, and emotion and to clarify and summarize information. Asking appropriate open-ended questions is an important communication skill, especially for trainers. Giving and receiving feedback enables the trainer to be assertive or nondefensive, as the situation requires. The use of self-disclosure can convey to the audience that the trainer is human and nonthreatening.

Key Points

- Effective communication requires skill in listening, questioning, feedback, self-disclosure, and assertiveness.

- Listening includes paraphrasing.

- The ability to ask appropriate open-ended questions is important.

- Giving and receiving feedback are essential.

- Assertion is appropriate in giving feedback; nondefensiveness is necessary in receiving feedback.

- Self-disclosure can dispel fear.

EIGHT TRAINING COMPETENCIES BROWN SHEET

Instructions: The first task of your group is to learn about the training competency ("Evaluation") described in this handout. Assume that the information is correct and do not add personal knowledge to this information.

Later you will be taught additional competencies; be an active learner in each instance. All tasks will have time limits, and the facilitator will keep you apprised of the time.

You may refer to this sheet at any time. The remaining instructions have been numbered for easy reference.

1. After you have examined the description and key points of "Evaluation," your group will have ten minutes to plan how to teach this information to the Purple group. When the facilitator gives you the signal, meet with the Purple group, which will spend ten minutes teaching you another competency ("Communication"). Then you will have ten minutes to teach the Purple group the competency you studied ("Evaluation").

2. At this point, your group and the Purple group will have learned two competencies. You will merge with the Purple group, and your new group (Purple-Brown) will spend twenty minutes designing a training program to teach both competencies ("Communication" and "Evaluation") to the Red-Pink group.

3. When the facilitator gives you the signal, meet with the Red-Pink group, which will spend twenty minutes teaching you two more competencies ("Motivation" and "Instructional Strategies"). Then you will spend twenty minutes teaching the Red-Pink group the two competencies you already have learned.

4. After that session, your new group and the Red-Pink group will have learned four competencies. Again you will combine groups, so that your new group is Red-Pink-Purple-Brown. This larger group will spend thirty minutes designing a training program to teach the other participants the four competencies you already have learned ("Motivation," "Instructional Strategies," "Communication," and "Evaluation").

5. The Blue-Yellow-Green-Orange group will spend thirty minutes teaching you four competencies ("How Adults Learn," "Planning Instruction," "Managing Instruction," and "Presentation Techniques"). Then you will have thirty minutes to teach that group the four competencies you already have learned.

6. At this point, all participants will have learned eight training competencies. Congratulations will be in order, and the facilitator will reconvene the total group for a discussion.

DESCRIPTION OF COMPETENCY: "EVALUATION"

Training can be evaluated in the following areas:

- The participants' satisfaction or dissatisfaction;

- The observable or measurable change that took place in the classroom;

- The new or changed performance at work; and

- The impact of the training at the organizational level.

Although there are many different methods for evaluating a training program, all methods should include the four areas listed above.

Participant reactions are easy to gather. The trainer should elicit feedback on his or her performance. Evaluation also tells the trainer how well the learning objectives were accomplished and whether it is necessary to make adjustments to or redesign the course.

Key Points

- It is important to evaluate training on four levels: (1) participant satisfaction or dissatisfaction, (2) observable change in the classroom, (3) changed performance at work, and (4) impact on the organization (Kirkpatrick, 1955).

- There are many different methods of evaluation.

- Trainers need to obtain feedback on their performance.

- Evaluation indicates how well the learning objectives were accomplished.

- Evaluation indicates whether it is necessary to adjust or redesign the course.

Reference

Kirkpatrick, D.L. (1955, a four-part series starting in November). Techniques for evaluating training programs. *The Training Director's Journal.*

580. Living Ethics: Meeting Challenges in Decision Making

Goals

- To offer participants an opportunity to make decisions in situations involving ethical challenges.

- To encourage participants to discuss situations that present ethical challenges.

Group Size

Sixteen to twenty-four participants, divided into four subgroups of four to six members each.

Time Required

One hour and ten to fifteen minutes.

Materials

- A copy of one of the four Living Ethics Situation Sheets for each participant (a different sheet for each subgroup).

- A copy of the Living Ethics Discussion Guidelines for each participant.

- Blank paper and a pencil for each participant.

- A clipboard or other portable writing surface for each participant (not necessary if tables are available).

- A newsprint flip chart and a felt-tipped marker.

- Masking tape for posting newsprint.

Physical Setting

A large room in which the subgroups can work without disturbing one another. Movable chairs must be provided. A table for each subgroup is useful but not essential.

Process

1. The facilitator states that the upcoming activity concerns *ethics* and defines that term as "moral principles." The facilitator then explains the goals of the activity and assembles subgroups.

2. The members of each subgroup are given copies of one of the Living Ethics Situation Sheets (a different sheet for each subgroup), blank paper, pencils, and clipboards or other portable writing surfaces (unless tables are available). The facilitator states that each participant is to work independently on the handout task. (Ten minutes.)

3. After the participants have completed the individual task, they are given copies of the Living Ethics Discussion Guideline Sheet. The facilitator tells them to spend no more than thirty minutes on their task: (1) using the guidelines to discuss their responses in subgroups, concentrating on the critical factors and issues that led to their decisions, and (2) selecting a spokesperson who will later share the situation with the total group, along with a summary of the critical factors and issues. *The facilitator emphasizes that the spokespersons are not to violate confidentiality by identifying who said what.* (Thirty minutes.)

4. The facilitator reassembles the total group. The spokespersons take turns reporting on the situations as well as critical factors and issues. As they report, the facilitator lists the critical factors and issues on newsprint and posts each sheet of newsprint. (Ten minutes.)

5. The facilitator leads the participants in a concluding discussion. The following questions may be asked:

   ■ How did you feel about having to choose an action?

   ■ How did you feel about discussing your responses to the situation?

   ■ In what ways were people's opinions changed as a result of the discussion?

   ■ What have you learned about differing ethical viewpoints? What have you learned about the factors and issues that affect decisions when ethical challenges are involved?

   ■ What have you learned about how to make ethical decisions?

- What types of ethical challenges have you faced recently or are you facing now?

- How can you ensure that you will weigh critical factors and issues in the future when you are faced with ethical challenges?

(Twenty minutes.)

Variations

- To shorten the activity, the participants may be polled to identify and vote on an ethical concern. Then they address that concern in subgroups, without completing the individual task.

- The final discussion may include how to take the insights gained from the activity into the participants' organizations.

- If more time is available, the activity may be conducted in two phases. In the first phase, the subgroups examine one situation without being given the discussion guidelines. In the second phase, the subgroups switch situations and are asked to follow the guidelines. The total-group processing then includes a comparison of the two discussions and any conclusions about group culture and dialogue on ethics.

- New situation sheets may be written to include situations that are more personal in nature or more specific to the experiences of the participant group.

Submitted by Gilbert Joseph Duran, Erna E. Gomar, Marianne Stiles, Christina A. Vele, and Judith F. Vogt.

Gilbert Joseph Duran is pursuing a master's degree in administration at the University of the Incarnate Word in San Antonio, Texas. He is also a cadet in the Reserve Officer Training Corps at St. Mary's University Rattler Battalion in San Antonio and expects to be commissioned a Second Lieutenant in the U.S. Army in 1997.

Erna E. Gomar is pursuing a master's degree in administration at the University of the Incarnate Word. While at Incarnate Word, she has served as a resident assistant, participating in a variety of leadership and team-building activities. Currently she is a resident director, a campus mediator, and a tutor in the university's Learning Center.

Marianne Stiles *received her M.B.A. from the University of the Incarnate Word. She is a C.P.A. with twenty years' experience working with the construction and oil and gas industries and with the U.S. government. In 1993 the 12th Comptroller Squadron at Randolph Air Force Base presented her with the Civilian of the Year award.*

Christina A. Vele *is pursuing a master's degree at the University of the Incarnate Word. She has been involved in tailoring her family's business to the ethnicity of its neighborhood.*

Judith F. Vogt, Ph.D., *is an associate professor of organizational studies at the University of the Incarnate Word. She teaches courses in the M.B.A./ management programs as well as interdisciplinary courses in leadership and organization development. She also consults to organizations.*

LIVING ETHICS DISCUSSION GUIDELINE SHEET

In your discussion with the other members of your subgroup, follow these guidelines:

- Commit to confidentiality. Later, when you participate in a total-group discussion, you may talk about the factors and issues that led to people's decisions, but *you may not use people's names.*

- Keep lines of communication open so that all members feel free to contribute.

- Be open and honest in describing the action(s) that you believe should be taken by the person in the situation.

- Actively encourage others to be open about their reactions.

- Be respectful of others' viewpoints.

- Keep an open mind.

LIVING ETHICS SITUATION SHEET 1

THE SITUATION

After delivering some materials to her boss, Mary returns to her office to find one of her coworkers, Bob, downloading a word-processing program from her computer. The company has only a site license for the use of this program. Bob explains that his home computer has no word-processing software and that his son Jeff, a high school senior, needs it to write a lengthy report on World War II. He further says that Jeff's final grade in history is on the line; if the grade isn't high enough, the boy's total grade-point average may make college acceptance impossible. Bob asks Mary to let him finish downloading the program.

THE TASK

Write answers to the following questions:

1. What ethical conflict(s) does Mary face?

2. In addition to Mary, Bob, and Jeff, who might be affected by Mary's decision?

3. What actions are open to Mary?

4. Which of these actions best meets ethical considerations while resolving the situation as positively as possible for the people involved/affected?

LIVING ETHICS SITUATION SHEET 2

THE SITUATION

Frank is a supervisor reviewing applications for an open position in his department. One of the company's standard procedures for the hiring process is a background check. Frank's friend Michael is one of the applicants and is well qualified for the position. Michael recently told Frank that twelve years ago he embezzled $4,000 from his employer. The employer pressed charges, and Michael was ultimately sentenced to one year of probation. According to organizational policy, this incident would disqualify Michael as a candidate for the position. Michael has convinced Frank that the embezzlement was a one-time error in judgment that will never happen again. He has asked Frank not to do the background check.

THE TASK

Write answers to the following questions:

1. What ethical conflict(s) does Frank face?

2. In addition to Frank and Michael, who might be affected by Frank's decision?

3. What actions are open to Frank?

4. Which of these actions best meets ethical considerations while resolving the situation as positively as possible for the people involved/affected?

LIVING ETHICS SITUATION SHEET 3

THE SITUATION

Ed works for Bionate International, a company that is trying to forge an alliance with Zentron, a firm based in another country. Some of Zentron's executives are visiting Bionate on an executive-exchange program designed to facilitate ties between the two firms.

Ed is leading a project team that includes one of Zentron's executives, Marina, as a member. In her role as a team member, Marina has twice violated Bionate's directives. After the first incident, Ed spoke with her about her behavior, and she attributed it to a misunderstanding. After the second incident, Ed again spoke with her, and she essentially said that she couldn't see what all the fuss was about. At this point Ed told his supervisor, Ralph, about Marina's behavior. Ralph, in turn, referred the matter to top management. Now Ralph has told Ed that top management wants Ed to drop the issue and say nothing further about it.

THE TASK

Write answers to the following questions:

1. What ethical conflict(s) does Ed face?

2. In addition to Ed, Marina, and Ralph, who might be affected by Ed's decision?

3. What actions are open to Ed?

4. Which of these actions best meets ethical considerations while resolving the situation as positively as possible for the people involved/affected?

LIVING ETHICS SITUATION SHEET 4

THE SITUATION

Susan is a front-line supervisor. One of her employees, Meg, has been in her department for eight months. Despite Susan's repeated efforts at training and coaching, Meg is performing below an acceptable level. Meg has been given average ratings in the past by the supervisors of three other departments. Susan has talked to these supervisors and has discovered that they acted as they did in order to avoid hassles resulting from Meg's reactions; they explained that Meg files grievances and Equal Employment Opportunity (EEO) complaints on a regular basis. Susan's boss, Barbara, has told Susan to give Meg a superior rating and a glowing recommendation for a vacant position in another division.

THE TASK

Write answers to the following questions:

1. What ethical conflict(s) does Susan face?

2. In addition to Susan, Meg, and Barbara, who might be affected by Susan's decision?

3. What actions are open to Susan?

4. Which of these actions best meets ethical considerations while resolving the situation as positively as possible for the people involved/affected?

Introduction

to the Inventories, Questionnaires, and Surveys Section

Inventories, questionnaires, and surveys are feedback tools that help respondents understand how a particular theory applies to their own lives. Understanding the theories involved in the dynamics of their own group situations increases respondents' involvement. Instruments allow the facilitator of a small group to focus the energies and time of the respondents on the most appropriate material and also to direct, to some extent, the matters that are dealt with in a session. In this way, the facilitator can ensure that the issues worked on are crucial, existing ones, rather than the less important ones that the members may introduce to avoid grappling with the more uncomfortable issues.

The contents of the Inventories, Questionnaires, and Surveys Section are provided for training and development purposes. These instruments are not intended for in-depth personal growth, psychodiagnostic, or therapeutic work. Instead, they are intended for use in training groups; for demonstration purposes; to generate data for training or organization development sessions; and for other group applications in which the trainer, consultant, or facilitator helps respondents to use the data generated by an instrument for achieving some form of progress.

Each instrument includes the theory necessary for understanding, presenting, and using it. All interpretive information, scales or inventory forms, and scoring sheets are also provided for each instrument. In addition, we include all of the reliability and validity data contributed by the authors of instruments; if readers want additional information on reliability and validity, they are encouraged to contact the instrument authors directly. (Authors' addresses and telephone numbers appear in the Contributors list, found near the end of this book.)

Other assessment tools that address certain goals (and experiential learning activities and presentation/discussion resources to accompany

137

them) can be located by using our comprehensive *Reference Guide to Handbooks and Annuals*. This book, which is updated regularly, indexes all the *Annuals* and all the *Handbooks of Structured Experiences* that we have published to date. With each revision, the *Reference Guide* becomes a complete, up-to-date, and easy-to-use resource for selecting appropriate materials from *all* the *Annuals* and *Handbooks*.

The 1997 Annual: Volume 1, Training includes three assessment tools in the following categories:

Individual Development
The Defensiveness Inventory, by Beverly Byrum-Robinson and B.J. Hennig

Communication
The Negotiation-Stance Inventory, by H.B. Karp

Leadership
The Managers for the 21st Century Inventory, by Gaylord Reagan

THE DEFENSIVENESS INVENTORY

Beverly Byrum-Robinson and B.J. Hennig

Abstract: Defensiveness affects a host of communication functions in organizations as well as individual understanding and perceptions, interpersonal effectiveness, work effectiveness, and organizational effectiveness. This article presents a new model of the defensiveness. The Defensiveness Inventory assesses four dimensions of defensive reactions: feelings of fear and sadness, feeling attacked, consequent behaviors, and sensitivity to flaw. Respondents rate twenty-eight items in respect to a critical incident in which they felt defensive. The inventory can be used for self-discovery and growth, team building, coaching in interpersonal relationships, process consulting, performance-appraisal training, and other applications.

Defensiveness—the act of protecting one's self—often is viewed as a serious threat to communication and the subsequent success of organizations (Argyris, 1986; Baker, 1980; Giacalone, 1987; Peterson, 1977; Sussman, 1991). Paradoxically, organizational change efforts breed defensiveness, which occurs when clear communication is most needed.

Baker (1980) cites communication as the most influential variable in organizational effectiveness. Clear communication leads to accurate perceptions and the efficient exchange of information between and among individuals. Messages can be analyzed objectively, which helps in making timely, high-quality, and accepted decisions, which leads to individual and organizational effectiveness. On the other hand, defensive communication can lead to inaccurate perceptions, misinformation, and ineffective decisions.

This article provides a framework for conceptualizing defensiveness and presents a Defensiveness Inventory for use by the HRD practitioner. The inventory can be used in both individual and group interventions.

THE IMPORTANCE OF DEFENSIVENESS

Defensiveness affects employee self-understanding, interpersonal effectiveness, and work effectiveness.

Self-Understanding

Self-understanding is an important prerequisite to understanding and relating with others. Self-understanding is enhanced when one can identify the reasons one becomes defensive and the behaviors one exhibits when defensive. If someone tells a trainer in a training session that he or she does not live in the "real world," so the skills he or she teaches won't work, the trainer feels defensive. The reasons may be:

- The trainer's credibility is being attacked, so he or she feels attacked.

- The trainer feels threatened (someone may think he or she is incompetent).

- The trainer feels angry because he or she thinks the skills being taught are very practical.

Because of these feelings, the trainer switches to a self-protective mode, which results in defensive behaviors. These may include:

- Responding with a sarcastic comment.

- Overexplaining and justifying.

- Asserting his or her status as an expert.

Unfortunately, behaviors such as these are unlikely to change the other person's mind or help the trainer to feel better.

Individuals need to know to what they respond to defensively and how they respond defensively. The focus needs to be on their own behaviors (which are under their control), not on the correctness or fairness of the other person's behavior. In the example above, if the trainer were more aware of the triggering behaviors, he or she could handle the situation better and contribute to a productive outcome.

Interpersonal Effectiveness

Interpersonal effectiveness is the ability to communicate effectively and to resolve problems with others. Controlling defensiveness enhances interpersonal effectiveness. Continuing with the example, if the trainer responds with a sarcastic answer to the person who tells him or her that he or she doesn't live in the "real world," the trainee may not participate for the rest of the session. If the trainer simply reasserts his or her explanation and justification, the trainee may not feel listened to. If the trainer reasserts his or her status as an expert, the trainee will feel discounted.

Thus, defensiveness results in deterioration of communication, which may lead to withdrawal, win/lose arguments, and/or standoffs. None of these situations allow relationships to be built or problems to be solved.

Work Effectiveness

Because defensiveness prevents individuals from establishing trusting relationships, issues cannot be openly discussed; valuable opinions are not offered; and information may be withheld. Problem solving then cannot address all necessary facts. Consequently, defensive behavior polarizes individuals and eliminates the possibility of arriving at creative and collaborative alternatives.

Organizational Effectiveness

To the extent that members of an organization are defensive, organizational productivity suffers. Intra- and interdepartmental communication may be distorted or nonexistent. When the corporate culture is one of protection, the ability to respond to change is reduced.

A MODEL FOR DEFENSIVENESS

The model used for the original defensiveness inventory was based on Ellis' (1974) rational emotive therapy, in which an activating event stimulates certain beliefs about the event, which lead to certain reactions. This model demonstrates that the event does not cause the consequence; what goes on in the mind does. For example, if the activating event is "these ideas won't work in the real world," and the consequence is anger, then the interceding belief may be that "these skills are great and anyone who disagrees is stupid." Ellis also includes a "D" for disputation of irrational beliefs, e.g., "maybe these skills are great in my perception; that doesn't mean that everyone is going to see the benefit in them; I can just try my best to present them as practical tools, and if someone doesn't agree, that's ok." The purpose of this approach is to teach people to control their thinking, so that their reactions and behaviors are more rational (i.e., less defensive).

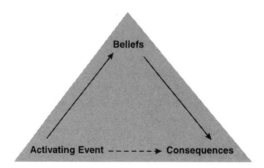

The model was further extended to include the following:

- activating event
- thoughts
- feelings
- physical reactions
- behaviors
- consequences

A situation stimulates defensive thoughts or interpretations, which stimulate emotions and physical reactions. The thoughts and feelings can intensify one another, resulting in behaviors that lead to consequences. For example, the event is an announcement of company downsizing. The thought is "I'm going to lose my job." The feelings are fear and anger. The physical reactions are tension and insomnia. The behavior is inability to concentrate and procrastination. The consequences are poor performance.

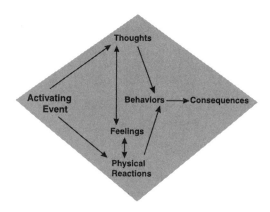

Based on this model, a survey was developed, with items divided into six sections, each section corresponding to an element of the model. Some examples for each follow.

Activating Event:

- I had a personality conflict.
- I thought someone had power over me.
- The other personal verbally attacked me.

Thoughts:

- I thought I was incompetent.
- I thought everyone was out to get me.
- I wanted to "get even."

Feelings:

- I felt ignored.
- I felt hurt.
- I felt scared.

Physical Reactions:

- I cried.

- My heart raced.

- I experienced a surge of energy.

Behaviors:

- I blamed someone else.

- I tried to justify my behavior.

- I lectured the other person.

Consequences:

- I could not perform my job.

- My relationship with the other person improved.

- I detached myself from others.

DEVELOPMENT AND TESTING OF THE INSTRUMENT

The instrument was administered to undergraduates at a large Midwestern university. Part 1 of the instrument consisted of a brief description of defensive behavior. Following this description, respondents were asked to recall and describe an incident in which they became defensive. (In its current form, respondents are asked to respond to a work situation in which they became defensive.) In this methodology, the feelings associated with defensiveness are recalled before the respondent reacts to the items. If a situation could not be recalled, subjects were provided with an incident.

The first step in the data analysis was a factor analysis of the items. A principal-components analysis of the items was conducted using an equamax rotation. An eigenvalue of greater than 4.0 was used to determine the optimal number of factors. The factor analysis yielded a 4 factor solution accounting for 40 percent of the variance in scores.

The first factor appears to cluster around items intended to measure the subjects' emotional reaction to the defensive situation. To a certain extent, the items intended to measure physical symptoms loaded on the same factor.

This may indicate a lack of independence between the physical symptoms and emotional reactions surrounding defensive behavior. This is not surprising, as these two aspects of interaction are highly intertwined and dependent on each other. The highest correlation, however, was among the emotional-reaction statements. Factor one accounted for almost 20 percent of the variance in responses. These items have been retained as a single scale.

Factor two clustered around statements that dealt with emotional feelings of injustice, being attacked, and holding a flawed viewpoint. These items reflect the view of defensive communication that holds that the element of perceived attack in the others' behavior is an antecedent to defensive behavior. Conflict, injustice, and discontent may reflect inner feelings, which give way to defensive behavior as a coping and/or defense mechanism. This scale would be supported in research on defense mechanisms and defensive communication. Factor two accounted for almost 10 percent of the variance in scores.

The third factor clustered around items dealing with both immediate and long-term consequences of defensive behavior. The element of aggression and emotional reaction remains salient in these items. This factor accounted for 8 percent of the total variance in scores.

The final factor clustered around items that tap into the individual's sensitivity to a flaw. In the literature on defensive communication, defensiveness is often instigated by an other's identification of a flaw in the self. The defensive situation may result only when that flaw is one to which the individual is indeed sensitive. This factor accounted for 2 percent of the variance in scores.

Table 1. Summary of Factor Analysis

Factor Loadings

Items	Factor 1 Feelings, Fear, Sadness	Factor 2 Feeling Attacked	Factor 3 Consequent Behaviors	Factor 4 Sensitivity to Flaw
I felt depressed	.7371	.1003	.1078	.0780
I felt scared	.6932	.1614	.0421	.1513
I felt alone	.6747	.0989	.0688	.0338
I felt uncertain	.6669	.0209	.2937	.2307
I thought I was not a good person	.6301	.2413	.0848	.3583
I felt guilty	.6108	.3082	.1242	.1459
I felt ashamed	.6016	.3520	.1809	.2327
I began to tremble	.5986	.3081	.0134	.1763
I felt sad	.5978	.0524	.4027	.1190
I felt hurt	.5953	.2842	.1279	.0115
I felt deflated	.5920	.0648	.0293	.0390

Items	Factor 1 Feelings, Fear, Sadness	Factor 2 Feeling Attacked	Factor 3 Consequent Behaviors	Factor 4 Sensitivity to Flaw
I felt flushed	.5909	.0804	.0957	.1396
I felt uninvolved	.5901	.1408	.2008	.1167
My voice became "shaky"	.5884	.3320	.0818	.2695
I felt inadequate	.5879	.1793	.1831	.1640
I felt disappointed	.5624	.2345	.0271	.0939
I had been wrongly attacked	.2371	.4770	.0258	.0800
I felt a sense of injustice	.0578	.4345	.0920	.0126
I had a "personality conflict" with someone	.1409	.4247	.3419	.1343
I felt discounted	.0787	.4225	.0571	.1773
I realized there was a flaw in my viewpoint	.3217	.4221	.0061	.0299
I wanted to hurt the person(s) that made me defensive	.3898	.0223	.6065	.1465
I wanted to damage something	.3889	.0319	.5745	.2313
I lectured the person	.1251	.1852	.5068	.4806
I wanted to get even	.3988	.1465	.2709	.0702
I became defensive toward person(s) similar to those involved in this situation	.3280	.0432	.4380	.0200
I screamed	.3010	.1152	.1107	.4723
I did not let the other person talk	.2359	.2913	.2136	.4055
I thought that I was different/did not belong	.2703	.1350	.0553	.4051
I cried	.2923	.1154	.1106	.4011
I thought my values/ beliefs were attacked/ challenged	.1231	.0024	.1310	.3209
I felt uncomfortable with my surroundings	.1904	.0302	.2206	.3050
I was emotional about the topic	.2756	.2718	.0617	.3032

Items with common factor loadings were retained for use in the final version of the instrument. Statements loading on more than one factor were discarded. The following are the remaining statements, grouped according to the four factors described earlier.

Factor 1: Feelings, Fear, Sadness

I felt depressed.
I felt scared
I felt alone.
I felt uncertain.
I felt ashamed.
I felt hurt.
I felt deflated.
I felt flushed.
My voice became "shaky."
I felt inadequate.
I felt disappointed.

Factor 2: Feeling Attacked

I had been wrongly attacked.
I felt a sense of injustice.
I had a "personality conflict" with someone.
I felt discounted.
I realized there was a flaw in my viewpoint.

Factor 3: Consequent Behaviors

I wanted to hurt the person(s) that made me defensive.
I wanted to damage something.
I lectured the person.
I wanted to get even.
I became defensive toward person(s) similar to those involved in this situation.

Factor 4: Sensitivity to Flaw

I screamed.
I did not let the other person talk.
I thought that I was different/did not belong.
I cried.
I thought my values/beliefs were attacked/challenged.
I felt uncomfortable with my surroundings.
I was emotional about the topic.

Based on the findings, an adjusted model of defensiveness was adopted, as follows:

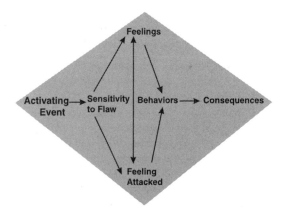

Gender Differences

The following are the gender differences from the original inventory, administered to 136 students in a university communications course (fifty-five males, eighty-one females). Differences in percentages by gender are rounded to the nearest whole number.

	Agree Male % Female %	Disagree % %

Agree **Disagree**
Male % %
Female % %

1. I thought my values/beliefs were attacked/challenged
   M 31   10
   F 46   14

2. I felt uncertain
   M 21   19
   F 33   27

3. I had been wrongly attacked
   M 33   7
   F 48   11

4. I wanted to damage something
   M 17   24
   F 27   33

5. I realized there was flaw in my viewpoint
   M 15   26
   F 20   40

6. I felt deflated
   M 27   14
   F 38   22

7. I felt uncomfortable with my surroundings
   M 19   21
   F 32   28

8. I felt scared
   M 14   26
   F 25   35

9. I felt a sense of injustice
   M 29   11
   F 50   10

10. I wanted to hurt the person(s) who made me defensive
    M 19   22
    F 28   32

11. I felt emotional about the topic
    M 34   7
    F 50   10

12. I felt disappointed
    M 28   13
    F 47   13

13. I felt discounted
    M 25   10
    F 54   11

14. I felt depressed
    M 19   21
    F 36   24

15. I lectured the person
    M 22   19
    F 32   28

16. I screamed
    M 13   27
    F 27   33

17. I felt inadequate
    M 14   26
    F 32   28

18. I cried
    M 7   33
    F 20   40

19. I wanted to get even
    M 19   22
    F 28   32

20. My voice became shaky
    M 18   22
    F 28   32

21. I did not let the other person talk
    M 17   23
    F 28   33

22. I felt alone
    M 22   19
    F 30   30

23. I had a "personality conflict" with someone
    M 23   17
    F 35   25

24. I felt hurt
    M 26   14
    F 46   14

25. I felt flushed
    M 20   20
    F 36   23

26. I thought that I was different/did not belong
    M 16   24
    F 20   39

27. I felt ashamed
    M 14   25
    F 20   41

28. I became defensive toward persons similar to those involved in the situation
    M 18   24
    F 37   21

Instrument Items and Scaling

The final version of the Defensiveness Inventory consists of twenty-eight items. The items ask participants to respond to each statement in terms of how often this statement applied to them in the critical incidents they are remembering. As an option, a critical incident can be given to participants so that they all have the same point of reference for responding. A six-point Likert scale ranging from (1) "never applied to me" to (6) "always applied to me" is used. Individual scores are then calculated for each of the four dimensions described previously.

The six-point scale is utilized because it has been shown that an even number of response options forces people to take a stand, as opposed to an odd number of responses, which encourages a tendency toward the mean. This information is not of the same value when attempting to compare responses to the mean (Paul & Bracken, 1995).

Potential Uses of the Instrument

In addition to being used as a self-discovery tool, the Defensiveness Inventory has the following uses:

- The inventory can be completed by peers and used in a feedback session. This would work particularly well in a team-building session focusing on interpersonal feedback.

- The inventory can be used as a coaching tool for an employee who wishes to improve interpersonal relationships. The coach may complete the form and/or have others complete the form for the person being coached before discussing results.

- The inventory can be followed by an experiential activity such as a role play. If the participants thought of their own critical incidents, various critical incidents can be role-played and processed. If a critical incident is given with the inventory, that also can be role-played. Additionally, the critical incidents could be reenacted to have more productive outcomes after the discussion of theory.

- The inventory can be used in process consulting. Behavioral parts of the inventory could be used by an observer, or the entire inventory could be administered during process-consultation interviews.

The results could be fed back to the team to increase knowledge of the incidents that stimulate defensiveness.

- The inventory can be used in performance-appraisal training to demonstrate how people become defensive in that type of evaluative situation.

- If the critical incidents are supplied, participants can rewrite them to show how the situation could have been avoided or how they could reduce defensiveness.

ADMINISTRATION OF THE DEFENSIVENESS INVENTORY

The Defensiveness Inventory should be administered before any lecturette on the topic of defensiveness is offered. Having participants complete the instrument before discussing the topic will lessen their tendency to react to the items in socially desirable ways.

To begin, provide each participant a copy of the Defensiveness Inventory and read the instructions aloud, telling the participants that they have ten minutes in which to complete the inventory, if given an incident, and fifteen minutes, if they are remembering and recording their own.[1]

Make certain that the participants understand that they are to respond to the items in terms of their feelings and behaviors that occurred during their personal incidents. If the critical incident is provided to the participants, instruct them to respond as if they were in that situation.

Scoring

After participants have completed the inventory, ask them to transfer the number they assigned to each item to the appropriate column on the Defensiveness Inventory Scoring Sheet and to total each of the four columns. After they have completed the totals, instruct them to plot their results on the Defensiveness Inventory Profile.

Interpretation and Presentation of Theory

A discussion on the interpretation of participants' scores may begin with the definition of defensiveness provided on the inventory. The facilitator may

---

[1] Some general critical incidents are supplied following this article for the facilitator's use. If training a homogeneous group, one can create critical incidents based on the group's work.

ask the participants how the definition fits for them. The facilitator may also ask how the incident(s) they used influenced their answers.

After the discussion, the model for defensiveness should be provided, accompanied by an explanation of each of the four dimensions of defensiveness. As an explanation of the model and its four elements is presented, the facilitator may ask the participants how they scored on each element. According to the results on their profiles, they will be more or less likely to exhibit the behaviors, feelings, or thoughts associated with each factor. The higher the score on each factor, the more likely the respondent is to display behaviors described by that factor. The percentages along each factor line indicate the total percentage of people, in a sample of 120, who were as likely as the respondent to display behaviors described by that factor.

The processing questions that follow will help lead participants to applications of the learnings from the instrument.

Processing Questions

To improve application, participants can partner with one another before the total-group processing session to discuss their highest and lowest scores and their reactions. The following questions can be asked of participants after they complete the inventory, score it, and hear the theory and interpretation presentations. Scores also can be posted to exhibit any intergroup differences (i.e., between genders, between personal/business situations, between real and provided critical incidents). Normative data follows this discussion.

- What was your highest score? Your lowest? What does that mean to you?

- How does your score fit with the norms? What does that mean to you? How do you feel about that?

- Did anyone notice any gender differences? How does that fit for you?

- How do you think your inventory would have been different if you had thought of a personal, rather than a professional, situation? What does that tell you?

- What have you learned about yourself and defensiveness?

- What have you learned about defensiveness in general?

- What is your hypothesis about how defensiveness affects work relationships? How does it affect the organization?

- What do you want to try to do differently in the future? What reactions or behaviors would you like to change on the job? At home?

- What have you learned about sending messages that engender defensiveness? How might you change your own messages to decrease the likelihood of defensive reactions from others?

References

Argyris, C. (1986). Reinforcing organizational defensive routines: An unintended human resource activity. *Human Resource Managment, 25*(4), 541-555.

Baker, W.H. (1980). Defensiveness in communication: Its causes, effects, and cures. *Journal of Business Communication, 17*(3), 33-43.

Ellis, A. (1974). *A guide to rational living.* Englewood Cliffs, NJ: Prentice Hall.

Giacalone, R.A. (1987). Reducing the need for defensive communication. *Management Solutions, 37*(9), 70-75.

Paul, K.B., & Bracken, P.D.W. (1995, January). Everything you wanted to know about employee surveys. *Training & Development,* p. 2.

Peterson, R. (1977). Are "self-defenses" keeping you from being a better manager? *Supervisory Management, 22*(9), 71-74.

Sussman, L. (1991). Managers on the defensive. *Business Horizons, 34*(1), 81-87.

Beverly Byrum-Robinson, Ph.D., is a full professor in the department of communication at Wright State University in Dayton, Ohio. She also is president of the Communication Connection. She conducts seminars on topics such as interpersonal skills, team building, stress and time management, and assertiveness and, as a consultant, she facilitates team-building sessions in organizations. She has written one book, has coauthored three others, and has published numerous articles on interpersonal and group communications and training.

B. J. Hennig is a manufacturing training specialist for the Iams Company in Dayton, Ohio. In addition to his training design and delivery responsibilities, he has implemented a variety of computer-based training programs, numerous needs assessments, instruction in strategic planning, and an acclimation process for international employees. He also is responsible for evaluating new technologies for use in training.

DEFENSIVENESS INVENTORY SAMPLE CRITICAL INCIDENTS

1. Chris enters Casey's office and puts a report on the desk saying, "I need to talk to you about this. There are a number of holes in the recommendations. If the report is presented the way it is now, we'll never gain acceptance. You need to do some more research to substantiate your recommendations. I'm not sure why you didn't do that in the first place."

   If you were Casey, you would:

2. Sue has just presented her proposed advertising plan to the other vice presidents The v.p. of engineering says, "You can't make those kinds of claims. We're nowhere near that target in our development. Where did you get your information? That'll play havoc with the company image."

   If you were Sue, you would:

3. Dale is conducting a performance appraisal for Jo. Dale says, "It seems that you have completed only half of your objectives for the year. What is your explanation for that?"

   If you were Jo, you would:

4. Tim and Tom are working together to assemble manuals in a last-minute rush for a course the next day. Tom says to Tim, "Can you speed it up? We'll never get out of here. Why was this left until the last minute, anyway?"

   If you were Tim, you would:

DEFENSIVENESS INVENTORY

Beverly Byrum-Robinson and B.J. Hennig

Introduction: Defensiveness is a feeling that almost everyone has experienced. It is human nature to defend ourselves against various types of psychological attacks, dangers, or injuries. Degrees of defensiveness may vary, as may the types of responses. In addition, we may feel more defensive on some days than on others. The purpose of this self-discovery inventory is to explore some of the characteristics of defensiveness so that you may better understand your communication behavior during situations of this kind. The inventory will take approximately ten minutes to complete.

Instructions: Think of an incident at work in which you became extremely defensive. What triggered it? Who was involved? How did you feel? What did you say and do? What was the outcome? Based on the experience, rate the extent to which the items presented below describe your reactions in the situation. Please read each statement carefully and respond by circling the appropriate number for each item. Your first response is usually the most honest.

Key to Ratings

Strongly Agree	Agree	Slightly Agree	Slightly Disagree	Disagree	Strongly Disagree
1	2	3	4	5	6

1. I thought my values/beliefs were attacked/challenged	1	2	3	4	5	6
2. I felt uncertain	1	2	3	4	5	6
3. I had been wrongly attacked	1	2	3	4	5	6
4. I wanted to damage something	1	2	3	4	5	6
5. I realized there was flaw in my viewpoint	1	2	3	4	5	6
6. I felt deflated	1	2	3	4	5	6
7. I felt uncomfortable with my surroundings	1	2	3	4	5	6
8. I felt scared	1	2	3	4	5	6

Strongly Agree 1	Agree 2	Slightly Agree 3	Slightly Disagree 4	Disagree 5	Strongly Disagree 6

9. I felt a sense of injustice   1   2   3   4   5   6

10. I wanted to hurt the person(s) who made me defensive   1   2   3   4   5   6

11. I felt emotional about the topic   1   2   3   4   5   6

12. I felt disappointed   1   2   3   4   5   6

13. I felt discounted   1   2   3   4   5   6

14. I felt depressed   1   2   3   4   5   6

15. I lectured the person   1   2   3   4   5   6

16. I screamed   1   2   3   4   5   6

17. I felt inadequate   1   2   3   4   5   6

18. I cried   1   2   3   4   5   6

19. I wanted to get even   1   2   3   4   5   6

20. My voice became "shaky"   1   2   3   4   5   6

21. I did not let the other person talk   1   2   3   4   5   6

22. I felt alone   1   2   3   4   5   6

23. I had a "personality conflict" with someone   1   2   3   4   5   6

24. I felt hurt   1   2   3   4   5   6

25. I felt flushed   1   2   3   4   5   6

26. I thought that I was different/did not belong   1   2   3   4   5   6

27. I felt ashamed   1   2   3   4   5   6

28. I became defensive toward persons similar to those involved in the situation   1   2   3   4   5   6

DEFENSIVENESS INVENTORY SCORING SHEET

Instructions: From your completed Defensiveness Inventory, transfer your responses to the appropriate squares below. For example, if you have circled a 2 on item 13, write 2 in the square numbered 13.

Once you have transferred your scores, calculate a total for each column on the line provided. These are your factor scores, to be transferred to your Defensiveness Inventory Profile Sheet.

F1	F2	F3	F4
Scoring Box			
#2 _____	#3 _____	#4 _____	#1 _____
#6 _____	#5 _____	#10 _____	#7 _____
#8 _____	#9 _____	#15 _____	#11 _____
#12 _____	#13 _____	#19 _____	#16 _____
#14 _____	#23 _____	#28 _____	#18 _____
#17 _____			#21 _____
#20 _____			#26 _____
#22 _____			
#24 _____			
#25 _____			
#27 _____			
Factor Scores F1 = _____	F2 = _____	F3 = _____	F4 = _____

DEFENSIVENESS INVENTORY PROFILE SHEET

Instructions: Transfer your factor scores from the Scoring Sheet to the boxes below. Once you have done this, plot each score at the appropriate point along the Factor Line. The lower your score (vertically), the more likely you are to display behaviors described by the factor.

The percentages along each Factor Line indicate the total percentage of people in a sample of 120 who were as likely as you to display the behaviors described by each factor.

	F1. Feelings of Fear	F2. Feeling Attacked	F3. Consequent Behaviors	F4. Sensitivity to Flaw
Factor Percent				
1	11 — 12%	5 — 26%	5 — 10%	7 — 10%
2	22 — 21%	10 — 23%	10 — 13%	14 — 20%
3	33 — 21%	15 — 22%	15 — 20%	21 — 19%
4	44 — 14%	20 — 12%	20 — 14%	28 — 13%
5	55 — 17%	25 — 14%	25 — 25%	35 — 23%
6	66 — 15%	30 — 3%	30 — 18%	42 — 15%

DEFENSIVENESS INVENTORY INTERPRETATION SHEET

Factor One

Scoring above the mean on factor one, **feelings of fear and sadness**, indicates that in a defensive situation, you experience the more "passive" emotions of anxiety and hurt. You may feel inadequate to deal with the situation and may find it difficult to argue for your point of view.

Scoring below the mean on factor one may indicate confidence in your viewpoint, regardless of disconfirming messages. You may also have the ability to avoid taking things personally.

Factor Two

Scoring above the mean on factor two, **feeling attacked**, indicates that in a defensive situation, you experience more "active" emotions of anger and conflict. You may tend to believe that the situation is being handled unfairly or addressed inappropriately. These feelings may lead you to defend your point of view.

Scoring below the mean on factor two may indicate the ability to see both sides of an issue without feeling threatened.

Factor Three

Scoring above the mean on factor three, **consequent behaviors**, indicates that, in a defensive situation, you want to take strong action toward the situation or person. You may tend to hold on to defensive feelings until your desired resolution is attained.

Scoring below the mean on factor three may indicate an ability to control aggressive emotional reactions.

Factor Four

Scoring above the mean on factor four, **sensitivity to flaw**, may indicate a variety of strong feelings and responses to the situation. The behaviors and feelings in this factor are emotionally extreme, from feeling different to emotional outbursts of crying and screaming. These extreme reactions may stem from a general oversensitivity when you are challenged.

Scoring below the mean on factor four may indicate a general self-confidence and ability to handle challenges with extreme reactions.

Scoring high on factors one and two and low on factors three and four may indicate that you hold your emotions of defensiveness inside, rather than acting them out or expressing them. Conversely, scoring high on factors three and four may indicate a tendency to act at the time on your emotional state.

SUGGESTIONS FOR IMPROVEMENT

Defensiveness may be reduced by learning any of the following skills:

- **Self-talk:** to view the other person's comments as information about his or her viewpoint rather than as information about you

- **Perception checking:** to determine if what you are perceiving the situation to be is correct

- **Paraphrasing:** to understand the other person's point of view

- **Calling time out** and setting an appointment to talk at a future time

- **Using "I" messages** to express to the other person how his or her messages affected you

- **Requesting** that the person word his or her concern in a way that is easier for you to hear it

- **Asking open-ended questions** to elicit the other person's real concerns, i.e., what the person wants/needs

- **Asking for** specifics, examples, or preferences

- **Using conflict-management skills** to move toward resolution of the issue, as opposed to focusing on the problem

THE NEGOTIATION-STANCE INVENTORY

H.B. Karp

Abstract: With the emphasis on both teamwork and individual empowerment in today's organizations, the development of negotiation skills is particularly important. However, there is an important step that precedes that skill development: learning how one views the process of negotiation. Some people see negotiation as an odious experience to be avoided at all costs; some see it as an opportunity to obtain essential resources, thereby benefiting themselves, their opponents in the negotiation, and the organization. There are also stances between these two extremes.

The author's contention is that some people may possess the necessary skills to negotiate, but they are unwilling to participate in the process. For these people, training in negotiation skills would be inappropriate. Therefore, the author has designed an instrument that helps the respondent to clarify his or her own attitude toward negotiation. This instrument would provide an excellent beginning to a workshop on negotiation: It can be completed in about ten minutes, respondents score their own inventories, and the instrument is accompanied by both an interpretation sheet and a rationale sheet.

INTRODUCTION

Organizations are becoming increasingly more team oriented and, at the same time, more focused on the empowerment of the individual worker. With this orientation, the need to negotiate from a position of strength and confidence has become extremely important to those who are accountable for decisions at all levels of the organization. Both teams and individuals are expected to be more effective in obtaining what they need in the work setting and less dependent on those in higher authority to simply grant or deny their requests.

A clear and easily understood definition of *negotiation* is "a process in which two or more parties, with common and conflicting interests, come together to discuss ways to reach agreement." The need to negotiate effectively has always been apparent in traditional situations such as management-labor relations or the purchase of supplies and equipment. Now, however, negotiation is becoming just as important in nontraditional situations. For example, it is used in dealing with customers' service issues, in setting prices, in bartering with fellow team members concerning the allocation of assets and opportunities (such as vacation times or work load), and in other situations in which resources or opportunities are limited.

People may have difficulty with the negotiation process because either (1) they do not possess the skills needed to engage others effectively or (2) they do not possess the fortitude or perspective to engage fully in the negotiation process. Those in the first category need to learn the tactics and strategies of effective negotiating and bargaining. Many excellent training programs address the needed skills; and many experts can show people how to engage in negotiations, maintain the upper hand, and determine where the pitfalls lie.

If skills were the only consideration, organizations could have all employees trained and ready to negotiate at a moment's notice. However, the greater problem is a lack of fortitude or perspective. Regardless of latent ability, many people avoid negotiating because they see themselves as weaker or less aggressive than the other party and/or because they are painfully uncomfortable with the negotiation process. For example, many people are willing to pay almost list price for an automobile because they want to escape from a conflict-ridden, pressure-laden encounter.

The option is to see the negotiation process from a more positive perspective. To do that, a person has to recognize how he or she presently views negotiation.

The Negotiation-Stance Inventory helps participants to discover how they experience the negotiation process and to what extent they resist it. A high score on the Negotiation-Stance Inventory indicates that regardless of the effectiveness of a negotiation-skills program, the participant is unlikely to internalize or value the learning. Consequently, the first step after completing the inventory is to establish a view of negotiating as a positive and essential process.

THE INSTRUMENT

The Negotiation-Stance Inventory helps a participant understand the extent to which he or she is comfortable in engaging in negotiations with another person. It consists of fifteen items, each of which the participant answers with a number on a seven-point scale, ranging from "Strongly Disagree" to "Strongly Agree."

The Negotiation-Stance Inventory Scoring Sheet allows participants to score the inventory themselves. They can then read the Negotiation-Stance Inventory Interpretation Sheet, draw their own conclusions about the implications of their scores, and use those conclusions as a basis for group discussion and for developing a positive attitude toward negotiation.

The Negotiation-Stance Inventory Rationale Sheet, which is based on Gestalt theory,[1] emphasizes the need for individual strength and self-support in the negotiating process. The preferred answer for each item is explained in terms of the participant's:

- Not taking responsibility for the other person's feelings or actions;

- Being willing to recognize his or her own right to be successful and obtain what is wanted; and

- Recognizing and respecting the other person as an opponent, instead of viewing the opponent as an adversary with evil intentions.

Validity and Reliability

No validity or reliability data are available on the Negotiation-Stance Inventory. However, the instrument has face validity, as its purpose is to make participants more aware of their views on negotiating.

---

[1] The facilitator does not have to be familiar with Gestalt theory to use the inventory.

Uses of the Instrument

The Negotiation-Stance Inventory was designed as part of a training module on negotiation and is valuable when administered as the opening activity. However, other uses are possible (for example, as a warmup activity prior to actual negotiations).

Administering and Scoring the Instrument

A copy of the Negotiation-Stance Inventory is distributed to each participant, who is given approximately ten minutes to complete the fifteen-item form.

After all participants have completed the instrument, the facilitator distributes copies of the Negotiation-Stance Inventory Scoring Sheet and explains the scoring process, *reminding participants that the scoring is reversed on items 2, 10, and 15.* Scoring takes about seven minutes.

Interpretation

When the scoring process has been completed, the facilitator distributes copies of the Negotiation-Stance Inventory Interpretation Sheet. Either the participants read this handout silently, or they follow along as the facilitator reads it aloud. If the participants read silently, the facilitator reviews the highlights of the sheet afterward.

Next the facilitator distributes copies of the Negotiation-Stance Inventory Rationale Sheet and asks the participants to read this sheet. Subgroups of three to five members each are then formed, and the members of each subgroup are asked to devise a list of ideas, issues, and questions that they would like to discuss in the total group. The facilitator clarifies that items on the list should be focused on how to improve attitudes toward negotiation.

One important point that the facilitator should make is that the participants' scores have to do with the way they feel about negotiating, not with their negotiation skills. Those who made the "poorest" scores (that is, those who had the highest numbers) may be the most effective negotiators—when they allow themselves to negotiate. The most important question for this discussion is "How are we stopping ourselves from negotiating when we already know how to do it?"

Once this point has been made, the balance of the training can take one of several directions, such as the following:

1. If the group is Gestalt oriented, the facilitator can link negotiation to the Gestalt-theory base of the inventory and demonstrate how

developing clear personal boundaries can enhance one's effectiveness as a negotiator.

2. The awareness gained from the inventory can support a discussion of various strategies and tactics of negotiating.

3. The participants may engage in role plays designed to provide practice in negotiating in a nonthreatening environment. After the role plays, experiential outcomes would be discussed.

H.B. Karp, Ph.D., is presently on the faculty of management of Christopher Newport University in Newport News, Virginia. He also is the owner of Personal Growth Systems, a management-consulting firm in Chesapeake, Virginia. He consults with a variety of Fortune 500 and governmental organizations in the areas of leadership development, team building, conflict management, and executive coaching. He specializes in applying Gestalt theory to issues of individual growth and organizational effectiveness. He is the author of many articles, of Personal Power: An Unorthodox Guide to Success, *and of* The Change Leader: Using a Gestalt Approach with Work Groups.

NEGOTIATION-STANCE INVENTORY

H.B. Karp

Instructions: This inventory consists of fifteen statements. You are asked how strongly you agree or disagree with each. Evaluate each statement as honestly as you can. Although you may realize that exceptions occur, use your best judgment and choose the response that describes your point of view most of the time. Use the following scale to indicate your choices:

> SD = Strongly Disagree
> D = Disagree
> DS = Disagree Slightly
> N = Neutral
> AS = Agree Slightly
> A = Agree
> SA = Strongly Agree

_____ 1. Negotiating is basically an undignified and messy process.

_____ 2. I am fundamentally comfortable with conflict and confrontation.

_____ 3. If I cannot have it all, I would just as soon have nothing.

_____ 4. I refuse to negotiate with people I do not like.

_____ 5. I do not like taking a strong stance with others, because it could hurt their feelings.

_____ 6. If people just knew why I wanted what I want, they would be more willing to give it to me.

_____ 7. If I am a good team player or organizational member, I should not have to negotiate for what I want.

_____ 8. When I am in a negotiating position with another person, part of my responsibility is to see that we both obtain as much of what we want as we can.

_____ 9. People who resist the rules and demands of the organization are just being selfish and do not have the organization's best interests at heart.

SD = Strongly Disagree
D = Disagree
DS = Disagree Slightly
N = Neutral
AS = Agree Slightly
A = Agree
SA = Strongly Agree

_____ 10. Resistance is a natural part of the negotiating process. It should be honored and dealt with openly.

_____ 11. In any negotiation, it is important for both sides to maintain a friendly, cooperative stance from the outset.

_____ 12. Going for a win-win outcome is the only way to approach a negotiation.

_____ 13. Negotiating is based on greed. It would be far better for people just to share equally in the resources.

_____ 14. If someone takes advantage of me in a negotiation, he or she cannot be trusted, and I will never negotiate with that person again.

_____ 15. My initial objective in any negotiation is to obtain all of what I want.

NEGOTIATION-STANCE INVENTORY
SCORING SHEET

Instructions: For all items *except numbers 2, 10, and 15,* the scoring is as follows:

$$SD = 1 \text{ point}$$
$$D = 2 \text{ points}$$
$$DS = 3 \text{ points}$$
$$N = 4 \text{ points}$$
$$AS = 5 \text{ points}$$
$$A = 6 \text{ points}$$
$$SA = 7 \text{ points}$$

For items **2, 10,** and **15** only, the scoring reverses and the points are assigned as follows:

$$SD = 7 \text{ points}$$
$$D = 6 \text{ points}$$
$$DS = 5 \text{ points}$$
$$N = 4 \text{ points}$$
$$AS = 3 \text{ points}$$
$$A = 2 \text{ points}$$
$$SA = 1 \text{ point}$$

Add the numbers you assigned to your responses for the fifteen items, and write the sum in the blank below.

Total Score _____

NEGOTIATION-STANCE INVENTORY
INTERPRETATION SHEET

Range of Scores	Interpretation
15-33	You have an excellent negotiation stance. You are strong and flexible and maintain a realistic perspective of the negotiating process. Your time-and-place orientation is "right now, right here." Although you respect others and acknowledge that they have just as much right to want what they want as you do, you realize that they will take care of themselves. You recognize that in a universe of limited resources, negotiating is the most effective and civilized way of obtaining what you want.
34-50	You are usually a willing negotiator, but a few areas (those items on which you scored 6 or 7 points) tend to be blind spots for you. You can and will negotiate, but you sometimes wish there were an easier way to obtain what you want. You are reasonably comfortable with conflict if it does not last too long or become too heated. You maintain good working relationships, for the most part, but prefer others to be a little more cooperative in helping you obtain what you want.
51-69	Negotiating is difficult for you. Although others may have needs, you believe those needs are, frankly, just not as important as yours. Although you can and will negotiate on some things, you believe you should not have to. You believe that you have earned the right to the resource; and, if others want to be considered, they should work as hard or be as entitled as you. You are uncomfortable with conflict and confrontation; you view negotiating as conflict producing and, therefore, harmful to those involved.
70-88	You consider negotiating to be compromising, and you want little to do with it. You view people who are competing with you for some resource or outcome as the "enemy" and untrustworthy. You abhor conflict and confrontation and will go to almost any length to avoid them. You believe that the most important thing is for you to be treated fairly; no one else should receive more of the resource or outcome than you. If resources have to be shared, then you believe they should be shared equally, as a point of policy.
89+	You refuse to negotiate. If you have to negotiate to obtain what you want, you will do without it. You do not want anyone but yourself to receive anything, but you are unwilling to "fight" about it. Your philosophy is "If, for some reason, I can't have it all, then I don't want any of it. That'll show them!"

NEGOTIATION-STANCE INVENTORY
RATIONALE SHEET

For each item of the Negotiation-Stance Inventory, the original statement is listed below, along with the preferred response and the rationale for preferring that response.

1. Negotiating is basically an undignified and messy process.

Preferred Response: SD

As long as people approach negotiation from this position, they will view the process as being beneath them. It is a way for them to avoid the difficulty of negotiating while maintaining an acceptable self-image.

2. I am fundamentally comfortable with conflict and confrontation.

Preferred Response: SA

Viewing conflict as a natural and positive condition among people who have different needs or perspectives is essential for developing creative solutions. Being hurt is not inevitable in a conflict situation.

3. If I cannot have it all, I would just as soon have nothing.

Preferred Response: SD

This position not only blocks any chance of coming out of the negotiation with anything of value; it also identifies the person who holds this position as a self-styled martyr. This position will also reduce the probability of positive outcomes in any future negotiations.

4. I refuse to negotiate with people I do not like.

Preferred Response: SD

Negotiation is not a social event. Liking or disliking should play no part in how one conducts a negotiation. In fact, liking an adversary too much can often lead a person to softening his or her position inappropriately, because a "friend" is being dealt with. At the minimum, negotiators need to achieve some social distance from each other.

5. I do not like taking a strong stance with others, because it could hurt their feelings.

Preferred Position: SD

In any conflict situation, there is a chance that someone's feelings will be hurt. Behavior that will hurt someone should be avoided whenever feasible, but fear of hurting should never be used as an excuse not to engage in negotiations. Once it is discovered that someone takes this position, all the other person has to do to "win" is appear to be emotionally injured.

6. If people just knew why I wanted what I want, they would be more willing to give it to me.

Preferred Position: SD

Unless there is a hidden benefit for the other person to receive what you want, this negotiating position is a myth. Once you attempt to convince the other person that your motivation is superior to his or hers, you immediately lower your position and take a defensive stance. In other words, once you begin explaining why you want what you want, the other person can easily say, "Sorry, not good enough." Rather than revealing your reasons, you can put the other person in a defensive position by demanding, "What is your objection to my having this?"

7. If I am a good team player or organizational member, I should not have to negotiate for what I want.

Preferred Position: SD

This position suggests that one is rewarded for good work by having the system anticipate and meet one's needs. That is not the way the system works. One is rewarded by pay, bonus, or opportunity for growth and development. The available resources, on the other hand, go to the people who can make the best case for receiving them. In fact, the "good team player and organizational member" is frequently identified by his or her ability and willingness to negotiate effectively.

8. When I am in a negotiating position with another person, part of my responsibility is to see that we both obtain as much of what we want as we can.

Preferred Position: SD

The objective of any negotiation is to come to an agreement that all parties can actively support. This goal is best accomplished by taking full responsibility for getting what you want and allowing the other person to do the same. Beware the salesperson who wants to make a deal on an automobile that is "fair" to both of you. If you are looking out for the salesperson's welfare and he or she is also looking out for his or her own welfare, then who is looking out for your welfare? Offer to pay the *list* price and see if the salesperson counters with "Oh, no, no, no! That's way too much! We can do *much* better than that!"

9. *People who resist the rules and demands of the organization are just being selfish and do not have the organization's best interests at heart.*

Preferred Response: SD

The most positive aspect of negotiating is that it provides a process for people who have different views to surface as much information as possible. Discussing or arguing these differences increases the number of options. If a win-win strategy is adopted, the broader the view the better.

10. *Resistance is a natural part of the negotiating process. It should be honored and dealt with openly.*

Preferred Response: SA

If receiving what is best for yourself and the organization is the preferred situation, then resisting what is worst is every bit as beneficial. People will naturally resist things that they view as harmful to themselves and their objectives, regardless of who says that they should or should not. Openly expressing that resistance gives you and the other person an opportunity to discover where the blocks occur and an opportunity to address them.

11. *In any negotiation, it is important for both sides to maintain a friendly, cooperative stance from the outset.*

Preferred Response: SD

The time to develop and maintain a friendly, cooperative relationship is after the negotiations have been concluded. Placing a value on warm relationships may ease the negotiating process, but it also softens the edges and diminishes the probability that all parties will emerge with the best possible outcome. Although hostile and aggressive positions should also be avoided, a reasonable amount of distance is desirable.

12. *Going for a win-win outcome is the only way to approach a negotiation.*

Preferred Position: SD

A win-win outcome is the preferred position in most negotiations but not in every case. A win-win solution is particularly important when there is an ongoing relationship between the negotiators, when there is a condition of mutual accountability for the outcome, or when this negotiation will have an impact on future negotiations. However, a win-lose outcome may be preferred if a fixed amount of resource is available with no options, if there is a tradition of competition between the parties, or if only a win-lose option is available (for example, when buying an automobile).

13. Negotiating is based on greed. It would be far better for people just to share equally in the resources.

Preferred Position: SD

This position, although appearing somewhat reasonable, is the ultimate strategy of the conflict avoider. Not only does it disempower people and keep them dependent; it also does not take into account the outcome. This position does not consider what is needed, why it is needed, and by whom it is needed. The inevitable result would be a mediocre to poor solution.

14. If someone takes advantage of me in a negotiation, he or she cannot be trusted, and I will never negotiate with that person again.

Preferred Response: SD

Although this position is an understandable response to being taken advantage of, it is an ineffective approach to negotiation. The painful reality is that if you were taken advantage of, you let it happen and you should assume responsibility for your behavior. A much better response is to learn from the experience and take a different approach next time. Rather than refusing to deal with the person again, let him or her know that you are aware of the past behavior, and point out that he or she is going to find it much tougher now to get anything from you as a result of it. Then demand some kind of collateral or escrow up-front to guard against that person's unethical tactics.

15. My initial objective in any negotiation is to obtain all of what I want.

Preferred Response: SA

The operative term here is "initial." The clearer you are about what you want in the beginning, the easier it will be to make reasonable concessions later. If you walk into the negotiations ready to compromise from the first word, you will have little left to bargain with when you arrive at the tougher points.

THE MANAGERS FOR THE
21ST CENTURY INVENTORY

Gaylord Reagan

Abstract: A search of the literature has revealed a new model of management for the 21st Century. This model encompasses new skills and behaviors that have not been taught in traditional management training programs.

Part One of the Managers for the 21st Century Inventory assesses individuals' awareness of and agreement with the new management behaviors; presents specific characteristics, activities, and tasks of modern managers; and helps respondents to develop action plans for improving their awareness of and skills in implementing new management behaviors. Part Two asks respondents to state the percentages of weekly time they spend on specific activities, presents research on the percentages of time that successful and effective managers spend on those specific functions, and helps respondents to develop action plans.

THE SEARCH FOR A NEW MODEL OF MANAGEMENT

Employers, trainers, and consultants attempt to teach managers the basic skills they are perceived to need. As a rule, curricula presenting these skills are built around a traditional model that emphasizes planning, leading, organizing, controlling, and staffing—often referred to as the PLOCS model (see Haimann, 1984). Countless exercises and simulations have helped new managers master the basics of these five skills. Thus fortified, the new managers enter the workplace, where they often find that their just-completed courses have not adequately prepared them for what they encounter there.

A list of major factors contributing to managerial failures makes scant mention of PLOCS skills. Instead, top factors include:

1. An inability to get along with others.

2. A failure to adapt to change.

3. Demonstrating a "me first" attitude.

4. A fear of taking action.

5. An inability to rebound from past failures.

6. Being overwhelmed by the pressure of "external catalysts."

Many authors attempt to remedy this situation by first identifying behavioral traits that are common to successful managers and then packaging the identified traits into models that can be taught in seminars. Classic examples of this approach can be found in Covey (1989); Bennis (1984); and Bennis and Nanus (1986). A useful discussion of the approach is found in Hersey and Blanchard (1993). Alas, as these approaches are based on other manager's styles, they quickly lose their impact once the seminars are completed.

Others publish works designed to chart new directions for indoctrinating managers in a more "practical" way. McCormack (1984, 1989) offers a body of nontraditional, "street smart" advice. After noting that most business training tends to overlook what he calls the "ins and outs of everyday business life," McCormack urges managers to become skilled at dealing with people, mastering sales and negotiating, and learning the basics of running a business. Although this offers a healthy dose of real-world political awareness to new managers, it and a follow-up volume by the same author ultimately fall short of providing an overarching, coherent theme. Studies such as these are worthy of being included in a curriculum, but they cannot stand as the curriculum itself.

What Do Managers Really Do?

A series of research studies combine to point the way toward a more useful approach for training new managers. Kraut (1989) studied over 1,400 executives/managers/supervisors, and identified seven key tasks that members of all groups performed, with varying degrees of importance attached to each task. This approach does come dangerously close to the older trait-based leadership approach, but differs in that skills *can* be learned, while it is arguable whether learned behavioral traits can ever appear genuine to others (i.e., subordinates).

The results of Kraut's study are supported by models that demonstrate that top-level managers need more conceptual skills than their lower-ranking counterparts. First-line supervisors require more technical skills, while the dwindling ranks of middle managers need a lot of human resource skills and smaller amounts of both conceptual and technical skills. The seven tasks identified in Kraut's study include elements of the older PLOCS model, plus newer components:

1. Managing individual performance: of high importance for supervisors, low importance for executives;

2. Instructing subordinates: of high importance for supervisors, low for executives;

3. Planning and allocating resources: of high importance for managers, low for supervisors;

4. Coordinating interdependent groups: of high importance for executives, low for supervisors;

5. Managing group performance: of high importance for managers, low for supervisors;

6. Monitoring the organization's environment: of high importance for executives, low for supervisors;

7. Representing one's employees: of high importance for managers, low for supervisors.

A second study by Keys and Case (1990) identified clusters of influence behaviors that managers use with their bosses, their peers, and their subordinates. Keys and Case found that when it comes to successfully persuading others to follow his or her advice/suggestions/orders, a manager's effectiveness is determined by that person's ability to match his or her influence behavior to the target individual's organizational level.

1. Effectiveness in influencing a boss depends on the subordinate manager's ability to accomplish things though his or her subordinates. When this ability is combined with more assertive influence

techniques (telling, arguing, talking, rational explanations, presenting complete plans, persistence, repetition), influence attempts are successful more than 50 percent of the time (Keys & Case, 1990).

2. Effectiveness in influencing a manager's peers depends on that person's ability to do so without formal authority in meetings and negotiations. Influential managers must demonstrate an ability to develop and show support of their peers (Keys & Case, 1990).

3. Effectiveness in influencing a manager's subordinates depends on that person's ability to demonstrate upward influence with his or her superiors. Managers who use formal authority alone greatly limit their options. They must learn to use methods of influence other than formal authority (Keys & Case, 1990).

In a study of general managers carried out over a five-year period, Kotter (1982) examined what his subjects "really" did, as distinguished from what management trainers tell new managers they should concentrate on. After collecting a list of apparently random behaviors within his subject group, Kotter discerned that only three common tasks actually consumed most of the managers' time. These three tasks mesh very well with the seven influence behaviors of successful managers identified in Keys' research:

1. Agenda development: Preparing loosely connected, largely unwritten, short-, medium-, and long-range goals and plans. This process facilitates the accomplishment of multiple goals through an incremental process.

2. Network building: Seeking out cooperative relationships with people who will help implement the managers' agendas. This is based on favors, lobbying, norm setting, environment shaping, etc. Larger networks enhance a manager's chance for achieving successful outcomes.

3. Execution: Moving the agenda forward by influencing network members to pay attention to multiple important items contained within that agenda. This process allows managers to save time by getting their networks to accomplish the managers' agendas.

Successful Managers and Effective Managers

Luthans, Hodgetts, and Rosenkrantz (1988) used a slightly modified version of Kotter's model to study more than 700 managers over a four-year period. The researchers found that their subjects performed four comprehensive categories of activities that expand on those identified in Kotter's work:

1. Routine communication: Paperwork, e-mail, memos, reports, letters, telephone calls, faxes, etc.

2. Traditional management tasks: Planning, leading, organizing, controlling, and staffing. This area incorporates most traditional training programs (based on the old PLOCS model) offered to new managers.

3. Networking: Interacting with outsiders, socializing, politicking, hall chats, chance meetings, etc. This area incorporates the nontraditional, political skills described by McCormack.

4. Human resource management: Motivating, reinforcing, disciplining, managing conflict, staffing, training, developing, empowering, involving others, etc. This area incorporates many of the "soft" skills found in newer models of management.

Luthans et al. found that, overall, real managers devote approximately 29 percent of their time to routine communication, 32 percent of their time to traditional management, 19 percent to networking, and 20 percent to human resource management. In addition, guided by the relative importance the managers attached to these four activities, the researchers identified three distinct types of managers: successful managers, effective managers, and successful and effective managers.

Successful managers are defined as those individuals who receive more rapid promotions, as compared to others in their organizations. They devote 28 percent of their time to routine communication (about the same as the overall average), 13 percent to traditional management (19 percent less than the overall average), 48 percent to networking (29 percent more than the overall average), and 11 percent to human resource management (9 percent less than the overall average).

Effective managers are defined as those individuals whose employees excel in quantity and quality of production and display superior levels of satisfaction and commitment toward the organization. These managers devote 44 percent of their time to routine communication (15 percent more than the overall average and 16 percent more than their "successful" counterparts), 19 percent of their time to traditional management (13 percent less than the overall average and 6 percent more than their "successful" counterparts), 11 percent of their time to networking (8 percent less than the overall average and 37 percent less than their "successful" counterparts), and 26 percent of their time to human resource management (6 percent more than the overall average and 15 percent more than their "successful" counterparts).

Successful and effective managers' percentages are almost identical to the overall averages. They devote 30 percent of their time to routine communication (1 percent more than the overall average), 30 percent to traditional management (2 percent less than the overall average), 20 percent to networking (1 percent more than the overall average), and 20 percent to human resource management (the same as the overall average).

In summarizing their study, Luthans et al. point out that the most "successful" managers engage in 70 percent more networking activities and 40 percent fewer traditional management activities than their "effective" counterparts. In fact, the authors found that managers seem to not be doing what management texts say they should be doing. Nor is the profile of a "successful" or "effective" manager particularly consistent with what actual managers say a manager should do. In addition, the authors encourage their readers to ask whether organizations are rewarding the wrong people ("successful" managers) or rewarding the right people ("effective" managers) in the wrong way. They also urge organizations to identify ways to encourage the development of more "successful and effective" managers.

Management Competencies in the Age of Hypercompetition

Finally, a study by D'Aveni (1995) identifies seven competencies that managers must demonstrate if their employers are to cope successfully with the challenges of hypercompetition in the mid-1990s. D'Aveni's framework mandates that managers become skilled at:

1. Satisfying customers before employees and investors.

2. Envisioning future trends and creating appropriate self-fulfilling prophecies.

3. Constantly disrupting the status quo.

4. Being the first to create new competitive advantages.

5. Continually shifting the rules of the gameplan and then updating the plan.

6. Announcing the organization's vision to everyone and being highly visible.

7. Utilizing competitive thrusts to upset the status quo and opening new opportunities (innovating).

This entrepreneurial call to arms reflects similar models contained in Reagan (1996), Peters (1994), and Pinchot (1985). These studies all urge managers and their employers to become more risk taking, innovative, rule bending, and—in Peters' case—"weird." The bottom line is that traditional

PLOCS-based, management-training programs show little ability to help managers obtain successful careers.

THE INSTRUMENT

Validity

The Managers for the 21st Century Inventory is designed to be used as a discussion-provoking training tool rather than as a rigorous data-gathering instrument. Applied in this manner, the inventory has demonstrated a high level of face validity when used with audiences ranging from executive managers to nonmanagement personnel.

Administration

The following suggestions will help facilitators administer the Managers for the 21st Century Inventory:

1. Before respondents begin completing the inventory, discuss the shortcomings of traditional new-manager training models. Answer questions pertaining to these bodies of information.

2. Distribute copies of the Managers for the 21st Century Inventory and read the instructions aloud as the respondents follow. Answer any questions.

3. Urge respondents to avoid overanalyzing their choices. After reading each of the statements on the inventory, respondents should check only those statements that accurately reflect their own beliefs. Respondents should complete both parts of the inventory.

Scoring and Interpretation

1. Ask respondents to wait to score their inventories until all respondents have finished both Part One and Part Two. This creates less confusion and repetition as inventories are being processed.

2. To score Part One of the inventory, add up the number of items checked and multiply the result by five.

3. Each respondent then should find the corresponding Part One bracket within which his or her score lies and read the brief, interpretive statement there.

4. Next, respondents should read the longer Part One discussion section, to gain a better understanding of the study that underlies the items to which they just responded. (This material contains Kotter's model.) The administrator may lead a discussion of the material as deemed appropriate and desirable.

5. To interpret Part Two of the inventory, respondents first compare their percentage estimates (which should add up to no more than 100 percent) with the results produced by the Luthans et al. research study and then read the background material for Part Two. This offers them a way of assessing the pattern produced by their estimates. Again, the administrator may lead a discussion of this material as deemed appropriate and desirable.

6. Respondents now should be ready to prepare Part One action plans to take back to their workplaces, in which they detail how they will implement the new model. It is useful for respondents to share their action plans with one another before they leave the session.

7. Finally, respondents use their Part Two patterns to respond to the action-plan questions. Again, it is useful for respondents to share their results with one another before they leave the session.

Option: The background materials for Parts One and Two may be combined. The action-planning activities for Parts One and Two also may be combined.

USES OF THE INVENTORY

The Managers for the 21st Century Inventory is designed to accomplish the following objectives:

1. To familiarize managers and their organizations with the short-comings of the traditional PLOCS model of management training.

2. To offer a constructive critique of management models that might currently be used in organizations that are seeking to improve their management training and development activities.

3. To identify the features of a new body of competencies that can be included in future-oriented management training and development programs.

4. To provide a basis for discussion about the relationship between the present competencies of an organization's managers and the

demands that the emerging business environment will place on those same managers.

5. To offer organizations a format to use as they assess their readiness to implement a more contemporary style of management.

References

Bennis, W. (1984, August). The four competencies of leadership. *Training and Development Journal*, pp. 15-19.

Bennis, W., & Nanus, B. (1986). *Leaders: The strategies for taking charge.* New York: Harper and Row.

Covey, S. (1989). *The seven habits of highly effective people.* New York: Simon & Schuster.

D'Aveni, R. (1995). Coping with hypercompetition: Utilizing the new 7S's framework. *Academy of Management Executives, 9*(3) 45-60.

Haimann, T. (1984). *Supervisory management for health care organizations* (3rd ed.). St. Louis, MO: The Catholic Health Care Organization of the United States.

Hersey, P., & Blanchard, K. (1993). *Management of organizational behavior* (6th ed). Englewood Cliffs, NJ: Prentice Hall.

Keys, B., & Case, T. (1990). How to become an influential manager. *Academy of Management Executive, 4*(4), 38-51.

Kotter, J. (1982). *The general managers.* New York: The Free Press/Macmillan.

Kraut, A. (1989, November). The role of the manager: What's really important in different management jobs. *Academy of Management Review, 3*(4), 286-293.

Luthans, F., Hodgetts, R., & Rosenkrantz, S. (1988). *Real managers.* New York: Ballinger.

McCormack, M. (1984). *What they don't teach you at Harvard Business School.* New York: Bantam Books.

McCormack, M. (1989). *What they still don't teach you at Harvard Business School.* New York: Bantam Books.

Peters, T. (1994). *The Tom Peters seminar.* New York: Vintage Books/Random House.

Pinchot, G., III. (1985). *Intrapreneuring.* New York: Harper & Row.

Reagan, G. (1996). U.S. style teams (USST) inventory. *The 1996 annual: Volume 2, consulting.* San Francisco, CA: Pfeiffer, an imprint of Jossey-Bass.

Gaylord Reagan, Ph.D., *is an independent consultant who provides public-sector and governmental clients with assistance in total quality management, management training, and organization development. He also serves as an adjunct instructor at Central Michigan University, the University of Oregon, the University of Nebraska at Omaha, Century University, the College of St. Francis, and Iowa Western Community College. He has also been a director of training and management development, manager of employee education and development, human resource manager, and internal consultant for organizational development. He is a member of the Academy of Management, the American Management Association, and the Society for Human Resource Management.*

MANAGERS FOR THE 21ST CENTURY INVENTORY

Gaylord Reagan

INVENTORY: PART ONE

Instructions: After reviewing the following list of activities, check those items that you believe best describe what "21st Century managers" do with their time. Don't overthink your responses; your initial reactions most accurately reflect your perceptions.

❑ Managers spend as much as 75 percent of their time being involved with other people.

❑ Managers go around the formal chain of command.

❑ Managers focus on building networks.

❑ Managers discuss anything and everything associated with their organization.

❑ Managers ask a lot of questions.

❑ Managers rarely make big decisions.

❑ Managers focus on developing agendas (goals, objectives, etc.).

❑ Managers joke, kid around, use humor, and talk about nonwork activities.

❑ Managers "waste" time discussing issues that appear to be nonsubstantive.

❑ Managers seldom tell people what to do.

❑ Managers frequently attempt to influence others.

❑ Managers frequently respond to others' initiatives.

❑ Managers focus on executing their agendas.

❑ Managers invest significant amounts of time in short and disjointed discussions.

❑ Managers work long hours (e.g., sixty hours per week).

❏ Managers rely on conversations with others for information, not on books, magazines, or reports.

❏ Managers realize that the size of their networks largely determines their degrees of success.

❏ Managers seek out cooperative relationships with people who will have to help implement their agendas.

❏ Managers seek to maximize teamwork and minimize politics.

❏ Managers' network members are chosen for their ability to help accomplish the managers' agendas.

Scoring for Part One

Instructions: Give yourself five points for each item that you checked in Part One.

Your total score is:

90-100 = You have a strong grasp of the behaviors that characterize "21st Century managers." Your main tasks for the future include patiently helping your organization and your colleagues to learn more about these behaviors, being sure to model and reward these new behaviors with your subordinates, and systematically coaching everyone around you to begin implementing leadership models appropriate to the 21st Century.

80-89 = You have a moderately good understanding of what it takes to be an effective manager in the 21st Century. Your main tasks for the future include strengthening your own familiarity with the behaviors, experimenting with the behaviors in low-to-moderate-risk situations, rewarding yourself when you are successful in using the behaviors, establishing goals for yourself that focus on increasing the frequency with which you use the behaviors, and letting others know about your efforts.

70-79 = You are aware of the 21st Century management behaviors but do not find them compelling, or you may work in a setting in which you cannot presently use the behaviors. Your main tasks for the future include continuing to learn about the new management behaviors, finding someone with whom you can talk about them, and identifying settings in which you can try out selected behaviors.

60-69 = Your have a below-average understanding of what it takes to be a successful 21st Century manager. Your main tasks for the future include looking around to see what your organization's top competitors or peer organizations are doing as they prepare to meet the challenges of the 21st Century. You also should consider the long-term needs of your organization: How will your employer become steadily more competitive while utilizing fewer resources and responding to growing customer demands for higher levels of product and service quality? Armed with responses to questions such as these, you are then ready to examine the degree to which your current leadership or management style will help you and your employer to be successful in the coming period.

0-59 = You have little or no awareness of 21st Century management practices. For a variety of reasons, you also may have little or no interest in altering that situation. Your main tasks for the future include taking time to reflect on where you want your career to lead, your effectiveness in working with other people, how you feel about yourself as a leader/manager, and how other people with whom you work seem to react to your present style of leadership or management.

Background to Part One

Kotter (1982) identifies specific activities or characteristics involved with each of the three common, overarching tasks of managers. These include:

1. Developing an agenda. This allows managers to react in an opportunistic manner, knowing that their actions will serve broader, long-term goals. It is important to note that agendas are not the same as formal plans. Agendas consist of loosely connected goals and plans. Compared to formal plans, the (usually unwritten) agendas contain less-detailed financial objectives, more-detailed strategies, and a broader time frame, and they articulate multiple and somewhat vague goals that will be accomplished simultaneously through an incremental process. Developed largely inside managers' minds, agendas address short-term (one year), medium-term (one-to-five years), and long-term (five-to-twenty years) goals. In order to gather the information needed to help them tighten their agendas, managers must be aggressive information seekers and must rely on conversations with others for information—not on books, magazines, studies, or reports.

2. Building a network to execute the agenda. Modern managers go outside their formal structures and build cooperative relationships with people (peers, boss, outsiders, vendors, boss's boss, subordinates' subordinates, etc.). Agenda-building managers also foster very strong ties to and among their subordinates; they do favors for others, encourage people to identify with them, consciously develop feelings of dependence in those around them, change suppliers, lobby, set norms, move/hire/fire subordinates, and actively shape their environments. Their tactical goals include encouraging others to feel obliged and dependent, enhancing their reputations in others' eyes, replacing incompetent employees, and maximizing teamwork while minimizing politics. The bottom line is that a larger network increases a manager's chances of successfully implementing his or her agenda.

3. Executing the agenda through exercising direct and indirect influence on members of their networks. Direct influence includes asking, demanding, cajoling, and intimidating. Indirect influence includes meetings, stories, language, space, time, and events. Doing this allows managers to save time by getting their networks to accomplish their agendas for them. Successful network managers are personally involved in choosing which agenda items will be acted on, making certain that all agenda items receive attention, selecting appropriate networks to get action on chosen agenda items, and selecting influence approaches that accomplish multiple agenda items at once.

Part One Action Plan

1. How strong a grasp of 21st Century management practices does your score suggest that you currently have? How do you feel about that result?

2. What management procedures are you currently using? Does your choice appear to be working well for you? What adjustments might increase the impact of your management practices?

3. Which management practices does your organization seem to reward? In what specific ways are they rewarded? Does it appear to be in the long-term interests of the organization to continue to reward these practices?

4. Does your first-hand experience tend to support or refute Kotter's findings?

INVENTORY: PART TWO

Instructions: Place an "X" on each of the following four scales to indicate the approximate percentage of your weekly time you believe should be devoted to each of the four indicated management activities. Your total should add up to 100 percent.

1. Routine communication (oral, written, electronic, symbolic)	0%	25%	50%	75%	100%
2. Traditional management tasks (plan, lead, organize, control, staff)	0%	25%	50%	75%	100%
3. Networking (socializing, influencing, ingratiating)	0%	25%	50%	75%	100%
4. Human resource management (training, coaching, supporting)	0%	25%	50%	75%	100%
Your percent total for the above categories:		%			

Background to Part Two

1. Of the "real managers" studied by Luthans, Hodgetts, and Rosenkrantz (1988), the average percentages of time the managers devoted to the four categories indicated on the scales above are:

   A. Routine communication: 29 percent

   B. Traditional management: 32 percent

   C. Networking: 19 percent

   D. Human resource management: 20 percent

2. Defining "successful managers" as those individuals who receive more rapid promotions relative to others in their organizations (successful managers are highly valued by their organizations, and their high value is rewarded most directly by promotions), Luthans' team found that the percentages of time these persons devote to each of the four categories are:

   A. Routine communication: 28 percent (nearly the same as the overall average).

   B. Traditional management: 13 percent (19 percent less than the overall average).

   C. Networking: 48 percent (29 percent more than the overall average).

   D. Human resource management: 11 percent (9 percent less than the overall average).

3. Defining "effective managers" as being those individuals whose employees excel in quantity and quality of production and who display superior levels of satisfaction and commitment toward the organization, the researchers found that the percentages of time these managers devote to each of the four categories are:

   A. Routine communication: 44 percent (15 percent more than the overall average and 16 percent more than "successful" managers).

   B. Traditional management: 19 percent (13 percent less than the overall average and 6 percent more than "successful" managers).

   C. Networking: 11 percent (8 percent less than the overall average and 37 percent less than "successful" managers).

   D. Human resource management: 26 percent (6 percent more than the overall average and 15 percent more than "successful" managers).

4. When they examined the percentages of time that "successful and effective managers" devote to the four categories listed above, the researchers found that the percentages are almost identical to the overall sample's averages.

   A. Routine communication: 30 percent

   B. Traditional management: 30 percent

   C. Networking: 20 percent

   D. Human resource management: 20 percent

5. The most successful managers identified in the Luthans et al. study engaged in 70 percent more networking activities and 40 percent fewer traditional management activities than their less successful counterparts. Overall, the authors found that many of their subjects are not doing what management texts say they do. Nor is the profile of a successful or effective manager particularly consistent with what working managers say a manager focuses on. The researchers encourage their readers to ask whether organizations tend to reward the wrong people ("successful" managers) or reward the right people in the wrong way.

Part Two Action Plan

1. Which of the three patterns ("Successful," "Effective," "Successful and Effective") most closely approximates the one(s) currently being rewarded in your work area or overall organization?

2. Which of the three patterns would most help personnel in your work area to increase the competitiveness of the overall organization?

3. Which of the three patterns most closely resembles your own? How do you feel about that?

4. In order to increase the impact of your managerial approach, what do you need to do? What goals can you identify for yourself? Be as specific as possible.

References

Kotter, J. (1982). *The general managers.* New York: The Free Press/Macmillan.

Luthans, F., Hodgetts, R., & Rosenkrantz, S. (1988). *Real managers.* New York: Ballinger.

Introduction
to the Presentation and Discussion Resources Section

Every facilitator needs to develop a repertoire of theory and background that can be used in a variety of situations. Learning based on direct experience is not the only kind of learning appropriate to human-interaction training. A practical combination of theory and research with experiential learning generally enriches training and may be essential in many types of cognitive and skill development. Affective and cognitive data support, alter, validate, extend, and complement each other.

The 1997 Annual: Volume 1, Training includes ten articles, in the following categories:

Individual Development: Personal Growth
Trainers and the Discipline of Personal Mastery, by Michael O'Brien and Larry Shook

Communication: Communication Styles, Modes, and Patterns
Training from the Transactional View, by Karen L. Rudick and William Frank Jones

Communication: Confrontation and Negotiation
Four Cultural Dimensions and Their Implications for Negotiation and Conflict Resolution, by B. Kim Barnes

Groups and Teams: Techniques to Use with Groups
From Vision to Reality: The Innovation Process, by Michael Stanleigh

Consulting: Consulting Strategies and Techniques
Creating Training Excellence for Organizational Change, by Irwin M. Rubin and Robert Inguagiato

Consulting: Interface with Clients
Training in Mexico and Central America, by Kevin M. Kelleghan

Facilitating: Techniques and Strategies
Training for Organizational Results: How to Get the Most Value for the Training Dollar, by Kevin Daley

Widening the Fast Track: Five Ways to Move from Exclusionary to Inclusionary Training, by Mindy L. Zasloff

Liability and the HRD Practitioner, by John Sample

Leadership: Top-Management Issues and Concerns
Strategic Conviction, by David Nicoll

As with previous *Annuals,* this volume covers a wide variety of topics. The range of articles presented should encourage a good deal of thought-provoking, serious discussion about the present and the future of HRD. Other articles on specific subjects can be located by using our comprehensive *Reference Guide to Handbooks and Annuals.* This book, which is updated regularly, indexes the contents of all the *Annuals* and of the *Handbooks of Structured Experiences.* With each revision, the *Reference Guide* becomes a complete, up-to-date, and easy-to-use resource for selecting appropriate materials from the *Annuals* and *Handbooks.*

Here and in the *Reference Guide,* we have done our best to categorize the articles for easy reference; however, many of the articles encompass a range of topics, disciplines, and applications. If you do not find what you are looking for under one category, we encourage you to look under a related category. Also, in attempting to balance the contents of both volumes of the *Annual,* we may place an article in the "Training" *Annual* that also has implications for "Consulting," and vice versa. As the field of HRD becomes more sophisticated, what is done in a training context is based on the needs of, and affects, the organization. Likewise, from a systemic viewpoint, anything that affects individuals in an organization has repercussions throughout the organization, and vice versa. We encourage you not to be limited by the categorization system that we have developed, but to explore all the contents of both volumes of the *Annual* in order to realize the full potential for learning and development that each offers.

TRAINERS AND THE DISCIPLINE OF PERSONAL MASTERY

Michael O'Brien and Larry Shook

Abstract: Organizations must embrace continuous learning—and the active sharing of learning among all parts of the organization—if they are to survive. The basis for organizational learning is individual learning, and the pursuit of personal mastery is the cornerstone of individual learning and growth. Moreover, it leads to the wise and beneficial use of what we have learned.

This article presents four, basic, adaptive skills of personal mastery and explains how individuals, especially trainers and HRD professionals, can transcend inherent and learned limitations to change and enrich themselves and their organizations through this discipline.

Peter Senge is a humble messenger. When he published *The Fifth Discipline: The Art & Practice of the Learning Organization* in 1990, he said that the ideas in the book were not his, that many of them were a century old, and that he was merely a recording secretary. Nevertheless, the professor from MIT struck a deep chord with U.S. business. There is general agreement today that Senge was onto something, that the learning organization is not just another fad, and that organizations composed of people who are not actively learning together probably will not be around long.

In the movie *Scent of a Woman,* there is a scene that subtly—even poignantly—reflects this aspect of our times. The colonel and his young aide are getting out of a cab in front of the Waldorf-Astoria Hotel, "the pinnacle," the colonel declares, "of all things civilized." Looming over the elegant tableau is the Pan Am building. Although the once-proud name still blazes in the night, it is only the reminder of a once-great company.

THE NEED FOR LEARNING ORGANIZATIONS

Learn or die. That is the message. We all know the grim statistics regarding the life expectancy of U.S. corporations; few survive past the age of forty. It is like an actuarial table from the Dark Ages and is a sad commentary on the status of learning in the U.S. workplace.

Even so, half a decade after Peter Senge added "the learning organization" to the U.S. business vocabulary, and although many organizational leaders are working hard to make elements of the learning organization a reality, we know of no organization that is a complete learning organization.

A learning organization, according to Senge, is one in which "people continually expand their capacity to create the results they truly desire...." The learning organization also can be described as a place in which people sit up, pay attention, and talk freely about what they learn. They do this because the organization's operational phenomena—values, systems, policies, and procedures—invite them to and reward them for it.

On the other hand, the typical organization expects employees to "sit down, shut up, and hang on" until the ride is over. The real difference between the two is that, in the learning organization, individual and collective learning amounts to a business within a business. The fruits of this learning enterprise—the gross learning product—lets the organization continuously anticipate and adjust to changes in the environment. This also makes the organization less likely to need a very expensive reengineering effort.

PERSONAL MASTERY: THE CORNERSTONE OF LEARNING

Senge identified *personal mastery* as one of the five disciplines of the learning organization. It may be the cornerstone. An organization is an intangible thing, an invisible repository of will and competence; organizations exist in the thin ether of our actions and values. But there is nothing abstract about the people who make them up. They dream, worry, attend meetings, call on customers, and phone home. You can weigh them, poll them, and clock them. It makes sense that when an organization learns, the locus of that learning is the individual and groups of individuals.

The term "personal mastery" may just be another way of saying "learning," but we must be clear about the kind of learning we mean. It is not just the accumulation of technical and functional information, but the wise and beneficial use of that information. This is an important qualification, because it introduces the issues of self-knowledge and personal values. Here is where we find the answer to the riddle of the learning organization and the reason that the learning organization (as a whole, functioning entity) is so important.

Transcending Our Inherent and Learned Limitations

When he was an old man, an attorney named Ben Kizer, one of the great civic leaders of the Twentieth Century, observed, "The last thing we learn about ourselves is our effect." Personal mastery entails honing our effectiveness in the world through brave self-observation. It also involves creating a high-tension energy field in one's life by facing the truth of current reality and boldly envisioning something different: a future of one's choosing. The creative tension is where the juice of mastery comes from.

Through the ages, sages have testified to the virtues of the examined life and lamented a mind left untended. The following are the observations of three of them.

> Those who know much about others may be smart, but those who understand themselves are even wiser.
>
> —*Lao Tsu*

You could drop a leaflet or a Hubbard squash on the head of any person in any land and you would almost certainly hit a brain that was whirling in small, conventional circles. There is something about the human mind that keeps it well within the confines of the parish, and only one outlook in a million is nonparochial.

—*E.B. White*

We have met the enemy and he is us.

—*Pogo*

We happen to believe that the "something" E.B. White was talking about amounts to a biological imperative faced by humanity, and that the imperative is as inescapable in the organization as elsewhere. Medical research reveals that within the first six months of life, the human brain doubles in neural capacity, doubling again by age four. No other creature on the planet experiences comparable brain expansion. The body has about a hundred billion nerve cells, and every time the brain thinks a thought, a record of the transaction is preserved in the archives of muscle, blood, bone, and organ. Experience shapes us. Events compose our lives.

Throughout childhood, the human brain is a frenzied construction site in which neural structures are assembled in response to stimulus. During this time, countless circuits in the brain are rushed to completion. In the course of construction, some connections are bolstered into massive conduits of habit. Others are systematically diminished, sometimes even dismantled.

This is not metaphysical speculation, but part of the best current explanation that science has to offer about what makes us tick. It is this process that lays the foundation for what Dr. Robert B. Livingston—a leading brain researcher and former faculty member in the medical schools at Stanford, Yale, Harvard, and UCLA—calls the human "world view" (Livingston, 1990). Each of us has one, says Dr. Livingston; it is the highly subjective image of reality presented to us by our senses, which are created by the interplay of heredity and the impressionistic sculpture of our life experience. But there is more.

Livingston reports that the intensive brain development of early childhood is followed by an amazing event. During a single three-week period of adolescence, power to the construction site of the brain is drastically cut back. The brain's metabolism falls to half its previous rate, and we are "biologically wired," as Livingston says, with the conclusions, attitudes, suspicions, biases, inklings, and anxieties of our most impressionistic years. This occurs in all of us, and it so profoundly impacts the ways in which we lead our lives, it might be the most important event in all of human history. It locks us into a way of being that will govern us more forcefully, more ruthlessly, than any tyrant, unless we learn to intervene.

Livingston concludes that this "biological wiring," this deceptive "knowing" about the world (which accounts for our pig-headedness) could threaten humanity more than any other factor. It can lead to dysfunctionally rigid ways of perceiving and interacting with the world around us. It can cause great companies, such as Pan Am, to become extinct; fuel holy wars; result in economic systems that jeopardize ecosystems; and lead us to misuse technology in the waging of wars that weapons can win but people cannot. The only hope, as Livingston concluded at the end of a long and distinguished career, is for humanity to learn a lesson about itself that has eluded us so far.

We believe that "personal mastery" is as good a name for the lesson as any. Liberating ourselves from the conditioned, automatic responses to life that endlessly loop us into the same frustrations is one of the hardest things that we can ever attempt. Accepting the need for this is not an admission of inadequacy but a recognition of what it means to be human. It is understanding that we possess a psyche on which the world has long been at work before we get much of a shot at responding to the world. Dealing with this reality is always worth the effort, because even the smallest successes are immediately rewarded with proportionally greater personal freedom. This, in turn, leads to greater creativity, productivity, satisfaction, joy, and expanded life possibilities.

Although the task is difficult, people regularly accomplish even greater goals. Changing one's world view, says Livingston, is actually easier than overcoming chemical dependence, and people break such deadly habits all the time.

The Ripple Effect in Organizations

One person inside an organization (e.g., a trainer) on the trail of personal mastery would be good news for that organization. Think of the ripple effect. Two people would be even better, and the implications of ten people struggling with the ways of personal mastery are even more exciting because of the dynamics of critical mass. The cumulative rate at which individuals within the organization change themselves in pursuit of personal mastery defines the rate at which the organization can change.

Personal mastery is very personal, revolving as it does around the unique mechanisms of the mind. It is challenging enough at the personal level. In the organization, the challenge is compounded not just by numbers but by the fact that no one can choose the pursuit of personal mastery for us; we must choose it for ourselves. Nevertheless, it is a challenge that people and organizations must face if they are to survive individually and collectively. Organizational leaders who have the courage to confront this issue will need all the help they can get from the training profession.

The challenge can be described as follows:

1. Because of the rapidity of technological change and global competition, becoming a learning organization is now the real ante of doing business.

2. The pursuit of personal mastery by individuals is the essence of the learning organization.

Unfortunately, the practice of personal mastery by an organization's employees remains a taboo subject for management. A manager who addresses an employee with, "Excuse me, but I think you need to improve your personal mastery" will likely be as welcome as a religious pamphleteer at the door on Saturday morning. As Peter Drucker says, managers have no business messing with their employees' minds.

We must disagree with Drucker. Although we believe that organizations should not stick their noses into the private lives of their employees, we do not think that you can separate the person's work from the person. The general manager of the Four Seasons Olympic Hotel in Seattle corroborated this view when he explained why his company screens new hires with exquisite care. "We can teach people what to do," he said, "but not what to be."

The notion that we have a work life and a personal life is a dangerous illusion. Each of us has one mind, one body, and one spirit, and we take them with us wherever we go. We do a lot of messing with one another's minds; it may constitute the majority of human affairs. Every time a manager says "Thank you" or "You did it wrong again" to an employee, the manager is messing with the employee's mind. Every bonus paid, every new team assembled, every reorganization effort is an exercise in messing with minds. The challenge, again, is to do it responsibly.

By practicing personal mastery as individuals, trainers and other HRD professionals will make their practice more forceful than any sermons they could ever preach on the subject. Happily, the discipline of it will almost inevitably confine one to constructive, ethical interaction with others.

Components of the Discipline

The question is "How do you pursue personal mastery?" The answer is that the biological and psychological force of habit is so great that you must have a discipline. To harness the incomprehensible power of your brain, you need a "technology" that equals the switching capacity of the entire U.S. telephone network and can store 100 trillion bits of information. Such power dwarfs the largest computer.

The personal-mastery technology we propose (O'Brien & Shook, 1995) rests on four adaptive skills:

- Raising consciousness,

- Imagining,

- Framing and reframing, and

- Integrating new perspectives.

"Raising consciousness" means not just thinking, but thinking *about* thinking: noticing and managing the workings of your mind so that your mind will not run away with you like a startled horse.

When you "imagine," you create a mental picture—the most vivid image you can—of an outcome you desire. It works, and you do it all the time. If you are typical, however, most of the imagining you do goes by the name "worry." This most common form of imagining leads not to something you want but to something you do not want, and it works depressingly well.

"Framing and reframing" are the foundation of human experience and the essence of personal freedom. They mean interpreting the world, deriving meaning, and assigning significance to the events of life. When the Greek Stoic Epictetus noted two-thousand years ago that it is not the events of life that matter but our opinion of them, he was talking about framing and reframing. You do not have to think about anything in any particular way, but some ways of thinking about things are more helpful than others. Learning to frame and reframe means learning to see things in the most helpful light.

When Livingston refers to changing one's world view, he is describing what happens when you "integrate new perspectives." What we see depends on where we stand. And where we stand—that is, the view of the world our senses present to us—is profoundly influenced by the biases of our families of origin and the hands that fate has dealt us. However, each of us is not stuck with just one world view. We can get new ones any time by learning to integrate the perspectives of others. In this sense, the points of view of other people rank among life's most priceless gifts.

This is not esoteric; in fact, the irony of personal mastery is that it rests on practices that are deceptively mundane. These practices employ a series of studies and exercises that methodically engage the individual in raising consciousness, imagining, framing and reframing, and integrating new perspectives.

In thinking about personal mastery and its application in the organization, two paradoxes are clear. The first is that the actual steps to personal mastery are so straightforward, it is tempting to *think* about them but not actually *take* them. This is like trying to flatten one's stomach by reading about situps.

The second paradox is that personal mastery cannot be taught, at least not like computer skills. It can only be modeled. What those who pursue personal mastery do is notice their mental models and change them as needed, which is not easy. They dream in living color about the results they want, which takes passion. Based on good will and high purpose, they assign the most constructive interpretations (rather than knee-jerk reactions) to the events of their lives. And they respect and incorporate the useful ideas of others. Genuine curiosity and humility help them to do this.

The Impact of Personal Mastery

It probably is not possible for someone to engage in these activities without impacting events around them, without creating powerful and effective relationships with others. But any words that someone who pursues personal mastery could speak about these things would be pale next to the things themselves. In the story of Pinocchio, it is the master's love and the behavior of love that brings the puppet to life. It may be that way with personal mastery. Only to the extent that we are willing to step into these practices and give them life do they have the potential to shape our destinies and those of the organizations we form.

All this is a matter of considerable importance to organizational leaders, to trainers, and to organizations. Many organizations currently are trying to change themselves from the outside in, by reengineering new organizational forms into existence in the hope that structure alone equals performance. We doubt that it does. The catalyst missing from such efforts is the inside-out change offered by personal mastery. We doubt that the best team players can be made by teaching the external strategies of teamwork alone. To be constructive members of a team, people must examine their attitudes about collaborating with others, resolving conflict, coping with mistakes (their own and others'), dealing with anger and fear, and so on. That comes from the never-ending pursuit of personal mastery.

When the leaders of an organization sincerely embrace personal mastery themselves, they will automatically begin shifting the parent-child relationship between management and workers to adult-adult relationships. Although the former is still the dominant organizational paradigm, it is the latter that holds the power to drive truly empowered workers and an organization that is capable of continuous learning and fluid response to a dynamic marketplace.

References

Livingston, R.B. (1990). Neurophysiology. In J.B. West (Ed.), *Best and Taylor's physiological basis of medical practice* (12th ed.). Baltimore, MD: Williams & Wilkens.

O'Brien, M., & Shook, L. (1995). *Profit from experience: How to make the most of your learning and your life.* Austin, TX: Bard Books.

Senge, P. (1990). *The fifth discipline: The art & practice of the learning organization.* New York: Doubleday Currency.

Michael O'Brien, Ed.D., is the president of O'Brien Learning Systems, an organization development consulting firm dedicated to helping organizations meet the challenge of continuous learning and improvement. He consults internationally with corporations such as AT&T, NYNEX, Xerox, Bayer, and Prudential. A former vice president with McLagan International, he specializes in executive coaching and executive team development. He also is the author of Profit From Experience: How to Make the Most of Your Learning and Your Life *and the* Learning Organization Practices Profile.

Larry Shook, a professional writer and journalist, is president of The Printed Word, a communications company. He is the author of The Quality Detective's Bedside Companion *and other books, a contributor to national publications such as the* Washington Post *and the* New York Times, *and a former editor of* San Diego Magazine *and* Spokane Magazine.

TRAINING FROM THE TRANSACTIONAL VIEW

Karen L. Rudick and William Frank Jones

Abstract: Trainers often view the training process, because of its one-to-many nature, as an action that one person takes toward others, not as a transaction between people. According to the action view, the trainer's role is to create a message and inject it into the listener's head. Although this is an "overly simplified view of communication, it is one that many people still accept" (Stewart & Logan, 1993, p. 39). However, a more effective and comprehensive view of the training event is the transactional view.

This article applies the *action, interactional,* and *transactional* views of the communication process to the training process and discusses the advantages of viewing training from a transactional model. It also presents the six components of the transactional model.

THE ACTION VIEW

Since Aristotle, scholars have viewed communication as something one does to an audience. A message is something that one transfers to the other (Gronbeck, McKerrow, Ehninger, & Monroe, 1994). Because early rhetoricians were concerned primarily with the training of orators, early communication theories stressed the role of the speaker (Berko, Wolvin, & Wolvin, 1992). This perspective of communication, commonly referred to as the action view, is analogous to the hypodermic needle. The sender inserts the medicinal message into the passive receiver. Recipients of the message are believed to be directly and heavily influenced by the sender.

In the early 1900s, this view was also referred to as the "magic-bullet theory" by mass-communications researchers (Sproule, 1989) or as "the conduit metaphor" (Reddy, 1979). Some of the first communication models, appearing around 1950, used this linear view of communication (Lasswell, 1948; Shannon & Weaver, 1949). It is still discussed in introductory communication textbooks (Berko, Wolvin, & Wolvin, 1992; Gronbeck et al., 1994), mostly for historical reasons and to provide a framework for later work (McQuail & Windahl, 1993).

Although most communication scholars today consider this view outdated, and educators recognize the importance of the receiver of the message, very little is done in educational curricula to reflect this realization. For example, many universities require a basic communication/public-speaking course but require no listening course. Also, the syntactical structure of the English language (subject-verb-object) promotes this view of communication (Fisher, 1980). As Fisher notes, we often describe communication as person A speaking to (persuading, informing) person B, or as the sender affecting a receiver.

This speaker-centered view of communication suggests that messages are unidirectional, from speaker to listener, and that the listener has a minimal role in the process. It assumes that communication occurs when the message is received accurately. This assumption ignores the listener's role in providing feedback. If communication is ineffective or unsuccessful, blame usually is placed on the speaker, rarely on the listener. It is the speaker who is boring, speaks in a monotone, does not repeat instructions, or talks too fast.

It is assumed that if the speaker were to improve his or her sending skills, the problem would be solved. Therefore, a person is told to do something about his or her communicative behavior, e.g., add vocal variety, repeat, slow down. As Sereno and Bodaken (1975, p.7) point out, "all of these are strategies designed to reinforce a one-way notion of communication, and often they also reinforce the problem because the source is dissuaded from hearing the receiver sending." This one-way, linear view is incomplete and oversimplifies communication.

Many trainers still view communication as an action. For example, one may say things such as "It's hard to get that idea across to him," or "I made sure they understood me; I drew it on a piece of paper and repeated the directions twice," or "No wonder we don't get along; she doesn't communicate well," or "That professor bores me." Each of these comments makes it sound as if communication is an action (Stewart & Logan, 1993).

THE INTERACTIONAL VIEW

Because the action view fails to take into account all the variables in the communication process, some communication theorists have presented a more sophisticated perspective of communication: the *interactional* model. The interactional model not only recognizes the importance of the receiver and includes the concept of feedback, it also attempts to demonstrate a more dynamic nature of the communication process. Most often noted for the interactional model, Berlo (1960, p. 24) states, "We view events and relationships as dynamic, on-going, ever-changing, continuous....it [the communication process] does not have a beginning, an end, a fixed sequence of events.... The ingredients within a process interact; each affects all the others."

Although Berlo originally intended this model to recognize the dynamic nature of communication, it does not meet these expectations. For example, Stewart and Logan (1993, p. 41) likened the interactional view to a table full of billiard balls. "One person makes an active choice to do something to affect another, passive person, who's [sic] direction gets changed by what the active person does. Then the person who was passive becomes active, and in turn affects either the first person (who's now passively waiting to be affected) or someone else... The process is all cause and effect, stimulus and response."

When applied to billiards, this way of thinking correctly assumes predictability of response. If you hit a ball in exactly the right spot, at exactly the right angle, with exactly the right amount of force, the next ball will go where you wish. However, the predictability assumption is false when applied to human communication. No two people respond to the same message in the same way. Viewing communication as active then passive, or all cause and effect, distorts the process.

Also, emphasizing cause and effect tempts the person, as Stewart and Logan (1993, p. 42) state, "to focus on who's at fault or who caused a problem to occur." Given both sides and a fuller understanding of the context, it is very difficult to tell who "started it" or who is to blame. The complexities of human relationships do not allow for such a simplistic explanation. Moreover, fault finding and blaming make improving a situation almost impossible.

Another problem with viewing communication from the interactional view is the failure to see people as changing while they are communicating (Stewart & Logan, 1993). Neither humans nor environments are constant over time. "Moreover," as Sameroff and Chandler (1975, p. 234) note, "these differences are interdependent and change as a function of the mutual influence on one another." One cannot ignore this mutuality of influence or interdependence.

When viewing communication from the interactional perspective, a person is not only concerned with the "proper" preparation and delivery of messages, he or she is also listening for feedback to alter future messages—thus making the process less speaker-centered and more message-centered. A more equal emphasis on the "encoding" and "decoding" processes acknowledges the problems "in translating our thoughts into words or other symbols and in deciphering the words or symbols of others into terms we can understand" (Gronbeck et al., 1994, p. 501).

The billiard-ball view of communication also suggests a series of actions and reactions, "a process that is somewhat circular: sending and receiving, sending and receiving, and so on" (Berko, Wolvin, & Wolvin, 1992, p. 52). Each communicator is seen as either sending *or* receiving. The ability to simultaneously send *and* receive is not recognized (Sereno & Bodaken, 1975; Burgoon, 1978).

The interactional framework implies that the speaker can manipulate the message. In other words, if he or she chooses the "right" words, the communication problems will be solved. Unfortunately, communication is not that simple. Even if both parties select the "right" words and agree on their meanings, misunderstanding can still occur because each person brings different experiences to the communication event. As Gronbeck et al. (1994, p. 501) point out, "even when a message is completely clear and understandable, we often don't like it. Problems in 'meaning' or 'meaningfulness' often aren't a matter of comprehension but of reaction; of agreement; of shared concepts, beliefs, attitudes, values."

THE TRANSACTIONAL VIEW

A more accurate view of the communication process takes into account the simultaneity of sending and receiving, mutual influence, and interdependence. It also takes into account the many changes that occur while people communicate and how meaning is created between the participants. Recognizing this, many communication scholars have used the term "transaction" (Barnlund, 1970; DeVito, 1994; Kreps, 1990; Sereno & Bodaken, 1975; Stewart, 1986; Verderber, 1993; Watzlawick, 1978; Watzlawick, Beavin, & Jackson, 1967; Wilmot, 1987).

According to Prizant and Wetherby (1990, p. 5), "in the transactional model, developmental outcomes at any point in time are seen as a result of the dynamic interrelationships" between the parties and the environment that may influence both parties. Viewing the training process as transactional allows the trainer to see several important factors that affect what is going on.

In the *transactional* framework, communication has numerous components. An understanding of all the components is needed to provide a basis for the design of training strategies. The remainder of this paper is devoted to describing the transactional nature of the communication process and to providing an understanding of the way trainers behave toward clients and vice versa. Major components of communication as a transaction—such as system, process, perception, meaning, fault/blame, and negotiation—are discussed.

COMPONENTS OF THE TRANSACTIONAL PROCESS

System

Rather than viewing communication as a message injected into a passive recipient or a billiard-ball, cause-and-effect model, proponents of the transactional model assert that a communication event is a system. A systemic view of communication acknowledges not just the importance, but the constant awareness, of key factors such as interdependence and environment.

The premise that individual behavior is a part of a system, rather than a characteristic of the individual, provides an expanded view of the training process. This expansion recognizes the influence of different levels of reciprocal effects. The trainee is seen as one system immersed in and inseparable from a "larger ecological framework of systems" (Simeonsson & Bailey, 1990, p. 430).

Holding this view of communication acknowledges that it is impossible to separate the client, the trainer, the setting, the community, and the organizations from which the trainee and the trainer come. These components do not act in isolation, but influence one another in a complex and reciprocal fashion. A change in one element of the communication event "may completely change the event" (Cronkhite, 1976, p. 53). All elements are interdependent, and one cannot be considered without considering the others. As Sereno and Bodaken (1975, p. 8) state, "to deal with any one element of communication—say merely to analyze the verbal message—to the exclusion of all the others falsifies the true picture of communication as a continuous interchange."

To consider simultaneously these multivariables and their interdependence, one must keep in mind the constant "interplay between the organism and its environment" (Sameroff & Chandler, 1975, p. 234). What makes the transactional model so innovative and unique is its equal emphasis on the communicators and the environments (Sameroff & Fiese, 1990). The experiences provided by the environment are not viewed as independent of the communicators.

When trainers ignore the systemic and interdependent natures of human communication (such as the impact of a nonsupportive work environment on trainees), training is ineffective. For example, employees cannot be expected to report potential safety hazards if this information is received negatively by their supervisors. Usually, trainees are well aware of the organizational environment that they must reenter. However, if the trainer does not acknowledge this environment and make allowances for it in the training design, the message communicated to the trainee is ignored, and the trainee feels frustrated and considers the material irrelevant. The end results are that trainees do not learn or do not apply their learnings and trainers discredit themselves and the training program.

Something very similar happens when training is mandated and does not address the problems that exist in the workplace. Consider, for example, a sudden increase in accidents despite the presence of employees who are knowledgeable and enforce safety regulations effectively. The safety problems may result not from a lack of training but from other environmental factors that have a bearing on accidents—such as improperly maintained equipment or overtime hours that result in fatigue. The employees are fully aware of the reasons, yet are forced to receive additional safety training. If the trainer does not acknowledge the factors that are beyond the control of the trainee, both become frustrated, and the training process is ineffective.

The environment within which the training occurs also impacts effectiveness. Therefore, the issue of onsite versus offsite training is not a light decision. Onsite training can be especially effective when training involves new equipment. However, when training is located onsite, employees—especially managers—typically use their breaks to go to their offices and check mail, return phone calls, or take care of problems. The trainees are unable and/or unwilling to separate themselves psychologically from the workplace distractions, and the trainer who is unaware of environmental factors cannot facilitate the needed psychological distance. Offsite training can encourage new ways of relating to peers, subordinates, and other members of the team.

Thus, the trainer and trainee may be powerful determinants of perceived outcomes, but potential outcomes cannot be realized without considering the effects of the environment on the communicators. Further, the communicative process is a function of neither a single individual nor of the environment alone. Rather, the "outcomes are a product of the combination of an individual and his or her experience" (Sameroff & Fiese, 1990, p. 122).

Process

The second major component of the transactional model—and probably the least understood—is *process*. Unfortunately, many people believe process to be linear and describe it as "method," "order," or a "step-by-step" or "systematic" approach (Johnson & Proctor, 1992). However, process is not linear. It implies ever-changing, flowing, dynamic entities with no beginning and no end.

Two essential elements of process, *ongoingness* and *simultaneity*, are neither as easy to construct nor as simple as the linear and interactional models. Instead of the hypodermic-needle or billiard-ball analogy, a systemic view provides a new analogy for the study of communication: the living organism. The human body never remains constant. Neither does communication. Because of this inconstancy and the interdependent nature of communication, the roles of encoder and decoder are inseparable and interchangeable throughout the act of communication.

To increase effectiveness, trainers must monitor the impact of their interventions constantly, as well as adjust their interaction, especially when facilitating activities that generate much affect or emotional data. For example, when group feedback is focused on a group member's behavior, the trainer must constantly monitor nonverbals to ensure that the person is not experiencing the feedback as a personal attack. Even while a trainer is encouraging feedback regarding a group member's behavior, he or she must be sensitive to the receiver's nonverbals (body language, skin tone, etc.) to ensure the psychological safety of the recipient.

The encoding and decoding of messages are not mutually exclusive. Communicators are both senders and receivers at the same time in the transaction. As Sereno and Bodaken (1975, p. 8) state, there are "no periods of passive receptivity on the part of any communicator....At all times the participants are actively exchanging either verbal responses (words, sentences) or nonverbal responses (gestures, glances, shrugs or other cues of their reaction to the ongoing conversation)." The encoding and decoding processes occur simultaneously, continuously, and multidirectionally (Berko, Wolvin & Wolvin, 1992).

Perception

When using a theoretical model, one is forced to consciously simplify in graphic form a piece of reality (McQuail & Windahl, 1993). Models are merely static snapshots that capture separate pieces of a whole within moments of time, but never the whole. No one snapshot can capture all that is going on. This also is true of the communication event. No one view can capture all that has taken place; a person's "view" can explain only what *that person* perceived.

As Sereno and Bodaken (1975, p. 14) state, "When we speak of communication as having 'taken place' or 'occurred,' we're speaking figuratively of the arbitrary, fictional freezing of the process." A perceptual process helps "freeze" the communication event and make sense of the surrounding world.

Perception, the third component of the transactional model, is an active, subjective, continuous, sense-making process. Because people are continuously interpreting the world, they sometimes overlook the active and subjective natures of perception. The active nature of perception implies choice, and the subjective implies the personal, one's own. People have choices about how they interpret the world, and this sense-making process of the present is accomplished through their past experiences, which are entirely their own.

For example, when a trainer notices that someone is glancing at a clock or watch, he or she may interpret this act as boredom or simply an interest in the time—depending on the trainer's past experience. When someone suddenly leaves the meeting room, the trainer can interpret it as a serious incident or merely as an urgent need for a cigarette. Trainers who are aware of the complexity of the perception process and who constantly monitor trainees will increase the accuracy of their interpretations.

The interpretations that people choose are affected by their past experiences and relationships. As Gronbeck et al. (1994, pp. 502-503) point out, communicators "will comprehend and understand each other to the degree" of similarity between their prior experiences. If a person does not understand the prior experiences being applied to a conversation, meaning is altered.

For example, one of the authors is hearing impaired and must stay focused and concentrate when being spoken to. She explains this to the trainees in her introductory remarks in order to eliminate some perceptions of being harsh or too intense. She tells trainees that people have said that in the training environment she is totally different from the person she seems to be in her office. She further explains that in her office she does not have to concentrate as hard to hear, because she has only one person to focus on, compared to twenty people in the training room. Knowing her prior experience (hearing impairment), trainees are able to interpret her behavior within a context.

No one person's reality is *the* reality. The subjective nature of perception can be illustrated in a variety of ways. One's perception of others is influenced, for example, by one's emotional state at the time of the event (Forgas, 1991), the others' physical characteristics and attractiveness, and one's own gender (Zebrowitz, 1990), personality characteristics (Verderber, 1993), and self-perceptions (Zalkind & Costello, 1962). Self-perception and the perception of others significantly affect communication (Verderber, 1993). The more conscious that people are of the subjectivity of their interpretations, of the choices they have in this interpretation process, and of the fact that no two people will interpret the same event in the same way, the better communicators they will become (Stewart & Logan, 1993).

Perception is one reason that trainers need to use humor very carefully. Someone could be offended by a seemingly harmless joke. It is also important to protect trainees' perceptions of one another. For example, in an active-listening activity that assigns a controversial subject to the speaker, the speaker's position may be different from the one held by the listener, who is trying to practice listening skills. If the listener feels very strongly about the topic, he or she may interpret the views as the speaker's own and form negative and adverse feelings about the speaker. The trainer with a transactional view of communication would realize the importance of perception and disengage the speaker from ownership of the views expressed. The trainer could say, "When talking about a controversial subject, you may argue for or against it. You do not have to believe the position you are taking."

Created Meaning

Acknowledgment that no two people interpret anything in the same way implies that the same message has different meanings for different people (DeVito, 1994). The transactional view not only recognizes that the same word has different meanings to different people, it also recognizes a fourth component: *meaning* that is created collaboratively between communicators (Stewart & Logan, 1993).

Whereas the action view is speaker-centered and the interactional view is message-centered, the transactional view recognizes the need for "a meaning-centered theory" (Gronbeck et al., 1994, p. 502). An action or interactional view assumes that a message has one meaning, held by the speaker, to be reproduced in the listener. The transactional view, however, acknowledges a "productive rather than a reproductive approach to understanding" (Broome, 1991, p. 240). The trainer and trainee are active participants in the construction and negotiation of meanings. From a transactional perspective, the meaning of the content is created in the interaction between people and the context within which the communication occurs.

The following illustration comes from a training-in-residence event that involved twenty trainees. A small space in a large room was marked off with tape. Two trainees at a time were asked to enter the room, and each was asked to visualize his or her ideal space within the marked-off area. The ideal spaces the trainees visualized were very different from one another and usually were based on the individuals' needs and desires.

Later, all the trainees were brought into the same marked-off area and were asked to build a community out of the different spaces created in their imaginations. They soon revealed that their projected desires and needs had different meanings and were in conflict with one another. While one person had visualized a tent in the woods, another had visualized an ocean, another a waterfall, and another an office in the city.

The next few days were spent working out these differences, processing the event, and highlighting what could be learned from it. After the group finished this intense, affective work, the room had taken on all kinds of affective meaning for the participants. The trainers could not ignore this phenomenon and moved the remaining training events to a different room.

This example demonstrates the importance of being aware of the created-meaning component of the transactional model and also illustrates many of the other components previously discussed, such as environment, interdependence, process, and perception. An environment takes on different meanings to the trainees as they go through their training, and this creation of meaning is ever changing. We cannot separate these components from one another, because they are interrelated.

Also, it is important to consider the *potential* meaning of a space, the *different* meanings of that space for the trainees, and the space's *ever-changing* meaning, which is created between the communicators. A trainer must not be fooled into thinking that he or she can look at something as a discrete piece, separated from the larger environment. Space and time take on meaning. Training brings out all kinds of affective and cognitive meanings associated with the past, brought to the present, and projected into the future. A transactional perspective helps the trainer to become aware of these dynamic forces involved in a training event.

No Fault or Blame

If the creation of meaning is shared by communicators, the responsibility for this creation is also shared. This sharing leads to the fifth component in the transactional model: *no fault* and *no blame*. When communicators are mutually responsible, the notion of blame is eliminated (Verderber, 1993). This does not mean that no one is responsible, but, rather, the term "responsibility" is redefined to mean "response-able" or "able to respond" (Stewart & Logan, 1993). If people are not responsive, they are not considering how their behavior is affecting others. They are not conscious of how their "choices are part of a larger whole" (Stewart & Logan, 1993, p. 51).

The trainer must create a community of learners with training structures that support everyone's sharing the responsibility for learning. One way is to assign a learning monitor whose role is to focus on how effectively the group is learning. The role of the other participants is to provide feedback to the monitor. If there are questions or concerns, the monitor may function as a liaison between the trainer and trainees. Learning monitors take the responsibility of voicing trainees' concerns and providing the trainer with input about trainees' needs and how effectively those needs are being met.

Another way to enact this element of no fault or blame is to ask participants at the beginning of the training event what they want to accomplish from the training event. Hearing these expectations makes the trainees aware of mutual responsibility in the learning process. However, their needs may change; therefore, the "want" list should reflect those changes throughout the event. The trainees must be given the responsibility for providing feedback on how effectively their needs are being addressed.

The transactional view requires a conscious and continuous attempt by the trainer to change the way he or she thinks about communication. This is not easy. It is human nature to want to point the finger at someone else when shared meaning is not successfully created. However, one of the major benefits of a trainer's attempt to view communication from a transactional view is a more complete and less simplistic explanation of communication. The trainer also will enhance his or her probability to improve communication.

Negotiation of Selves

Using the term "transactional" to describe human communication implies "that each person is changing, being defined and redefined in relation to the other persons involved" (Stewart & Logan, 1993, p. 45). This process of constructing and responding to definitions of oneself and others is the sixth component of the transactional model, the *negotiation-of-selves* process (Stewart & Logan, 1993). Research shows that people who are more aware of this negotiation-of-selves process are perceived as more effective communicators (Applegate & Delia, 1980; Burleson, 1987; O'Keefe & McCornack, 1987).

This process acknowledges several factors, including the importance of feedback, simultaneity of sending and receiving, and interdependence. First, feedback is paramount. If definitions of selves and others are negotiated and created between communicators, shared meaning is not necessarily created. Meaning is shared through feedback. The more one recognizes that sending and receiving processes are simultaneous and cannot be separated, the more he or she will recognize that feedback is continuous and ongoing.

The trainer who views communication from the transactional model will pay attention to the continuous flow of feedback from and to trainees and not wait until the end of the training event for an evaluation. Nor will the trainer wait until the actual training event begins to seek input about the client and client system. To determine the appropriateness of the content, the client must be involved as much as is practical in the analysis of the problems and the design of the training solution.

Definitions of self and others are not determined by one person but are interdependent. Interdependence means that one communicator may affect the other, but no one individual controls or determines the other. In other words, what I do may affect you and what you do may affect me, but neither of us determines the outcome (Stewart & Logan, 1993).

From the beginning of the training event, a trainer needs to make clear to the trainees how he or she will function; for example, what the trainer's role is and what kind of self the trainer will project. The trainer's role is not that of a lecturer. The trainer should tell the participants that he or she will not just present information, that an active learning approach will be used, and that the trainee's role is necessary to make this approach successful.

Defining the roles expected of the trainees is also important. One way to help them to start thinking about their roles is to ask, "What are the worst and the best things that could happen, and what can you do to encourage the best?" Responses will give the trainees some insight into what kind of "selves" they are going to be during the training event and will reinforce the idea of shared responsibility.

As a person goes through training, he or she is continually negotiating who the trainer is, who the trainees are, and who each is for the other. So everything the trainer can do to facilitate the negotiation process is important. When a trainer asks a trainee to role play something in new ways, he or she is asking that person to be a new self. The trainer must give that person sufficient feedback about how to fine tune the role or self he or she is assuming.

              The 1997 Annual: Volume 1, Training/© 1997 by Pfeiffer

The trainer also should redefine his or her own role so that it is appropriate to the task that is assigned. For example, if a trainer facilitates a group activity in which trainees assume the roles of practicing professionals in occupational therapy (O.T.), the trainer may need to interact with the trainees while they are still in role. This interaction could cause the trainees to shift in and out of the assigned roles.

To avoid this problem, trainers can redefine the facilitative role in a way appropriate to the roles assigned trainees. In the present example, a trainer could say, "My role in this activity is to be your O.T. consultant. If you have a problem in working with your O.T. client and don't know what to do, you may call on me to give you some input." Assuming the role of consultant to the activity assists the participants in maintaining the roles essential to their learning.

Giving trainees positive feedback about the new roles they are about to assume is helpful. Statements like "You are really effective when you're an active listener" are positive reinforcements to help them maintain the newly negotiated selves that they have discovered during the training event. Support during the training event will help them to continue their new roles when they return to their work environments.

CONCLUSION

The transactional communication model has been applied to a variety of training situations, such as gerontology (Litterst & Ross, 1982), intercultural communication (Broome, 1991), child care (Prizant & Wetherby, 1990), and child development (Sameroff, 1975). This model is not limited by any area of training expertise, and the possibilities of application are limitless.

The transactional view requires that a more integrated perspective of multiple variables be considered, including system, process, perception, meaning, no fault or blame, and negotiation of selves. This approach recognizes that focusing only on isolated aspects of training without considering the interrelationships among and between these different variables may be of limited value and may not be true to the realities of the training. This view also requires consideration of the complex interdependencies among trainers, trainees, and organizational and situational contexts.

When the transactional model is applied to training, it helps us to see the complexity of factors in successful training. The more we take these factors into consideration, the more likely we are to be successful in our training endeavors.

References

Applegate, J.S., & Delia, J.G. (1980). Person-centered speech, psychological development, and the contexts of language usage. In R. St. Clair & H. Giles (Eds.), *The social and psychological contexts of language* (pp. 114-131). Hillsdale, NJ: Erlbaum.

Barnlund, D.C. (1970). A transactional model of communication. In J. Akin, A. Goldberg, G. Myers, & J. Stewart (Eds.), *Language behavior: A book of readings in communication* (pp. 43-61). The Hague, Netherlands: Mouton.

Berko, R.M., Wolvin, A.D., & Wolvin, D.R. (1992). *Communicating* (5th ed.). Boston, MA: Houghton Mifflin.

Berlo, D.K. (1960). *The process of communication.* New York: Holt, Rinehart & Winston.

Broome, B.J. (1991). Building shared meaning: Implications of a relational approach to empathy for teaching intercultural communication. *Communication Education, 40,* 235-249.

Burgoon, M. (1978). *Human communication.* New York: Holt, Rinehart & Winston.

Burleson, B.R. (1987). Cognitive complexity. In J.C. McCroskey & J.A. Daly (Eds.), *Personality and interpersonal communication* (pp. 86-109). Newbury Park, CA: Sage.

Cronkhite, G. (1976). *Communication and awareness.* Menlo Park, CA: Cummings.

DeVito, J.A. (1994). *Human communication: The basic course* (6th ed.). New York: HarperCollins.

Fisher, B.A. (1980). *Small group decision making: Communication and the group process.* New York: McGraw-Hill.

Forgas, J.P. (1991). Affect and person perception. In J.P. Forgas (Ed.), *Emotional and social judgments* (p. 288). New York: Pergamon Press.

Gronbeck, B.E., McKerrow, R.E., Ehninger D., & Monroe, A.H. (1994). *Principles and types of speech communication* (12th ed.). New York: HarperCollins College.

Johnson, S.D., & Proctor, R.F., II. (1992, September). We cannot not process—or can we? *Spectra,* p. 3.

Kreps, G.L. (1990). *Organizational communication* (2nd ed.). White Plains, NY: Longman.

Lasswell, H.D. (1948). The structure and function of communication in society. In L. Bryson (Ed.), *The communication of ideas* (pp. 37-51). New York: Harper and Row.

Litterst, J.K., & Ross, R. (1982). Training for interpersonal communication: A transactional perspective. *Educational Gerontology, 8*, 231-242.

McQuail, D., & Windahl, S. (1993). *Communication models for the study of mass communications* (2nd ed.). New York: Longman.

O'Keefe, B.J., & McCornack, S.A. (1987). Message design logic and message goal structure: Effects on perceptions of message quality in regulative communication situations. *Human Communication Research, 14*, 68-92.

Prizant, B.M., & Wetherby, A.M. (1990). Toward an integrated view of early language and communication development and socioemotional development. *Topics in Language Disorder, 10*(4), 1-16.

Reddy, M. (1979). The conduit metaphor. In A. Ortony (Ed.), *Metaphor and thought* (pp. 284-310). New York: Cambridge University Press.

Sameroff, A. (1975). Early influences on development: Fact or fancy. *Merrill-Palmer Quarterly, 21*, 267-294.

Sameroff, A.J., & Chandler, M.J. (1975). Reproductive risk and the continuum of caretaking casualty. In F.D. Horowik (Ed.), *Review of child development research* (Vol. 4, pp. 187-244). Chicago: University of Chicago Press.

Sameroff, A.J., & Fiese, B.H. (1990). Transactional regulation and early intervention. In S. Meisels & J. Shonkoff (Eds.), *Handbook of early childhood intervention* (pp. 119-149). New York: Cambridge University Press.

Sereno, K.K., & Bodaken, E.M. (1975). *Trans-Per understanding human communication*. Boston, MA: Houghton Mifflin.

Shannon, C.E., & Weaver, W. (1949). *The mathematical theory of communication*. Urbana, IL: University of Illinois Press.

Simeonsson, R.J., & Bailey, D.B., Jr. (1990). Family dimensions in early intervention. In S. Meisels & J. Shonkoff (Eds.), *Handbook of early childhood intervention* (pp. 428-444). New York: Cambridge University Press.

Sproule, J.M. (1989). Progressive propaganda critics and the magic bullet myth. *Critical Studies in Mass Communications, 6*, 225-246.

Stewart, J. (1986). Interpersonal communication: Contact between persons. In J. Stewart (Ed.), *Bridges not walls* (pp. 15-32). New York: Random House.

Stewart, J., & Logan, C. (1993). *Together: Communicating interpersonally* (4th ed.). New York: McGraw-Hill.

Verderber, R.F. (1993). *Communicate!* (7th ed.). Belmont, CA: Wadsworth.

Watzlawick, P. (1978). *The language of change: Elements of therapeutic communication*. New York: Basic Books.

Watzlawick, P., Beavin, J.H., & Jackson, D.D. (1967). *Pragmatics of human communication: A study of interactional patterns, pathologies, and paradoxes.* New York: Norton.

Wilmot, W.W. (1987). *Dyadic communication* (3rd ed.). New York: Random House.

Zalkind, S.S., & Costello, T.W. (1962). Perception: Some recent research and implications for administration. *Administrative Science Quarterly, 9,* 218-235.

Zebrowitz, L.A. (1990). *Social perception.* Pacific Grove, CA: Brooks/Cole.

Karen L. Rudick, Ph.D., *is an assistant professor of organizational communication in the department of speech communication at Eastern Kentucky University. She also provides training for a variety of organizations in the areas of conflict, negotiation, professional presentations, and interviewing, and she consults in the areas of communication audits and small-group communication.*

William Frank Jones, Ph.D., *is a professor of philosophy at Eastern Kentucky University, where he initiated the university's faculty development program. He was the director of the Corporate Training Center for the Begley Company and is on the faculty of the American Laundry & Linen College for managers. He has trained every level of management in over one hundred companies. He specializes in leadership/managerial training, communications, and team building. He also has published articles on the improvement of adult learning through experiential instruction.*

FOUR CULTURAL DIMENSIONS AND THEIR IMPLICATIONS FOR NEGOTIATION AND CONFLICT RESOLUTION

B. Kim Barnes

Abstract: Geert Hofstede (1980) has identified four important cultural dimensions. These dimensions are particularly relevant to anyone who is involved in negotiation with people from different cultural backgrounds or in conflict resolution around issues of cultural diversity. This article describes the cultural values and conditions that result from high and low prevalence of the four dimensions and presents implications for negotiation and conflict resolution in regard to each.

In his book *Culture's Consequences: International Differences in Work-Related Values,* Geert Hofstede (1980) identifies four different cultural dimensions that have implications for anyone who is working with people from cultures other than their own. Other cultural factors have been identified by other researchers, including attitudes about time and the structure of national or professional languages that orient their speakers toward certain concepts and make others difficult to grasp. Because of the great numbers of people from diverse backgrounds in the United States and other countries, and with today's increasingly global marketplace, knowledge of cultural preferences and differences, including Hofstede's research, is needed—or soon will be needed—by members of almost all organizations.

A major use of Hofstede's findings is in cross-cultural negotiation and conflict resolution. This may occur in international negotiations, in business relationships, in diversity training in organizations, and in a host of other situations. Following are a few indicators for estimating where a group (national cultural group, organization, or subgroup) lies on each of the four dimensions and some implications for negotiation and conflict resolution.

The four dimensions of culture identified by Hofstede are:

- Power distance,

- Uncertainty avoidance,

- Individualism, and

- Competitiveness.[1]

For each dimension, a group can be rated on a scale from "low" to "high." It is important to note that neither position is intended to be presented as "good" or "bad." Any such implication is a result of the author's cultural limitations.

You are invited to compare your own preferences on Hofstede's dimensions with the preferences that characterize organizations in (or with) which you work. Note any differences between your own preferences and a party or group with whom you are working or negotiating. Add your

---

[1] Hofstede calls this dimension "masculinity." The author has taken the liberty of renaming it for greater specificity.

own observations to the "implications for negotiation and conflict resolution" for each of the four dimensions. Then adjust your approach, taking the differences into account.

FOUR DIMENSIONS OF CULTURE

Power Distance

Power distance is the degree of fixed inequality of power between the more and less powerful members of a group.

Low Power Distance

When power distance is low, the following conditions exist:

- Decisions are made after consultation with all parties.

- Inequality is seen as bad. Hierarchy exists for convenience, not for the routine expression of power of one group over another.

- Those in lower-status roles may disagree with those in authority and may express their disagreement.

- Trust among members of one's peer group is high. Those in authority are often mistrusted.

- Personal power is emphasized. Expert power is accepted.

- Change occurs by redistributing power.

High Power Distance

When power distance is high (i.e., there is a high degree of fixed inequality of power between the more powerful members and the less powerful members), the following conditions exist:

- Decisions are made by those in authority.

- Everyone has a rightful place. The hierarchy represents reality.

- Those in lower-status roles are reluctant to disagree openly with those in authority.

- Trust among peers is low. Those in authority are often trusted.

- Positional power is emphasized. Referent power also is important.

- Change occurs by dethroning those in power.

Implications of Power Distance for Negotiation and Conflict Resolution

In low power-distance cultures, negotiators should specify ground rules that equalize power during the negotiations. Expert power will be accepted, but "pulling rank" may make agreements difficult. Proposals that involve the redistribution of existing power may be considered. Negotiators are more likely to be able to make agreements without gaining approval from their superiors.

In high power-distance cultures, one should expect authority to be an issue. Defer to and protect the positions of those in power. Use or borrow authority to press for a solution. Make proposals that protect existing control of power while bringing a better balance to the situation. Seek or provide formal methods for the redress of grievances.

Uncertainty Avoidance

Uncertainty avoidance is the degree to which members of a group prefer to avoid uncertainty or ambiguity.

Low Uncertainty Avoidance

Cultures that have low uncertainty avoidance are typified by the following:

- More risk taking and less resistance to change.

- A preference for broad guidelines but few rules.

- An appreciation of generalists and of "common sense."

- A view of conflict as natural, and a resultant acceptance of dissent.

- A willingness to make decisions and to take action based on less evidence.

- A high prevalence of innovation and informality.

High Uncertainty Avoidance

In cultures where avoidance of uncertainty is high, the following is typical:

- More resistance to change and less risk taking.

- A preference for clear requirements and specific regulations.

- An appreciation for specialists and expertise.

- The view that conflict is undesirable; therefore, consensus is sought.

- A requirement for more evidence before making a decision.

- A prevalence of ritual, tradition, and formality.

Implications of Uncertainty Avoidance for Negotiation and Conflict Resolution

Where uncertainty avoidance is low, negotiators can make broader, more flexible agreements. Informal agreements may be acceptable. Innovative ideas for exchange will be considered.

In situations where uncertainty avoidance is high, it is necessary to use more structure and to emphasize one's expertise. Agreements must be made specific and enforceable. (It is helpful to stress a past history of success with similar agreements.) One should be extremely careful in planning and should be prepared with back-up options to deal with every possible contingency.

Individualism

The dimension of individualism reflects the degree to which members of a group prefer to operate and make decisions independently, as opposed to collectively.

Low Individualism

When there is a low degree of individualism, the following conditions exist:

- There is dependence on and identification with the group.

- Group decisions are considered superior to individual decisions.

- A high value is placed on security, conformity, and duty.

- There is an emphasis on belonging—a "we" consciousness.

- Opinions and values are considered to be predetermined by one's reference group.

High Individualism

A high degree of individualism produces the following conditions:

- Self-reliance and independence are valued.

- Individual decisions are considered superior to group decisions.

- Autonomy, variety, and freedom are valued.

- There is an emphasis on individual initiative.

- Opinions and values are considered to be personal and individual.

Implications of Individualism for Negotiation and Conflict Resolution

Where individualism is low, negotiators should stress common interests and the interests of the larger community when making proposals. It is wise to emphasize organizational needs and traditional solutions.

Where individualism is high, a thorough exploration of differences is acceptable. Encourage individual initiative in finding creative solutions. Identify and respond to individual needs.

Competitiveness

Competitiveness is a measure of the degree to which members of a group are motivated by achievement and competition, as opposed to service and cooperation.

Low Competitiveness

In cultures with low competitiveness, the following are typical:

- Relationships, service, and social atmosphere are valued.

- There is a preference for cooperation and interdependence.

- Intuition and feelings are trusted.

- Sex roles are more fluid and more equal.

- Conflict may be avoided or win-win solutions sought.

High Competitiveness

In cultures with high competitiveness, the following are typical:

- Achievement, recognition, and advancement are valued.

- There is a preference for autonomy.

- Analyses and data are trusted.

- Sex roles are more defined; men dominate.

- Confrontation is common, and win-lose situations are accepted.

Implications of Competitiveness for Negotiation and Conflict Resolution

Where competitiveness is low, the need for harmony in relationships is probably high. Your tactical attitude should reflect this. Cooperation is valued, and attentive listening will be appreciated.

In more competitive cultures, achievement is highly valued. Anything that you can do to "save face" for your opponent will be helpful in achieving agreement. Benefits should be tangible and clear. Time limits should be respected. "Toughness" is respected as long as you are perceived as being fair.

Reference

Hofstede, G. (1980). *Culture's consequences: International differences in work-related values*. London/Beverly Hills, CA: Sage.

B. Kim Barnes is the founder and president of Barnes and Conti Associates, Inc., a training and development firm in Berkeley, California, for which she has developed programs in the areas of influence, negotiation, innovation, creativity, risk taking, team skills, communication, conflict resolution, and managing change. She also is managing partner of The Influence Alliance.

FROM VISION TO REALITY: THE INNOVATION PROCESS

Michael Stanleigh

Abstract: Innovation is a collaborative process by which organizations abandon old paradigms and make significant advances. Innovative ideas come from several sources, including "unreasonable" demands or goals and time pressures. However, there are many blocks to innovation. An innovative idea is not helpful to an organization unless it is tested and implemented. This article presents the six steps in the innovation process and tells how a team can implement each of the steps.

The perfect solution is sometimes there: as a vision, a thought, a dream, or just a wish. But it is often far too complex for an individual to take it into reality.

An example of this is found in the story of Mary Peter, who is in charge of the inventory department of the Steel Plate Company. Mary had a thought: What if it were possible to put all her company's inventories into a system? Then it would be easier to match inventories with orders, immediately confirm stock availability, and take back-order requests. It would add a new level of customer service and generate time savings.

Perhaps this was not a brilliant idea by some standards. However, at the Steel Plate Company, order entry, work in progress, inventory, accounts, credit, etc., were all separate functions with their own, largely unrelated systems. Therefore, integration of the separate functions into one system had many benefits to offer. It was an innovation for both Mary and her organization. Unfortunately, the idea died; it died because Mary killed it! She soon realized that her job would be eliminated if her idea were implemented. Furthermore, she rationalized that no one would ever agree on how to structure such a system or pay for it.

This example illustrates how many innovative ideas go nowhere because they do not link to an overall business-improvement strategy. In order to protect innovative ideas, organizations need to create a forum for the innovation process.

WHAT IS INNOVATION?

Innovation is not the following:

- The result of a lone genius inventor.

- Just about ideas. (The problem is that people often do not know where to go with ideas or how to implement them, which is sometimes a problem with suggestion-box systems.)

- About individuality in thinking (which is what suggestion-box systems tend to focus on).

Rather, innovation is:

- A collaborative process in which people in many fields contribute to implementing new ideas. (Teams are very important to the process.)

- About products and reengineering and processes—both future processes and present processes.

- Involving of people who will challenge the status quo. The person who moans and complains may be the source of the next great innovation.

WHERE DOES INNOVATION BEGIN?

Innovation begins with an idea. Ideas come from the following:

- Nowhere: Such ideas usually die unless a fertile ground exists to develop them.

- A goal: An outlandish or unreasonable demand or goal, one that a continuous improvement process will not reach, often may spark innovation.

For example, the City of San Diego, California, held a team competition among its construction trades to build a house in eight hours and still meet strict building codes. For some, this seemed to be an impossible task, but not to a team of innovative construction workers, who rose to the challenge. They decided to completely rethink the entire process of building a house; they challenged the status quo. As a result, they managed to complete the task at lightning speed—in just under three hours. This was an unprecedented achievement! When the City of San Diego examined the winning effort, it learned that the team applied a combination of sensible strategies and creative techniques to achieve its goal. These included minute-to-minute planning, simultaneous construction, training and practice, reengineered processes, teamwork, and new technology.

All these elements are at the core of reengineering the ways in which we do our work. When we "think outside the box" about our own work processes and retool them, who knows what we can accomplish? That is innovation.

Innovation often springs from pressure. Being "under the gun," with a deadline, adds a sense of consequence to the task and a purpose to spur it. Facing a challenge—even a seemingly unreasonable one (like building a house in three hours)—spurs innovation. Studies show that positive thinkers rise to a challenge. The more they are likely to face defeat, the more they want to beat it.

Innovation is a result of abandoning old paradigms, the status quo, such as rules, policies, and set procedures. Only when you leave the rules behind can you be free to create. This is critical to successful innovation. An organization that is innovative, creative, and willing to take risks has a higher likelihood of creating organizational effectiveness.

BLOCKS TO INNOVATION

The following are blocks to or killers of innovation:

- We can't do that.
- That's stupid.
- That's not in the rules.
- It's against our policy.
- We don't have the budget.
- We don't have the time.
- We'll never get it approved.
- That's not what they're looking for.
- You've got to be kidding.

Even innovators themselves sometimes block innovation. Consider these historic examples:

- In 1880, Thomas Edison said that the phonograph was of no commercial value.
- In 1920, Robert Milliken, Nobel prize winner in physics, said, "There is no likelihood man can ever tap into the power of the atom."
- In 1927, Harry Warner, of Warner Brothers Pictures, said (in reference to the desirability of adding a sound track to silent movies), "Who the hell wants to hear actors talk?"
- In 1943, Thomas Watson, chairman of IBM, said, "I think there is a world market for about five computers."
- In December of 1977, Ken Olsen, president of Digital Equipment Company, said, "There is no reason for individuals to have computers in their homes."

THE INNOVATION PROCESS: SIX STAGES

There are six stages in the process of innovation: generating ideas, capturing ideas, beginning innovation, developing a business-effectiveness strategy, applying business improvement, and decline.

1. Generating Ideas

Generating ideas is the exhilarating part of the process. It is best to do this in teams, rather than individually—which is what suggestion-box systems tend to promote. Innovative ideas generally come from a vision, an unreasonable demand, or a goal.

To get innovation going in an organization, ask, "What is impossible to do in your business now, but, if it could be done, would fundamentally change what your business does?" The answers to this question will help you to see the boundaries of a new organization. That is where innovation begins.

2. Capturing Ideas

Capturing the ideas from the first stage is done by means of team discussion or discussion among peers. It is important to record the ideas. A great brainstorming technique is to ask each team member to silently brainstorm individually. Have each team member write each idea he or she comes up with on a separate sticky note. Then have the team create an "affinity diagram" on the wall or whiteboard by collectively organizing all ideas into columns of similar ideas.

3. Beginning Innovation

Review the entire list of ideas and develop them into a series of statements of ideas. The team members then need to agree on which ones to explore further. Next, quantify the benefits of each idea to be pursued. Do this in reference to the department, the organization, and/or the customer. Describe how the statement fits with the organization's strategy, mission, and objectives. Finally, estimate the business potential—the expected outcomes of implementing the idea. These steps are designed to capture the idea and have the team members agree on a statement of feasibility before presenting the suggested innovation to management.

4. Developing a Business-Effectiveness Strategy

Innovation implementation begins here. It usually means rethinking an existing process, product, or service. This is not the same as looking at an existing process and improving it. It is describing what a future process (such as building a house in three hours) will look like.

The team first develops this "picture of the future." This usually is where the innovation resides. The easiest way to start is to have the team members list their basic assumptions about the way things are now done (which the innovation is intended to overcome). Then they brainstorm, record, and discuss every idea that arises about a possible future process. It helps to use yellow self-stick notes to record ideas individually and then to consolidate them all. The team concludes by writing a paragraph that describes the inovation and illustrating it on a flowchart. This provides the team with a look at the entire future process.

Essentially the team will have detailed how to go about the process without concern for current thinking or typical procdedure. This is similar to what Mary Peter did with her inventory system in the example at the beginning of this article.

5. Applying Business Improvement

Once the innovation is applied, it is necessary to continuously examine it for possible improvements (to the process or product or service). In the example of building a house in three hours, how could the team improve the process by using fewer people or less money?

The team starts this process by identifying the business-process gaps between what is done in the present and what is done in the innovation. This is followed by identifying the blockages and barriers to implementing the innovation. Estimating the difficulties, benefits, costs, support required, and risks is necessary before the team can refine the innovation process. Then it will be ready to apply the improvements identified.

6. Decline

In time, it often becomes obvious that what was once an innovation no longer fits. Continuous improvement of the existing process, product, or service is no longer of value; the former innovation has become outdated or outmoded. It is time to let it go, abandon the existing thinking, and set a new goal to start the innovation process once again. It is time for new innovations in response to external pressure.

INNOVATION AND ORGANIZATIONS

Every organization undergoes innovation, or else it is not successful. It is just a matter of degree. The essence of innovation is discovering what your organization is uniquely good at, what special capabilities it possesses, and how it can take advantage of these capabilities to build products or deliver services that are better than anyone else's. Every organization has unique strengths. Success comes from leveraging these strengths in the organization's service or product market place.

Today, many organizations operate globally. They find that innovation can occur anywhere, in any country or culture. Traditionally, innovation has been a local issue, not transferred to other corporate locations. But today, innovation teams, similar to improvement teams, work on innovation in regard to a product or service and then develop a centrally planned roll out. For process innovations, the local organization implements them and then, because of enhanced communication, the innovation moves from location to location. This is accomplished by using the technology available today, including teleconferencing, videoconferencing, and the World Wide Web.

Innovation is an action. To encourage yourself to take action, consider the words of George Bernard Shaw: "You see things and you say, why? But I dream things and I say, why not?"

Michael Stanleigh is the president of Business Improvement Architects. He has been a contributor to the field of corporate human resources for over fifteen years. Specializing in the areas of strategic planning, project management, performance management systems, quality systems management, leadership, and the customized design of executive, management, and staff development programs, Mr. Stanleigh creates effective learning environments and brings about significant change through his process reengineering methods.

CREATING TRAINING EXCELLENCE FOR ORGANIZATIONAL CHANGE

Irwin M. Rubin and Robert Inguagiato

Abstract: Collaborating with senior executives in developing training programs to effect behavioral change that would create win-win cultures within their organization led to a new way of designing training. This effort resulted in input into the training from organizational members, the use of prototype training groups, and other unique approaches. The training allowed individuals to practice behaviors that they believed would create a climate of excellence in their organization and that were typical of situations in their organization. This article describes the approaches used, the learnings that resulted, and the implications for managers who want to develop excellence-oriented organizational cultures.

The Goals of Senior Executives

Collaborating with several senior executives who approached training in a unique manner has reconfirmed the importance of several old truths and uncovered some new truths. An organization that employs these insights will increase the likelihood that its training investment will add value to its bottom line.

The senior executives all believed that quality training is synonymous with creating excellence-oriented cultures. They wanted to ensure that behavioral-skills training programs would empower their people to engage in day-to-day behaviors that reflected their organizations' value-driven mission statements. They wanted to implement behavioral training that focused on organizational cultural change.

The organizations' mission statements emphasized creating win-win work cultures. They described what the organizations would like to be in relation to what they currently were.

To design and implement training systems that supported major changes in their organizations' cultures, the senior executives developed three broad considerations: collaboratively developing training versus buying package training; using inside trainers versus using outside trainers; and employing modeling versus mockery.

Collaboratively Developing Training Versus Buying Packaged Training

No off-the-shelf training program is likely to meet the unique cultural and behavioral requirements of a particular organization in creating large-scale changes in the organization's work environment. This does not suggest that publicly available educational programs or off-the-shelf training programs are without value. They certainly can result in individual development. However, education that supports organizational change differs substantially from education that supports individual development.

The senior executives were looking for training that would empower people to alter their day-to-day behaviors so that, over the long term, a different feeling would characterize the way in which business was conducted internally in their organizations. To ensure that any programs we developed collaboratively would fulfill each individual organization's specific behavioral requirements, we established two criteria. First, the program must give

The 1997 Annual: Volume 1, Training/© 1997 by Pfeiffer

individuals the opportunity to practice behaviors they agree are critical to achieving excellence in their organization. Second, the program must give individuals the opportunity to practice these new behaviors in situations that occur regularly in their organization.

Over the past ten years, we have asked more than 2,000 managers to identify the specific behaviors they associate with win-win relationships. We have synthesized their responses into forty-eight discrete, observable behaviors. To establish the foundation for the behavioral model to use within a specific organization, we surveyed senior executives and other members of the organizations to determine which of these behaviors they believed were most likely to create excellence in their relationships with one another. By defining the behavioral content of the program it was developing, each organization fulfilled our first criterion.

To fulfill the second criterion, each organization defined the contexts, the practice cases, and the experiential simulations that individuals would confront during the training program.

Achieving this level of reality in a program to accomplish organizational cultural change requires that the organization become an active, collaborative partner. We have had good success in developing this collaboration by using "prototype design and test groups." Senior management hand picks and personally invites the members of a prototype design and test group—a clear signal of its importance.

A prototype group has three objectives. As the first group to participate in the new program, the prototype group evaluates the program and provides in-depth feedback on the program's strengths and weaknesses. Then the group describes situations and events that typify the organization's day-to-day reality. We interview these participants about situations they have recently or regularly encountered that did not result in the win-win outcomes the organization seeks. After the participants have completed the prototype program, they provide a detailed briefing to their senior managers and, possibly, to other members of the organization.

The number of prototype test runs necessary varies according to the organization. In one organization, we were able to iron out the bugs after only one prototype program. In a second organization, four prototype groups were necessary, and they involved the entire head-office staff of sixty persons. The number of necessary revisions is only one of several factors that determine the number of prototype groups that go through a program. The size of the training population and the internal marketing that must take place also are important considerations.

By using the concept of prototype design, we hope to communicate three important messages. First, prototype design indicates that development of the program is flexible, not rigid. Second, the prototype participants are responsible for contributing the situations that enable the program to reflect organizational reality. Third, striving for excellence means stretching a prototype beyond normal limits, uncovering possible weak spots, and learning from experience how to increase the quality of the final version of the program. Only the inhabitants of a culture can change that culture, and they can do so best with tools that they have had a hand in creating.

USING INSIDE TRAINERS VERSUS USING OUTSIDE TRAINERS

Once the behavioral training program has moved beyond the prototype phase, the organization must give serious thought to who will conduct the program. We espouse the need to have actual inhabitants of the organizational culture as trainers. No matter how skillful outside trainers may be, they will always be outsiders to the culture.

Each of the organizations became comfortable in assuming this level of accountability at a different time. In one organization, we, as outside consultants, had delivered the program to all the senior managers before the essential transition to inside trainers took place. We collaboratively designed a spin-off version of the original program, then selected and trained two in-house managers to present the program to the organization's high-potential managers. When these participants receive promotions to upper-management positions, they will have little difficulty fitting into and reinforcing the emerging culture.

In a second organization, the best model proved to be a blend of inside and outside trainers. The inside trainers included both full-time trainers from the human resource department and line managers. This arrangement worked well because significant time passed between programs. The inside trainers could link program concepts to concrete situations in the organization, and, because the outside trainers were doing training for a living, they kept their presentation skills finely tuned.

The experience in the third organization demonstrated the potential power of using line managers to present programs. Senior managers had already demonstrated their commitment by making themselves the members of the first four prototype groups. The organization carried this commitment one step further by releasing six prototype participants from their line responsibilities to become full-time trainers for the next six months. Their goal was to carry the training message to the 400 or so people just below them in the organization and to select from those they trained the next group of line-management trainer candidates. The line-management trainers also received an extensive train-the-trainer program to prepare them for their upcoming role.

This organization has trained twenty-four line managers as trainers, and these inside trainers have devoted six months full-time to presenting the program to almost 2,000 participants. As a result of the intensity of their involvement, these twenty-four people—who have all rotated back into significant line-manager positions—have the potential to model and reinforce the aspects of cultural change they have spent six months teaching to others. Tracking the effects these people have on the cultural change in their organization reinforces our belief in the most powerful training program we know: modeling ourselves after leaders we respect.

MODELING VERSUS MOCKERY

Senior executives are responsible for ensuring the maximum return possible from the organization's investment in its most important asset: its people. People often say one thing and do another. Senior executives, in particular, must practice what they preach. Most senior managers with whom we collaborated understood the importance of leading by example. They knew that to tell others to attend a behavioral training program whose goal is organizational cultural change, and not to attend the program themselves, would make a mockery of the training effort.

Leadership by example (modeling) offers great potential for cynicism. We all have heard examples of training on Friday reverting to "business as usual" on Monday. This brings us back to the theme of quality training being synonymous with creating excellence-oriented cultures.

CREATING EXCELLENCE-ORIENTED ORGANIZATIONAL CULTURES

One of the central themes of the behavioral-skills training programs was developing win-win relationships. Recognizing when someone is doing something right, and learning from mistakes rather than blaming, are inherent in this theme. Managers and executives must learn to acknowledge and nurture employees who are demonstrating good returns on the training investment. In our experience, there is a tendency not to celebrate and learn from individual success. (Perhaps blowing someone else's horn is only slightly more culturally acceptable than blowing one's own.) Similarly, when a well-intentioned but fallible and imperfect human being does not yield a return commensurate with an organization's expectations, responsible persons in the organization must attempt to see what they can learn from the mistake, rather than blaming someone for it. These learnings are part of what made our collaborative efforts with the organizations we have discussed so refreshingly unique.

Two of our experiences demonstrate how some managers behave when they are committed to the belief that quality training is synonymous with creating excellence-oriented cultures.

The Case of the Crisis

One of the organizations found itself confronting a series of work-related crises during a period of intense training. If it had followed the standard routine, the organization would have pulled key managers from the training programs so that they could be available in their offices to handle the crises. Instead, senior management took a dramatically different approach.

The CEO wrote a case briefing for one of the real crises the organization was facing, and several of the programs that took place during this turbulent period used this case. The real-life-crisis case took the place of several of the cases that were normally used in the program. Consequently, training participants had the opportunity to practice new behaviors in a real work crisis and yet remain in the learning environment. They videotaped their work so they could review their behaviors and case outcomes as part of their learning.

Learning from experience, with or without the assistance of videotape, is just the habit we hope to instill on the job to create an excellence-oriented culture. This CEO had the courage of his convictions to use quality training to tackle problems of real and immediate consequence.

The Case of the Overenthusiastic Manager

The second example points out some important limitations of our own beliefs and convictions as program designers. A highly visible and influential senior executive from one of the organizations attended a training program and became quite enthusiastic about its potential effect on his behavioral patterns. His motivation and enthusiasm continued to grow back on the job, but his attempted integration of the behavioral skills was so dramatic that he increasingly rubbed people the wrong way. This senior executive's manager mentioned to us that he had not only taken the program "on board" but had gone overboard!

This situation reflects an important blind spot that we human resource development professionals sometimes have. We believed that the training programs we were collaboratively designing would make a difference in people's lives, and we hoped that participants would take the programs fully on board. However, we could have spent more time during the program helping the participants learn not to go overboard with their new behavioral skills.

The thing that reinforces the uniqueness of this organization and its desire for an excellence-oriented culture is how it handled this senior executive once it recognized the problem. The traditional response would have been to slap the person's hand, pull him up short, or, worse, cut the organization's losses by cutting him loose. The organization chose none of these options. Instead, it offered him the opportunity of one-on-one, on-the-job support from us to enable him to make better use of the skills the organization had asked him to learn and which he had so enthusiastically embraced.

CONCLUSION

Certain conclusions can be drawn from our experiences with these organizations that are relevant to human resource development professionals and organizations that wish to establish excellence-oriented work cultures. First, quality training goes hand-in-hand with establishing excellence in an organization's work culture. Second, collaborative design results in a behavioral-skills training program that reflects the organizational realities experienced by inhabitants of the culture. Third, when people from the work culture can serve as trainers within the organization, the likelihood of the organization's taking the program on board increases dramatically. Finally, the behavior of senior managers speaks louder than any behavioral-skills training program. The members of an organization will mimic the behaviors of their leaders; consequently, to teach one set of behaviors and to display another will only make a mockery of the training investment.

Irwin M. Rubin, Ph.D., is the president of Temenos, Inc., in Honolulu, Hawaii, a firm that provides organization development and training consulting services to organizations in the public and private sectors. Dr. Rubin is a former faculty member of the Sloan School of Management at MIT and of Harvard University, and has received several awards for outstanding teaching. He is a charter member of ISPI and is the coauthor of eight books and over thirty published articles in organizational psychology, health care, and other areas.

Robert Inguagiato, an independent consultant, specializes in designing, developing, and implementing executive and management training courses and organizational development systems. He has formerly served as the director of Educational Services for Astra Merck; executive vice president of Temenos, Inc.; head of management development and training for the international office automation firm NBI; director of Operations Division Human Resource Planning and Development for Crocker Bank; and staff vice president of Human Resources and director of Sales Training for Citicorp.

TRAINING IN MEXICO AND CENTRAL AMERICA

Kevin M. Kelleghan

Abstract: Training in Mexico and Central America offers exciting training opportunities, but it is necessary for consultants to inform themselves about the history and background of the Latin American countries that they will work in. Brief reviews of the economies and training climates of Mexico, the six countries of Central America (Costa Rica, El Salvador, Guatemala, Honduras, Nicaragua, and Belize), Panama, and other countries in South America are offered. Success for U.S. trainers or consultants in Latin America may well depend on whether they are able to adapt to doing business "the Latin way."

The article addresses the importance of relationships, the "*mañana*" perspective, reservations about language difficulties and payment, travel preparations and considerations, handling materials, audience expectations, and special challenges offered south of the border.

Quick tips on doing business in Latin America and a list of further resources add to the practical information in the article.

During the thirteen years that I have managed and presented training programs in Mexico and Central America, I have spoken before motivated, knowledgeable, and exacting audiences of middle and senior executives and commanded the same fees (or higher), in U.S. dollars, that I receive in the United States.

And that's just about where the similarity ends.

Knowing some background about Latin America before you go can help you succeed in your consulting efforts. Invest several hours to gain a working knowledge of the history, recent politics, economy, and culture of the country or countries in which you will be working. Your Latin hosts will appreciate your interest and extra effort and will be more receptive to your message.

BACKGROUND

Mexico

Although Mexico's economic woes have captured headlines, particularly following the North American Free Trade Agreement (NAFTA), trainers should not write off opportunities there. Of the six countries between the Rio Grande and the Panama Canal, it is by far the most attractive market. Devaluation of the peso and its consequences may be a primary concern right now, but devaluation has burdened every administration in Mexico for two decades. Since 1976, each president has dealt with devaluation and subsequent economic distress. Yet after every recession, Mexico, like the phoenix, restores itself to new heights of growth.

Prior to 1976, Mexico had enjoyed a 20-year reputation as a stable, emerging third-world economy, and investors gorged on Aztec stocks and bonds. Business enjoyed tariff protection, availability of investment capital, an incentive tax structure, and labor peace. All of this gave rise to the so-called "Mexican miracle," fueled by basic industries and manufacturing, especially steel and automobiles.

The automobile industry, as an example, spawned suppliers producing engine parts, batteries, tires, radios, plastics, glass, and other components. But Mexico's prize is oil, managed by state-owned Petroleos Mexicanos, or Pemex. The nation boasts about 5 percent of the world's crude oil reserves and ranks eighth among the world's oil-rich nations— those that each have at least fifty billion barrels of the world's reserves.

These eight nations have a stunning 80 percent of all the oil reserves on earth.

Mexico's economy has expanded dramatically during the past twenty years, as a result of the discovery of those vast oil reserves. Promising young managers study for advanced degrees at Ivy League business schools. They can afford to; business is booming and companies are mushrooming to conglomerate size.

Although the country is undergoing another recession, the nation has a strong manufacturing and service base, abundant natural resources, and an intelligent and progressive work force. Some of Mexico's most prominent business titans rank among the richest men in the world. Mexican business people admire U.S. management techniques and are eager to learn them. Recent topics have focused on management skills in manufacturing, human resources, and sales.

One final and important note: Mexicans consider themselves just as "North American" as U.S. citizens do, since the country is on the North American continent. As a matter of fact, the full name of Mexico is United Mexican States *(Estados Unidos Mexicanos),* which is quite similar to United States of America. To avoid offense, refer to yourself (and other compatriots) as *North* Americans, rather than as "Americans."

Central America

Six countries compose Central America: Costa Rica, El Salvador, Guatemala, Honduras, Nicaragua, and Belize. Panama, which would be included in this group by many Americans, is not considered part of Central America by its neighbors. You will demonstrate your knowledge of the region by treating Panama separately when discussing it with your Central American clients.

Costa Rica

Costa Rica draws thousands of U.S. tourists and investors every year. A nation at peace with its neighbors, it has no army and boasts a 92 percent literacy rate. Managers there have told me they are interested in advanced management techniques. The Instituto Centroamericano de Administracion de Empresas (Central American Institute of Business Administration), referred to by its initials, INCAE, boasts superb training facilities. Nestled near a village just outside San Jose, INCAE is associated with Harvard. During the weeks I conducted workshops there, I stayed in a two-bedroom cottage supplied with servants, dined with students in a dining room next to a large swimming pool, and was chauffeured each day to modern, luxuriously equipped classrooms.

El Salvador

El Salvador's attraction is a peacetime economy after a lengthy war with guerrillas. Government-financed construction is booming, and Salvadoran consumers are flocking to malls on balmy nights, something they were deprived of during the conflict. The owner of a restaurant chain asked me to write a program on cutting-edge advertising and promotion techniques, an indication that consumers are a key to the thriving economy. Another of my clients, based in Miami, organizes workshops for the Salvadoran government and has been providing agricultural training for several years. As an example of Salvadoran motivation, the owner and publisher of the country's largest newspaper sat in as a participant during my week-long seminar on business writing skills for mid-career journalists.

Guatemala

Guatemalans, who are exceptionally friendly and generous, may need some introduction to the fundamentals of any area you may teach before you move on to more advanced concepts. I have presented training sessions in resorts, some of which are located near Guatemala City. The country is popular with Americans, both retirees and investors, who live in sumptuous residences in charming towns (in which you might conduct workshops).

Honduras

Unlike other Central American countries in which the capital is virtually the only important city, Honduras has two major cities: the capital, Tegucigalpa, and an industrial center, San Pedro Sula. Of the two, I prefer to work in San Pedro Sula. There is an entrepreneurial spirit in San Pedro. When I was brought in from Chicago to provide management consulting for a spanking new, full-color daily newspaper, I found the staff knowledgeable, industrious, and eager to absorb more knowledge. For example, they invested extra hours in overnight assignments.

Nicaragua and Belize

Nicaragua currently offers limited opportunities for U.S. trainers because of its struggling economy. Nevertheless, my week-long program in Managua was held in a modern, sprawling conference center that provided every amenity, including a white-tablecloth restaurant. Many attendees spent several hours at work before the day-long session, then returned to their jobs after the workshop.

Belize, the smallest nation in Central America, nestled next to Guatemala, is a mecca for tourists and is less likely than other Central American countries to provide consulting opportunities.

Panama

Panama is especially attractive to U.S. trainers. Although the United States has a roller-coaster reputation because of U.S. control of the Panama Canal and U.S. intervention in the country's internal affairs, most sophisticated Panamanian executives leave their personal feelings about the United Sates outside when they walk through the training-room door. Only one person has ever revealed antagonism toward the U.S. during the many training sessions I have conducted. Panama is enjoying a construction boom. Interest is keen in the issue of the management of the Panama Canal when it reverts to Panama in the year 2000.

Background on South America

Although the focus of this article is on Mexico and Central America, several South American countries may be of interest to trainers and are mentioned briefly here.

Venezuela

Travel time is a consideration to the central and southern countries of South America, although flights to northern countries are not much longer than journeys to Central America. My flight time from Miami to Caracas, Venezuela, was about the same as a flight to Central America. Although a banking problem rocked its businesses last year, Venezuela's oil wealth is apparent in its high-rise office buildings. There is a strong U.S. business presence.

Colombia

Colombia's economy has been growing rapidly. My work for a multinational publisher took me to an impressive, thriving, office and commercial complex in Bogota.

Argentina, Chile, and Brazil

These are the three most interesting countries for U.S. trainers in the southern part of the hemisphere. Argentina has been struggling with recession following the impact on investment after the Mexican peso crisis in 1994.

Chile, with an 8 percent growth rate, is attracting investment around the world. Both countries reflect strong European influence. Brazil, the only nation in Latin America that speaks Portuguese, finally managed to control inflation in 1994. The computer industry is attractive for information systems trainers.

DOING BUSINESS THE LATIN WAY

Success for U.S. trainers and consultants who are examining opportunities in Latin America may well depend on whether they are able to adapt to doing business "the Latin way." You need to be aware of significant differences between U.S. and Latin American cultures, especially in areas of acceptable business practices and negotiation styles.

Relationships

For example, never begin a sales call by getting right down to business. People in Latin America are less direct than their U.S. counterparts. Manolo Santibanez, originally from Spain and CEO of an information systems consulting firm in Mexico City, describes this characteristic:

> If you want to sell peanuts to your potential client, for example, you would first talk about everything but peanuts. You might discuss the weather or your flight to Mexico City. You could talk about your plans to tour the city. But you would never begin a sales call by telling your client that you are interested in selling peanuts.

Relationships are critically important. Latin American clients want to get to know you first and then discuss business. Plan to spend a portion of your first phone call or visit just getting to know your client before you discuss training or consulting. Moreover, although you may become impatient, never pressure Latin Americans for a decision.

Get used to shaking hands with everyone in the room when you meet with Latin Americans. Every time you meet someone, you shake hands. Every time you leave, you shake hands again. Women greet and depart by bussing one another on the cheek. When you say good-bye to one person in a group, custom requires you to say good-bye to everyone else, no matter how long this takes. Carry a full box of business cards to hand out freely as you shake everyone's hand.

Mañana

Another characteristic that is significantly different from U.S. culture is the tendency in Latin America to put things off. You will need to gain a new understanding of the word "tomorrow," or *mañana*. It really means "at some point in the future," which may not necessarily be tomorrow.

During a consulting assignment in Honduras, for example, I was asked by a client to recommend a motivational trainer. I suggested a friend, an international trainer and author, and also offered to contact him. When I called him, he was interested and immediately faxed a proposal to the Honduras contact, including available dates. He heard nothing for several days. When he called me to ask for advice, I pointed out that Latin Americans generally take longer to respond than North Americans. He was impatient to fill that date but never got the immediate response he was used to in the U.S. The solution: set a date that is far enough in the future for the Latin American client to make a final decision.

On another occasion, a client from Mexico City asked me to submit an outline for a seminar on long-range sales planning. That was followed by an urgent request for a complete outline and suggestions for the brochure copy. Everything seemed to be flowing smoothly. But after all that, I did not hear from the client for several weeks. I called the program coordinator, who said that the seminar would definitely be presented in a public program and she would soon confirm the date. When she finally got back to me, it was to tell me that the seminar would be presented a year later! (The seminar went extremely well, with fifty-five participants.)

Although such experiences may not be uncommon in the United States either, they happen with much more frequency in Latin America. This *mañana* characteristic is referred to as *informal* in Spanish. Latin Americans lament this characteristic in their culture, but they are used to others being late for appointments and they compensate by arriving late themselves—a sort of chain reaction. Actually, the *informality* of the business people you will be dealing with is not the problem; most executives begin and end appointments on time. The problem is the people around the executives you will deal with. Many of these people continue to do things the old-fashioned, *mañana,* way.

Sometimes a delay is caused by conditions beyond your client's control. Latin Americans occasionally have to scramble for hard currency, for example, and may put off a final decision until they are certain that the dollars are in hand to pay your fee, travel expenses, and program costs.

Reservations

Trainers and consultants should not hesitate to present workshops south of the border because of concerns about the language barrier or payment, which are the reservations I have most frequently heard. Neither of these has been a problem for me.

If you are not fluent in Spanish, you can speak English in every Latin American country you work in. If some members of the audience are not comfortable with English, the client may arrange for simultaneous interpretation. This will require that you wear a lavaliere microphone so that the interpreter can hear you through earphones. The interpretation takes longer—Spanish uses 20 percent more words than the English equivalent. If you are a fast talker, you may be asked to speak more slowly. There also will be times when you will have to stop speaking entirely until the interpreter catches up with you.

TRAVEL TIPS

Preparations and Considerations

Mexico and Central America are easy to get to. Direct flights to Mexico City depart from a number of U.S. cities, and you can travel directly to Monterrey, Mexico, an industrial city, from Dallas/Fort Worth. However, for most flights to Central America. you will change planes at the Miami airport. On your return flight through Miami, you will need to walk a considerable distance from your arrival gate to baggage handling, take your bags through U.S. customs, and then go back to your domestic flight gate; so allow forty-five minutes or more between flights.

Because of long flights, try to schedule workshops or consulting in several countries below the border. For example, on one trip, I worked my way down one coast—beginning in Bogota, Colombia, then to Guayaquil, Ecuador, next a short flight to Lima, Peru, and finally to Santiago, Chile. I returned on a nonstop flight to Venezuela for a meeting with a client in Caracas.

A passport is essential, and some countries also require a visa. You generally will not need a business visa, but check with the country's consulate to be sure. The country in which you will be working may require that the visa be stamped in your passport. Arrange for that well in advance. The procedure is simple: call the country's consulate nearest you for requirements and then mail in your passport, along with any fee. (Some visas are free, but Bolivia charged me $50.00.) Generally, the visa-stamped passport will be returned within a few days.

For guidelines on vaccinations needed for a specific country, check with your county health department. Nurses also usually have up-to-date information.

Materials

You can carry participant workbooks and handouts with you, but this is usually unnecessary, unless there are special circumstances such as proprietary materials. I prefer to send a master copy of my workbook to the client. If you send the materials well in advance, the client may even arrange to have them translated and copied in Spanish. This is always preferable but not always necessary. There may be a few members of your audience who are not fluent in English, and a translation is a nice courtesy.

PRESENTING IN MEXICO AND CENTRAL AMERICA

Demanding Audiences

Audiences are sophisticated and demanding, a characteristic I have found especially true in Mexico. Many participants take extra time to write extensive critiques on their evaluations after a seminar. These extremely helpful comments also reveal their high expectations. In one workshop I presented two years ago in Mexico City, a participant sitting near the front of the room followed the brochure outline with great care, ostentatiously checking off each topic as it was delivered. He was not the only one, I learned later.

Challenges

Training in Latin America offers excitement and challenges you may never experience in a workshop in the United States. On one occasion, in San Salvador, a bomb exploded while I was presenting *When the Press Picks You for an Interview* to a group of fifty senior-level executives. Although the war was in its last throes, the guerrillas still planted bombs occasionally. On that second day of the week-long workshop, guerrillas knocked out a power station just six miles from our training site. Although electricity was cut off, a generator kicked in to maintain air conditioning. Unfortunately, the generator was just behind me at the front of the meeting room. It was so loud the audience could barely hear me.

The executives were apprehensive, and, although it was never mentioned, I had visions of guerrillas holding hostage this high-powered group, which included a cabinet secretary and the mayor's wife.

That afternoon the client came to me and asked if I wanted to cancel the program because of the danger. "I didn't come all this way to turn around and go back home just because a power station was blown up," I responded. "If the group wants to continue, I will too." Apparently my bravado impressed the attendees. Every one of them decided to continue with me. There was no further guerrilla activity, and the workshop was even extended by a day.

Quick Tips on Doing Business in Mexico and Central America

1. Do not show exaggerated interest. You may very much want this contract for the experience or to expand your résumé, but be prudent in your negotiations.

2. Use humility to your advantage. A trainer may feel that he or she is delivering advanced technology, "American know-how" that Latin Americans ought to be grateful for. Remember, Latin Americans put personal relationships before business relationships. A more gracious and empathic approach would be: "I'm flattered that you're doing me the favor of hiring me for your training needs."

3. Put everything in writing. Prepare your contract in English if you like so that the content is just as you wish, but then have it translated into Spanish. This is when you should spend a little more to get the best translator available.

4. Do not sign a contract that you receive by fax. Negotiate by fax, make changes or suggestions, but sign and airmail a hard copy of the final agreement.

5. Dress formally, always. Business dress is always correct in Latin America. Although you might dress in jeans or shorts and sneakers in your own office, always wear modest and conservative clothing when conducting business in Latin America.

6. Use titles. Anyone who has graduated from college has earned the right to the title *Licenciado*. Lawyers are addressed as *Licenciado* as well, which may appear in its abbreviated form, *Lic.*, before the person's name on business cards. Engineers are addressed as *Ingeniero*, which appears as *Ing.* before the person's name.

7. Accounting methods are different in Latin America. Ask your host, or an attorney in the country, for specific advice. Your client may be required to withhold local income tax. Remember that overseas income must be reported to the IRS.

With a bit of preparation and knowledge, you will find that Latin American countries hold many rich, exciting, and satisfying opportunities for your consulting expertise.

Resources for Further Information

You may find some of the following listings useful in your search for additional information:

- *Background Notes* is a series published by the U.S. Department of State. They are my first source for easy-to-read background information on any country. Available at nominal cost from the Superintendent of Documents, U.S. Government Printing Office, Washington D.C. 20402, Tel (202) 783-3238. Updated frequently.

- The National Trade Data Bank Compact Disk (NTDB CD), released monthly, with more than you will ever want to know about every country, is available nationwide in some local libraries, Federal depository libraries, and many college libraries. To order one CD or an annual subscription, for the address of the library with the CD nearest you, or for further information, call (202) 482-1986. Or call or write Denise L. Wood (who contributed to this resource guide), International Trade Coordinator, Rockford Area Council of 100, Rockford, IL 61103; Tel (815) 987-8128.

- *Commercial Guides* by country are full reports on trade conditions and best prospects for trade, the business climate, and trade resources. Each ranges from forty to one hundred pages. They are included in the NTDB CD, or call the Department of Commerce export office: 1-800-USA Trade (1-800 872-8723).

- The *CIA World Factbook,* also on the NTDB CD, contains extensive demographic information. Call (202) STAT-USA (202- 782-8872).

- The Internet address for information is www.stat-usa.gov, and the ftp address is ftp.stat-usa.gov. There is a fee for access to the NTDB. The most recent price was $25 for three months and $100 for one year of unlimited access; check for the current price.

- *Market Research Reports* provides industry reports by country, project-bid information, and economic trends, and other reports on the NTDB CD.

- If you are exploring opportunities to establish a business in any Latin American country, Price Waterhouse World Firm Ltd. publishes an excellent soft-cover series called *"Doing Business In..."* Each publication profiles the business environment, foreign investment, trade opportunities, investment incentives, restrictions on foreign investors, the regulatory environment, banking and finance, exporting, labor relations, and other topics. The books also cover taxation and setting up joint ventures and partnerships. Available for $20 per copy: 1251 Avenue of the Americas, New York 10020; Tel (212) 819-5000; Fax (212) 790-6620.

Kevin M. Kelleghan, *a bilingual trainer and consultant, is president of CED Seminars International, an executive-development and business-writing consulting company. He has worked in Mexico for 25 years and currently trains and consults in the U.S. and Latin America on communication skills and Latin America's business culture for business and government clients. His books include* How to Invest or Retire in Mexico *(Inversiones Alba S.A., 1972),* Dealing with Mexico's Business Culture—So Near and Yet So Foreign *(1994), and* Effective Business Writing *(in press, Fall, 1996). He is a member of The Authors Guild Inc. and the American Society for Training and Development, Rock Valley, Illinois, Chapter.*

TRAINING FOR ORGANIZATIONAL RESULTS: HOW TO GET THE MOST VALUE FOR THE TRAINING DOLLAR

Kevin Daley

Abstract: Training no longer can be regarded as a luxury in organizations. These days, trainers must demonstrate that what they do improves performance and contributes to organizational success. This article offers new insights into approaching training from this viewpoint. Examples include identifying training needs using the technique of Socratic questioning, training a critical mass to effect organizational change, considering various forms of training, using managers and individual follow-up to reinforce training, and evaluating training in terms of organizational results. Examples of innovative solutions in actual organizations also are presented.

Changing Organizational Realities

Organizational realities are changing the ways in which professional trainers approach their jobs. Senior management is looking at training expenditures with a more critical eye than ever before. Under these conditions, training cannot be regarded as merely an added expense or a luxury to be undertaken when time and budgets allow. Nor will it do to have managers think of training as remedial, as a matter of shoring up weak employees or fixing problems. Successful trainers will act less like physicians who administer to organizational ills and more like agents of change who understand the organization's strategic direction and who can design and implement creative ways of moving people in that direction. The necessity of gaining the full support of senior management cannot be emphasized enough. This is a crucial foundation that allows trainers to provide training to a critical mass, which will effect change within the various organizational cultures. Above all, today's trainers must be focused, able to take risks, and willing to put a business agenda before their personal ones.

Many organizations have already shifted their thinking about the training function. They have seen for themselves that training is where ideas and attitudes are changed and skills are developed. In the course of learning the skills that will increase sales, promote customer satisfaction, or build effective teams, employees learn the attitudes and aptitudes that will revise the corporate culture even as they improve operations.

The Monsanto Protiva Answer

When the stakes of training are so high, and the benefits so critical, it becomes imperative to provide the most for each training dollar. At Monsanto's Protiva division, for example, where virtually all salespeople have received selling and communication-skills training, there is emphasis on the needs of the individual. Different classifications of employees, including administrative staff, are given budgets of between $2,000 and $5,000 each for training. Each employee selects the training to meet his or her particular needs. One individual may take an organization development course while others study time management, media relations, or computer operations. The organization recognizes how to maximize its training impact through individualized instruction.

What Is Good Training?

Of course, almost every organization has war stories about training that just did not work. Everyone gave the personable and perky communications trainer top ratings, but communication is still the primary problem, or the customer service people came out of their telephone-skills training feeling insulted because the course was so rudimentary that virtually any of the attendees could have taught it. In another scenario, a change-management training session backfires because all it accomplishes is the fueling of rumors about plant closings.

Professional trainers know that training that makes people feel warm and good is not necessarily effective training. Training that makes people feel uncomfortable is not necessarily ineffective training. How employees evaluate the training is not the most important gauge of how successful the program is. The only thing that really counts is what happens afterward.

Good training is based on having fully answered the following questions:

- Is there actually a need for training? What is the need?
- Who needs to be trained?
- Who will provide the training?
- What form will the training take?
- How will the training be transferred from the session to the job?
- How will the training be evaluated?

When training is regarded as a strategy for effecting change, different answers come up than when training is regarded as a cure for perceived weaknesses.

Identifying Training Needs

Training needs can be expressed at the organizational, divisional, departmental, team, or individual levels. Much of the best training is "just-in-time," in response to a felt need. For example:

- A cross-functional team sees that it is becoming bogged down in miscommunication and arguments and asks for training in communication skills. A needs assessment verifies that the problem is a lack of good communication skills among the membership, not a deeper group issue.

- A sales manager realizes that her group is losing out to the competition because of poor presentation skills and asks for training.

- The corporate communications group sees that it could cut costs and save time if its staff had some training in desktop publishing.

It is important to remember that when there is no immediate need to practice and use what is learned, training is almost doomed to fail.

Using Socratic Questioning

The first, important step in the training process is clearly identifying needs. A useful tool in gleaning such information involves the technique of Socratic questioning. This technique is derived from Socrates' ancient philosophy, which held that asking a series of simple, easily answered questions would ultimately lead to a mutually beneficial conclusion. Whether it is used by an in-house human resources manager surveying his or her various business groups or an outside trainer interviewing a potential corporate client, this technique is an excellent means of uncovering real needs.

In Socratic questioning, the information gatherer constantly plays back information that is given in the conversation to ensure understanding. Probing phrases such as "What else should I know?" and "Why did you ask that?" are used to uncover the real issues and needs.

The following is a hypothetical conversation between a trainer and a potential client. The two have been discussing human resource consulting services when the client suddenly moves to a specific area:

Client: Do you provide prepackaged training programs?

Trainer-Consultant: That is one of several services we offer. Why do you ask? (Instead of launching into an in-depth description of this one area, the consultant probes for further information.)

Client: Well, last year we tried that approach with another consultant and it just didn't work.

Trainer-Consultant: Tell me more about what happened.

Client: Well, we were trying to teach computer skills that were specific to the telecommunications industry, and the trainer didn't really cover them.

Trainer-Consultant: So what you are saying is that the trainees didn't learn the kind of skills they needed in order to do their jobs better? (The consultant plays back what has been said in order to obtain clarification and begins to uncover the real concern.)

Client: Exactly, and they got frustrated, lost their motivation, and tuned out early in the session.

Trainer-Consultant: Perhaps a customized training approach is something you might want to consider. We can develop a program suited to your particular industry that would give your employees the specific skills they need.

The use of Socratic questioning throughout this conversation allows the questioner to get at the crux of the problem. By digging deeper, the trainer is able to obtain more information about the past and uncover the client's real concern, the need for a tailored training program. Ideally, the two parties will end up at the same place with a potential solution.

Training a Critical Mass of Employees

Once training needs have been clearly defined, the trainer needs to decide which people will receive the training. In order to create change, a critical mass of employees needs to receive the information. Getting a lot of people on the same wavelength accelerates desired change. Instead of viewing the new methods and attitudes with suspicion, the employees will be able to make them "the way we do things here." It also is vital that the managers of the employees who will receive the training also receive it. Nothing kills new learning as fast as the failure of the boss to understand and support it. Newly promoted and newly hired members of a group should also receive any training that was provided to the original group.

The Example of Penske Truck Leasing

When all members of a critical mass receive the same training, the benefits almost invariably extend beyond the acquisition of the skills taught. At Penske Truck Leasing, for example, all salespeople receive communication training, and the training does more than improve their communication skills. Being better communicators increases the confidence levels of sales representatives and, with more confidence, they can take on more responsibilities. Providing communication training has effectively created a pool of potential managers and enhanced the company's ability to realize its goal of promoting from within.

Deciding Who Will Deliver the Training

The choice of who will deliver the training requires much creative and strategic thinking. Is there a time constraint? Even if the internal training department is large, the time it takes to develop a program may not meet the pressing need to have a group of employees trained in a new method or skill. Human resource managers need to evaluate whether developing a new program is the best use of the internal trainers' time. Particularly if large numbers of newly hired people need to be trained on an ongoing basis, the use of an outside trainer should be considered.

Using Outside Trainers

An outside training consultant can efficiently develop programs that can be implemented quickly. Particularly if they are familiar with the specific industry, most such consultants have a quick learning curve when it comes to assimilating business information and developing appropriate programs. The human resource manager must evaluate whether the materials a consultant uses fit the organizational culture and the skill levels of the employees to be trained. A great deal of training misses the mark because employees are unable to relate to the people shown in videos or to examples provided in activities and discussions. Bringing in outside training services is not like buying office supplies; it is not about getting a good product at a good price. It is establishing and maintaining a productive relationship that will accelerate change.

Determining the Form of the Training

The form that training will take is another crucial issue. One recent, positive trend is focusing on training of individuals. This sometimes is based on assessments completed by the employee, his or her manager, and his or her peers or subordinates (360° feedback). This process, which is usually an accompaniment to broad-based training, allows the individual to choose skills that he or she wants to improve. This affects the form the training will take. Recognizing that different individuals learn in different ways, good training departments offer a variety of ways of acquiring skills, including computer-assisted learning, self-study programs, books, videotapes, seminars, and mentoring/apprenticeship programs such as shadowing an employee who excels at a particular skill. When employees understand how their performance impacts the strategic direction of the organization, their wisdom can be tapped by enabling them to help to choose what, when, and how they will learn in order to improve their performance.

Transferring the Training to the Job

Perhaps the most important consideration is how the learnings and insights from the training will be integrated into each individual's day-to-day job.

Working on real tasks and problems as part of the training can help to ensure that the training "takes." Spreading out training over several months or weeks gives employees adequate time to practice and solidify each new technique or skill.

More radically, making an actual, pressing problem the basis of the training program and devoting the training activities to working on and solving the problem not only meets a corporate goal but also teaches people skills that will transfer to future performance. At the very least, it may be advisable to include an individual action plan, delineating the steps the employee will take when he or she is back at work. Following up on the action plan helps to monitor results in terms of the employee and the overall training program.

Management Must Reinforce the Training

The managers of the employees who are receiving the training should be completely familiar with the content of the training and committed to supporting and reinforcing the new learnings. This means being able to answer employees' questions and concerns, allowing extra time to do things in a different way, praising and rewarding the use of new skills, and creating environments in which the new ways can take hold.

Chadbourne & Parke's Experience

Chadbourne & Parke, a leading New York law firm, recognizes that training must be supported. All the partners and associates receive individualized follow-up training with the firm's marketing director at predetermined intervals after they participate in presentation-skills training as a group. This allows each of them to work on potential "trouble" areas they may encounter after their initial instruction.

Evaluating the Training

Ultimately, training must be judged on its impact on the organization. This requires hard data on measurable objectives such as increased sales, market share, reduced operating costs, lower rates of absenteeism, or whatever the training was designed to achieve. Although it is recognized that other forces affect these measurable criteria, it is nonetheless important that training be tied to corporate objectives all the way through to the payoff stage.

"Temperature taking" during and immediately after the training is also important. If the trainer is dull or "puts the trainees off" in some way, if there is too much information to absorb, or if the material or the approach is off-target, this needs to be known immediately. Using this information to modify the training already in progress and to make the next round better will maximize the investment in training. Participants and their managers all should be involved in the evaluation—in ways more meaningful than filling out little checklists at the end of the day. Group evaluation sessions and discussions not only reinforce what was learned, they also underline the serious purpose of the training and stimulate employee ownership of the results.

Kevin Daley is the president and CEO of Communispond, Inc., a comprehensive communications and skills training resource that partners with its clients to help them reach their strategic goals. Headquartered in New York, the firm is the world's largest training company in business communications skills. Mr. Daley is the author of Socratic Selling, *which reflects his intent to transform the sales process from verbal maneuvering to communicating for mutual rewards. He also is an international speaker and is the current president of the Instructional Systems Association.*

WIDENING THE FAST TRACK: FIVE WAYS TO MOVE FROM EXCLUSIONARY TO INCLUSIONARY TRAINING

Mindy L. Zasloff

Abstract: Little note has generally been taken of a form of discrimination in organizational training policies. Often organizations focus mainly on their high-potential employees—the "stars"—and miss the benefits of broadening training to include all employees.

The article gives five steps necessary to an inclusionary, instead of exclusionary, training strategy for widening the "fast track" to a "mass transit lane": survey the landscape (broaden the scope), pave the way (do a cultural assessment), give directions (help employees help others), keep on the path (maintain the new pattern), and provide roadside assistance (develop measurement and reward systems). A chart outlines the necessary cultural shifts in order to create an organization full of high-potential employees.

Training that includes the majority of employees will help everyone prepare for a challenging future.

Given all the emphasis placed on diversity training these days, it's remarkable how little note is generally taken of a deep-seated form of segregation in organizational training policies themselves. But the truth is that by giving the main emphasis of training to high-potential employees—"shining stars" and "fast trackers"—many organizations turn the majority of their employees into second-class citizens.

Discrimination in training undermines several core values of organizational effectiveness. Teamwork takes a backseat to preferential treatment, and the commitment and self-esteem of the "halo-less" majority suffer. Flexibility decreases when the best opportunities go to those most likely to replicate the characteristics of current leaders, rather than to all employees charged with facing the challenge of an ever-changing future in which employability is key.

Truly inclusionary training is built on a foundation that rewards team development and shares information that nourishes the growth of relevant skills. It emphasizes concepts of personal mastery (Senge, 1990), in which special levels of proficiency are rewarded and recognized.

Personal mastery cannot be achieved unless training processes are created that map learning opportunities against competencies needed in the future. This mapping process helps ensure that employees will learn the necessary skills to thrive in their roles and to remain employable. To guarantee that these skills get learned and used, members of the workforce, including managers, must be trained in the coaching and mentoring practices that bring out the star qualities in all employees.

FIVE STEPS TO INCLUSIONARY TRAINING

Inclusionary training involves five steps for encouraging equal participation, by widening the fast track into a mass transit lane that allows as many employees as possible to travel on it.

1. Survey the Landscape

Many companies write a vision, articulate their mission and goals, and possibly identify their core competencies. But they stop short of the real challenge, which is to link these competencies to organizational learning and skill development. Instead, everyone in your organization can be encouraged to act as a savvy surveyor.

Spread the Mission

Spread the mission, vision, goals, and core competencies to everyone through word and deed. Ask employees to identify how they can personally contribute to the goals of the company, and reward them for putting those ideas into action.

Dialogue Sessions

Host dialogue sessions between department heads and employees for the purpose of identifying the skills that the organization will need in the future. A competency is not a single skill or technology, but an integrated group of processes providing benefit to customers (Hamel & Prahalad, 1994). It is necessary for everyone to share perspectives to determine what is needed to keep those customers in a perpetual state of delight.

Use these sessions to personalize corporate goals, so that employees understand their own accountability for acquiring the skills that will enable them to make a valuable contribution. During these sessions, have department heads list the skills that they see being needed in the future and ask employees to focus on how they can work together to develop these skills and others that the group may identify.

Next, have employee subteams meet to compare notes on the managerial and technical skills, as well as personality traits, that the organization will need to support the employee competencies of the future. These recommendations are like the traffic signals on the mass transit track: management must heed them carefully to avoid crashing.

Identify Learning Opportunities

Next, identify learning opportunities available to develop these skills. Learning opportunities include special employee teams and volunteer groups, existing formal training, informal training, and developmental assignments that encourage utilization and development of each specific skill.

Publish Skills

It is important to communicate and publish the skills needed for the future, along with behavioral examples and some suggestions for methods to acquire these skills.

2. Pave the Way

Recognize and act on the cultural and business changes that will need to take place to support the new competencies. Do a cultural assessment to identify an action plan for creating an environment that enables employees to be involved in inclusionary training. Examples of cultural changes that may need to take place in your organization are outlined in Chart 1.

3. Give Directions

Help employees and managers gain the coaching and mentoring skills needed to guide others toward achieving their goals. Typically, training is done by the human resources staff or "training experts." Instead, employees from each department can work together as training teams to train others. Mentoring skills such as active listening, advising and influencing others, giving feedback, networking, presentation skills, and organizational "truth-telling" need to be taught and nourished.

4. Keep on the Path

Despite careful planning, organizations may slip back into the old, comfortable, exclusionary training patterns. To make sure that the paving on the wider track remains in good repair, emphasize on-the-job learning opportunities that build skills. Most organizations, for example, have job posting systems, but few post opportunities for developmental assignments or explain how the posted job will lead toward acquiring a valuable skill.

5. Provide Roadside Assistance

Develop measurement and reward systems that encourage the use of inclusive training methods. Gear performance evaluations to recognize the new, useful skills employees obtain. Rewards and recognition need to benefit those who share their knowledge, not those who hoard it. It is important to emphasize that encouraging everyone's high performance is truly at the core of competence.

CONCLUSION

Organizations need to use inclusionary training to empower all employees to become a part of the team. Employees who have opportunities to learn and are encouraged to do so will become more accountable for their own skill development. Training that includes the majority minimizes the effects of downsizing and prepares everyone for a challenging and rewarding future.

References

Hamel, G., & Prahalad, C.K. (1994). *Competing for the future.* Boston, MA: Harvard Business School Press.

Senge, P. (1990). *The fifth discipline.* New York: Doubleday.

Mindy L. Zasloff is an organizational change consultant with over twenty years of experience specializing in communication skills, employability, coaching and mentoring, supervisory development, and self-directed work teams. Prior to becoming a consultant, she managed the training and administration functions of Fortune 500 auto and computer companies and affirmative action for a large utility. She regularly presents innovative topics, ranging from "Dealing with Difficult People" to "Making Teams Work," at conferences and universities.

CHART 1. SUBSTANTIAL SHIFTS TO CREATE AN ORGANIZATION FULL OF HIGH-POTENTIAL EMPLOYEES

SUBJECT	FROM	TO
Training Focus	Train the fast trackers/ high-potential employees. Training is an event.	Train everyone to work in high-potential teams. Training is an integrated process connected to acquiring competencies.
Training Approach	Most learning takes place in a classroom away from the job.	Learning is largely experiential with an emphasis on a variety of methods including develop-mental assignments.
Training Assessment	Training is planned by human resources. A select few make decisions about course content and structure.	Training is planned by everyone at all levels; HR organizes and supports the process. Employees routinely participate in design of learning opportunities.
Leadership	Individuals are empowered. The goal is swift action of a select few.	Teams are empowered. The goal is action combined with patience.
Communication	Skills needed in the future are left to guesswork. Employees don't understand how to avail themselves of learning opportunities.	There is active communication about projects and skills needed in the future. Employees are aware of devel-opmental opportunities and how to "sign up" to learn.
Change	A few select superstars drive change.	Everyone drives change; change agents are trained and encouraged.
Processes	Change in processes via reengineering and restructuring are driven from the top of the organization and left to the high-potential employees.	Employee teams drive change with coaching from employees with change-management skills.

SUBJECT	FROM	TO
Diversity	High-potential employees are like those at the top. Leaders are younger, more "ambitious" employees. Emphasis is on the "right" education (e.g., an Ivy League school).	High-potential employees offer different perspectives from those at the top of the organization. Leaders are a combination of junior and senior employees. Life education as well as scholastic education is emphasized.
Rewards	Individual incentives and recognition exist for fast trackers.	There are rewards and incentives for everyone who builds needed skills.
Culture	The emphasis is on selecting and separating out high-potential employees. An individual commitment to the organization is fostered.	Building a high-performance culture that uses all of its human resources is emphasized. A shared commitment to the organization is encouraged.
Information Technology	Systems focus on succession planning. Information is hoarded for a few select fast trackers. Systems do not support training processes.	Systems reinforce and enable learning for all employees. Shared information helps support skill growth. On-line systems routinely communicate upcoming learning opportunities and provide on-line training and support.

LIABILITY AND THE HRD PRACTITIONER

John Sample

Abstract: Organizations should be prepared for civil and criminal litigation relating to a variety of areas in human resource development. The article discusses areas of potential liability for HRD professionals: negligent training and OSHA; EEO and training; adventure and experiential training programs; and corporate due diligence for criminal activity.

General concepts and practices as they apply to HRD programs in business, government, and associations are discussed; suggestions on how organizations can meet governmental and legal requirements and avoid litigation are offered. Particular attention is paid to a case involving an adventure-based program, including areas of potential liability that organizations offering such programs may face.

INTRODUCTION

The passage of the Civil Rights Act of 1964 drastically changed the process of human resource management (HRM). During these past three decades, human resource development (HRD) professionals and their managers have been seemingly exempt from the long arm of the law and judgments in civil and criminal courts.

Unfortunately, that trend is reversing, and organizations should expect litigation well into the next century. HRD professionals must add a new set of skills to their list of competencies. This article will summarize areas of potential liability for the HRD profession. The following topics will be reviewed:

- negligent training and OSHA
- Equal Employment Opportunity (EEO) and training
- adventure and experiential training
- corporate due diligence for criminal activity

Tables 1 and 2 provide a partial summary of who may recover damages and who may be liable for damages (Sample, 1993).

In the previous era, the *primary reason* for providing training was to increase the probability of correct and consistent performance on the job. Managers of HRD units in business and government are now becoming concerned because of a *second reason* for training: to prevent or reduce an organization's legal liability. In this context, training becomes a defense against the charge of failing to adequately train employees and their supervisors and managers. *If employers more consistently and effectively attended to the primary reason, the need for the secondary reason would be significantly diminished* (Sample, 1995, 1996).

NEGLIGENT TRAINING AND OSHA

Negligence is generally defined as "unintentional conduct that falls below the standard of care that is necessary to protect others against exposure to an unreasonable risk of foreseeable injury" (Blackburn & Sage, 1991, p. 3). The elements of negligence include a legal duty, a breach of the duty, proximate cause, and injuries resulting in damages.

Table 1. Who May Recover Damages

EEOC/ADA Violations	Recovering Damages
• **EEOC/ADA Violations** Privacy and freedom of religion issues (nontraditional and "new age" training) Discrimination in selection of trainees for advanced and specialized training Training that results in a disparate effect on a federally protected class of employees Testing that unfairly discriminates against employees who are non-English speaking or culturally diverse Failure to provide assistive devices or to reasonably accommodate trainees with disabilities • **Injuries to Trainees** Training facility Unsafe simulation/laboratory equipment Unsafe workplace (OJT) • **OSHA Regulatory Requirements** General duty to train to standard Warning of workplace hazards & toxins	• **Recovering Damages** State Government: Workplace health hazards Safety violations Criminal negligence Federal Government: OSHA violations Industry regulations (Nuclear Regulatory Commission, etc.) Environmental Resources Act • **Loss of Benefits** Anti Drug Abuse Act of 1988 Workers' Compensation Third Parties • **Personal Injuries** Training facility Workplace Off-site location • **Property Damages** Real or personal property in the vicinity

Used with permission from Sample, J. (1993). *INFO-LINE Legal Liability & HRD: Implications for Trainers.* Alexandria, VA: American Society for Training & Development.

Table 2. Who May Be Liable

Trainers

- Negligent design of program, delivery of program, vendor selection, trainer selection, and/or facility supervision

Owner/Employer

- Negligent program design, supervision of training and facility, instructor selection, implementation of mandated training, and/or vendor selection
- Course content that is discriminatory
- Vicarious liability
- Invasion of privacy

The Employer

- Negligent program design, selection of instructors/vendors, supervision of training activities
- Failure to implement training mandated by statute
- Discriminatory course content
- Discriminatory selection of trainees
- Vicarious liability - intentional acts of supervisors or trainers
- Invasion of privacy

Outside Contractors/Vendors

- Negligent program design, supervision of training facility
- Misrepresentation of a safety record, credentials, experience, or other requirements, such as bond or insurance
- Contractual agreement - failure to meet specifications or breach of an indemnification agreement

Reproduced with permission from Sample, J. (1993). *INFO-LINE Legal Liability & HRD: Implications for Trainers.* Alexandria, VA: American Society for Training & Development.

An example of negligent training involves a medical center and its duty to train nurses in their expected performance if an emergency, such as a fire, should occur. In *Stacy v. Truman Medical Center* (1992), the medical center had a policy on fire safety and evacuation procedures; however, the nurses in this instance were not trained on the policy. A breach of duty occurred in not removing a patient from a room that was on fire. The proximate causal link between the death of the patient and the duty to train the nurses was adequate to sustain a judgment against the medical center.

A related area of responsibility for employers concerns compliance with OSHA, the Occupational Safety and Health Act (1970). OSHA has promulgated a general duty requirement of an employer

> to furnish to each of his employees employment and a place of employment which are free from recognized hazards that are causing or are likely to cause death or serious physical harm to his employees.... (OSHA, 1970)

The general duty clause "includes training of employees as to the dangers and supervision of the work site *(General Dynamics v. OSHARC, 1977).* This requirement speaks clearly to the special case for training supervisors, for they must always be regarded as the first-line trainers for their employer. Sage (1990, p. 10) sums it up best when he recommends that "If there is a failure to exercise reasonable care in performing this duty, either in the commission or omission of an instructional act or training activity, and that failure results in an injured trainee, the trainer or...[supervisor] is assumed liable."

Training and Job Performance

The following suggestions will assist employers and trainers in linking training directly to job performance:

- Review the organization's mission, strategic plan, corporate values, principles of service, operational goals and objectives that are related to training, and train for impact (Robinson & Robinson, 1991).

- For training requirements, complete a job-task analysis and performance criteria for the knowledge, skill, and attitudes needed at the micro level. Review macro-level goals and objectives for functional areas (customer service, quality improvement, manufacturing, sales, new product design, etc.) to determine job-related training requirements.

- If necessary, use systems and process documentation, survey questionnaires, interviews, or observations to document training requirements at the macro level. This is especially important for moderate- to long-range change requirements (i.e., corporate restructuring, downsizing, etc.).

- Use a logically structured analysis, design, development, implementation, and evaluation approach. Link instructional methods and media to job-related requirements at both micro (Dick & Carey, 1996) and macro (Rothwell & Kazanas, 1993) levels within the organization. Consider the importance of learning styles in the development of regulatory training (Eshelman & Woodacre, 1996).

EQUAL EMPLOYMENT OPPORTUNITY (EEO) AND TRAINING

Selection Procedures

Managers throughout a business must understand that selecting an employee for training, development, or education falls within Equal Employment Opportunity Commission (EEOC) guidelines. Consider for a moment the following EEOC mandate from the Code of Federal Regulations (CFR):

> These guidelines apply to tests and other selection procedures which are used as a basis for any employment decision. Employment decisions include...promotion, demotion, membership (for example in a labor organization), referral, retention. Other selection decisions, such as selection for training or transfer, may also be considered employment decisions if they lead to any of the decisions listed above. (Underlined for emphasis. 29 CFR 1607.2B)

Significant employment decisions must be job-related! Deciding who will or will not attend training may be an "employment decision," and such decisions must conform to EEOC requirements. If training and development are a prerequisite for promotion to higher-level positions, then such decisions are probably "employment decisions," and procedures for selecting trainees should conform to EEOC requirements. Adverse impact, also known as differential treatment, could be the result of poorly designed and managed procedures for selecting trainees (Cascio, 1991).

Good and honorable intent is not the issue in this context; impact is the bottom line. Well-intentioned attempts to meet EEOC guidelines are incidental to the adverse impact that occurs because of poor analysis and design of selection procedures for determining who will attend training.

Training as a Selection Component

A second guideline impacting the training arena has to do with validating selection procedures when training is a significant component of the selection process. For example, performance in training may be used as a criterion (or standard) by which future performance on the job is predicted. Again, EEOC guidelines are useful in guiding managerial decisions:

> Where performance in training is used as a criterion, success in training should be properly measured and the relevance of the training should be shown either through a comparison of the content of the training program with the critical or important work behavior(s) of the job(s), or through a demonstration of the relationship between measures of performance in training and measures of job performance. (Underlined for emphasis. 29 CFR 1607.14B(3))

According to EEOC requirements, measures of success in a training program include instructor evaluations, performance samples, or tests (but note that paper and pencil tests will be closely reviewed for job relevance). Bartlett (1978, p. 181) states that "unless training could be demonstrated empirically to make a difference in job performance, training requirements if showing adverse impact can be ruled discriminatory. Thus, training measures would be required to have demonstrated relationship to later performance before they could be used for any employment decisions."

ADA Implications

The Americans with Disabilities Act (ADA) of 1990 is another example of federal legislation that impacts human resource development. The following implications are suggested (Sample, 1995):

- Determine the "essential functions" for HRD positions and use them to recruit, select, train, and supervise training and development personnel. Although affirmative action to recruit and hire is not a requirement of ADA, role modeling by hiring disabled trainers demonstrates leadership.

- Accommodate those with disabilities in their training and development requirements. Expect employees to request reasonable accommodations when attending organization-sponsored HRD programs. Large-print type for the visually impaired and listening devices for the hearing impaired are examples.

- Teach supervisors how to work with employees returning to work with a disability. Supervisors may fear managing the disabled employee, carrying out performance appraisals, and making work assignments.

- Train company recruiters and supervisors in what types of interview questions are legal. From an attitudinal perspective, interviewers will be expected to feel comfortable in interviewing the disabled job applicant.

ADVENTURE AND EXPERIENTIAL TRAINING

Certain constitutional issues, such as the rights to privacy and religion, and issues about personal safety have a possible impact on the design and delivery of adventure-based and experiential types of programs (Vogel, 1991). Included in this category is classroom instruction of an experiential nature, such as role plays; ice breakers (e.g., improvisational theater); small-group strategies that promote anger, stress, or conflict; and adventure-based experiential programs. Adventure programs typically involve wilderness treks, off-shore jaunts, or other forms of individual or group survival experiences. These experiences are designed to instill self-confidence and promote team building.

Three civil court cases involving adventure and experiential approaches have been reported. In *Hiatt v. Walker Chevrolet Company* (1987), the plaintiff alleged wrongful discharge for refusing to participate in an experiential training program. Hiatt, the plaintiff, believed that the program countermanded his religious views and he refused to fire sales personnel who would not adopt the tenets of the company's program as delivered by a vendor. Although the state court summarily ruled in favor of the auto dealership, the plaintiff has appealed the lower court ruling

The *Dong Shik Kim, et al., v. The Dekalb Farmer's Market, Inc.* (1988) case was settled out of court, thereby precluding a determination on the facts by a state civil court. In this instance, managers who participated in an outdoor adventure program were terminated when they refused to require lower-level managers also to participate. The terminated managers alleged wrongful termination and constitutional infringement of their rights of privacy and religion.

The third case involved a contract trainer who, while working for a large telecommunications company, became a codefendant in a civil negligence case (Sample & Hylton, 1996). During a trust-building and planning exercise in which participants were balancing on a swinging log, a 59-year-old female employee fell from the log and broke her leg. The company-sponsored program was mandatory; however, the contract trainer testified that any participant not comfortable with a particular exercise could "challenge out" of direct participation.

The plaintiff alleged negligence on the part of the contract trainer and her employer, the telecommunications company. During the civil trial, the contract trainer was on the witness stand for over eight hours. He convinced the jury that he had followed the requirements of safe implementation for the swinging log exercise. His ability to educate the judge and jury on his credentials and experience and on the purpose of each exercise, coupled with his extensive record keeping, resulted in no finding of negligence on the part of the contract trainer.

The telecommunications company, however, was not so fortunate. A civil judgment in excess of $800,000 was found against the company. Two issues seemed to be in the minds of the jury members as they deliberated this case: the nature of injury sustained by an older woman and the fact that attendance was mandatory. (The judgment was later ruled excessive and reduced.)

Potential Liability

These cases suggest several potential areas of liability:

- Personnel injuries could occur, leaving the corporation and its insurance company liable for damages due to negligence and for workers' compensation claims.

- Stress-related illness may result in workers' compensation claims or civil suits for "emotional distress" or "intentional infliction of distress."

- Constitutional rights to privacy and religious freedom may be infringed on when participants are forced to discuss personal values and religious convictions. Pressure to adopt values inconsistent with individuals' personal values and religious convictions may place an organization legally at risk.

- Termination of employment for failure to participate in organizationally mandated programs could result in wrongful termination suits.

- Federally protected rights could be abridged if participants are not selected because of a handicap or for reasons based on race, nationality, sex, age, etc.

The following suggestions will help prevent or minimize potential litigation (Sample, 1994):

- Make participation voluntary in extensive experiential (overnight wilderness adventure) training. Require a written consent that discloses the contents of the program. Any other type of consent may not be interpreted as "informed" and is therefore unenforceable.

- Provide nonpunishing alternatives for employees who do not wish to participate in experiential activities that may intrude on constitutionally guaranteed rights, such as privacy, religion, or handicap. Design alternative developmental approaches that result in the same learning and performance outcomes.

- Never force an unwilling employee to continue an experiential activity or exercise, and make every effort to avoid embarrassing an employee, both during training and back on the job. This caution includes general classroom facilitation as well as extended residential or other forms of extensive experiential training.

- Do not punish those who do not volunteer for such programs when their performance appraisals are due or when promotions are being considered.

- Choose your private vendors/contractors carefully. Check their references, program content, and if possible observe one of their programs in progress for safety and emergency precautions. State in writing how you expect the vendor to handle instructional content and conflict. Based on job-related data, expect the vendor to modify the design and development of media and the content of the curriculum to meet the work-related requirements of the organization. Consider requiring performance bonds for vendors and contractors.

- Educate senior management and corporate legal counsel on the potential legal pitfalls of experiential approaches that are not linked to micro or macro job requirements.

CORPORATE DUE DILIGENCE FOR CRIMINAL ACTIVITY

White-collar crimes, such as tax evasion, deception, embezzlement, and other forms of business fraud, have forced the federal government to take an active role in preventing and curtailing such business practices (Albrecht, Wernz, & Williams, 1995). Powerful criminal sanctions now exist for a business convicted of a felony or serious misdemeanor under the Federal Sentencing Guidelines (Title 28, ss 994 United States Code). These sanctions would be levied against an individual business's corporate officers, board members, and other employees for violations of the law, depending on the culpability of the business as measured on a culpability index (Gruner, 1993).

In 1991, chapter eight was added to the Federal Sentencing Guidelines to provide for sentencing of businesses whose employees commit crimes, because the companies are "vicariously liable for offenses committed by their agents," i.e., employees. The guidelines are used by judges for assessing criminal penalities when individuals are convicted of violating federal law. Chapter eight of the Sentencing Guidelines is designed to provide punishment, adequate determent, and incentives for businesses to maintain internal mechanisms for preventing, detecting, and reporting criminal conduct.

Directors of HRD services may be called on to assist in the development of a unique and highly specialized type of program for their employers. Such program development will require collaboration with human resource management, security personnel, corporate attorneys, and senior management.

Example of Criminal Activity

If an employee, while acting on behalf of the business as a loan officer in a bank, violates the law by intentionally discriminating against qualified applicants, the business is automatically linked as a co-defendant to criminal penalities if charges are brought and a conviction obtained. The position that the employee was acting on his own will not by itself absolve the bank from being sanctioned under chapter eight of the Federal Sentencing Guidelines.

Criminal Fines

Depending on the culpability, nature, number, and history of prior convictions, criminal fines range from court-ordered community service and simple restitution to fines in the range of $70 million, including the possibility of prison terms. A sliding scale assists the federal court judge in assessing monetary penalities. The Sentencing Guidelines also allow for higher fines than the published amounts. If the convicted party is a threat to the environment or the economic market, an upward departure from the published penalties is warranted and possible under the Guidelines.

Elements of a "Program" Under the Sentencing Guidelines

The Sentencing Guidelines describe in detail how culpability will be determined: in part by the measures to prevent and detect criminal conduct that the organization took prior to the offense; the level and extent of involvement in or tolerance of the offense by certain personnel; and the organization's actions after an offense has been committed (Federal Sentencing Guidelines).

The requirements for an organizational program to prevent criminal activity, according to the Sentencing Guidelines, are stated in Table 3.

Table 3. Requirements for Training Under the Federal Sentencing Guidelines

An "effective program to prevent and detect violations of law" means a program that has been reasonably designed, implemented, and enforced so that it generally will be effective in preventing and detecting criminal conduct. Failure to prevent or detect the instant offense, by itself, does not mean that the program was not effective. The hallmark of an effective program to prevent and detect violations of the law is that the organization exercised due diligence in seeking to prevent and detect criminal conduct by its employees and other agents. Due diligence requires at a minimum that the organization must have taken the following types of steps...

(4) The organization must have taken steps to communicate effectively its standards and procedures to all employees and other agents, e.g., **by requiring participation in training programs or by disseminating publications** that explain in a practical manner what is required.

Source: Federal Sentencing Guidelines Manual, Chapter Eight, Sentencing of Organizations, Sec. 8A1.2 (p. 341).

In addition to the requirement of training and publication, the sentencing guidelines require the development of compliance standards and procedures and the assignment of responsibility to high-level corporate employees; they must provide monitoring and auditing to achieve compliance through consistent internal enforcement, including appropriate discipline for those responsible for infractions and those who fail to detect an offense. Finally, if an offense is discovered, the business must take reasonable steps to respond appropriately and to prevent future similar offenses.

DEVELOPING A CORPORATE COMPLIANCE PROGRAM

The advantages of developing a corporate compliance program for due diligence include the prevention of criminal activity by agents and employees of the business, lowered penalties and reduced legal costs, positive public relations, and improved morale. Disadvantages to such a program may include the existence of an auditable paper trail that may force a mandatory response if criminal activity surfaces, and the adverse publicity that follows such a revelation (Davis & McFarland, 1996).

The following suggestions are designed to guide a business in developing a compliance program:

- Determine the business's level of risk and potential legal problems. Interviews and focus groups of senior management and key personnel are a good starting point. Consider industry standards and regulatory requirements of state and federal agencies. Require that corporate legal counsel provide a legal assessment based on statutory requirements and case law.

- Based on an assessment, prioritize issues according to risk potential. For some types of businesses, safety issues could be a pressing issue, especially if compliance with the Occupational Safety and Health Act is mandated. For other businesses, compliance with environmental regulations, sexual harassment, or mergers and acquisitions could be the highest priority.

- Having prioritized issues, select the most expedient medium for communicating clearly the position and expectation of the business relative to criminal activity. For some businesses, publication of policies and procedures in employee handbooks and other distributed documentation will be sufficient. The use of classroom instruction may be necessary in some settings. If training is required, utilize a standard instructional systems approach (Dick & Carey, 1996). Especially important will be documentation of who attended each training program and the extent to which the instruction was evaluated for effectiveness (Sample, 1995).

- Monitor the compliance program for compliance, just as business practices are monitored for compliance. The potential for liability will change with the passage of time, and the program will have to be adapted to comply with new laws, regulations, and evolving case law.

- Document all phases of the program: the development of policy statements and training programs, investigations, and follow-up disciplinary reports for violation of compliance requirements. If compliance documentation becomes a financial and practical burden—assuming no laws or regulations to the contrary—consider a documentation retention program that allows for the destruction of records after a period of time.

CONCLUSION

Managers of HRD programs can expect more intrusion by the law and courts as time passes. Balancing employee rights with the mission of the organization is a responsibility of senior management and the organization's human resource management and training professionals. The safest strategy is always to link training and development to job tasks and the corporation's vision, mission, and strategic and quality initiatives.

There is a caveat to the concern about liability as presented in this article. One way to interpret the potential for liability is to adopt a conservative posture that precludes risk taking or creative individual and team performance. However, it is important to remember that "meeting the vision and mission of a dynamic business enterprise requires a certain amount of risk taking. Employees must not be frightened into non-performance of their jobs because of the potential for litigation" (Sample, 1995, p. 205).

Note to Readers: This article is designed to provide descriptive and illustrative material on general concepts and practices as they may apply to HRD programs in business, government, and associations. While the information in this article is accurate and timely, it does not constitute legal advice. *Readers are advised to consult competent legal counsel for specific advice on situations involving their organizations.*

References

Albrecht, W.S., Wernz, G.W., & Williams, T.L. (1995). *Fraud: Bringing light to the dark side of business.* Burr Ridge, IL: Irwin.

Bartlett, C.J. (1978). Equal employment issues in training. *Human Factors,* 20(2), 179-188.

Blackburn, J.D., & Sage, J.E. (1991). Where is training and the law heading during the 1990's. *1991 Technical and Skill Conference.* American Society for Training and Development, Washington, D.C.

Cascio, W.F. (1991). *Applied psychology in personnel management.* Reston, VA: Reston Publishers.

Davis, G., & McFarland, J. (1996, January). Corporate compliance programs: Protecting the business from the rogue employee. *The Florida Bar Journal,* pp. 34-37.

Dick, W., & Carey, L. (1996). *The systematic design of instruction.* Glenview, IL: Scott Foresman.

In re Dong Shik Kim, et al., v. The Dekalb Farmers Market, Inc. Civil Action No. 1-88CV2767HTW (D. Northern District of Georgia, filed December 7, 1988).

In re Equal Employment Opportunity Commission. (1995). *Guidelines on Employee Selection Procedures,* 29 CFR 1607.

Eshelman, C.K., & Woodacre, C. (1996). Reviving your regulatory training. *Technical and Skills Training,* 7(3), 18-21.

Federal (U.S.) Sentencing Commission Sentencing Guidelines, Chapter Eight, Sentencing of Organizations, 56 Fed. Reg. 22,786 (1991).

In re General Dynamics v. OSHARC, 599 F 2d 453 (1977).

Gruner, R.S. (1993). Beyond fines: Innovative corporate sentences under federal sentencing guidelines. *Washington University Law Quarterly,* 71, pt 1. 1, 261-328.

In re Hiatt v. Walker Chevrolet Company, 822 P. 2d. 1235 (1987).

In re Occupational Safety and Health Act, 29 U.S.C.A. 654 (1970).

Robinson, D.G., & Robinson, J.C. (1991). *Training for impact.* San Francisco, CA: Jossey-Bass.

Rothwell, W., & Kazanas, H.C. (1993). *Human resource development: A strategic approach.* Amherst, MA: HRD Press.

Sage, J.E. (1990, December). Safe attitudes minimize trainer liability. *Technical and Skills Training,* pp. 9-13.

Sample, J.A. (1993). *INFO-LINE legal liability & HRD: Implications for trainers.* Alexandria, VA: American Society for Training and Development.

Sample, J.A. (1994). How experiential training can land you in court. *Training Today,* pp. 4-9.

Sample, J.A. (1995). Liability and the technical trainer: An overview of issues and prevention strategies. In L. Kelly (Ed.), *The ASTD technical and skills training handbook* (pp. 178-210). Alexandria, VA: American Society for Training and Development.

Sample, J.A. (1996). Liability and the technical trainer: Recent cases and comments. In L. Kelly (Ed.), *Supplement 1 to the ASTD technical and skills training handbook* (pp. 131-147). New York: McGraw Hill.

Sample, J.A., & Hylton, R. (1996, May). Falling off a log and landing in court. *Training,* pp. 66-69.

In re Stacy v. Truman Medical Center (Unpublished, Supreme Court of Missouri, July 21, 1992).

Vogel, J. (1991). Manufacturing solidarity: Adventure training for managers. *Hofstra Law Review, 19,* 657–724.

John Sample, Ph.D., *is principal in the human resource development and consulting firm of Sample & Associates. His firm specializes in the assessment, development, and evaluation of human resources. He also provides case analysis and preparation assistance and testimony for attorneys in legal matters relating to negligent training and supervision. Dr. Sample is a past scholarly reviewer for the* Human Resource Development Quarterly, *and he currently reviews submissions for the* International Journal of Training and Development.

STRATEGIC CONVICTION

David Nicoll

Abstract: Conviction is an essential quality of key executives, organizational decision makers, and organizational teams. It provides the basis for direction and alignment in implementing organizational strategy. Most people agree that conviction is a feeling, but there are two distinct ways of describing it. There also appear to be five basic routines that people use to gain conviction. This article describes these very different routines and presents a means by which executive teams can identify their members' routines and take steps to generate the conviction necessary for alignment of strategic goals.

INTRODUCTION

Conviction is an essential quality in executives who are responsible for implementing their organizations' business strategies. Conviction is a bit like the wings of an eagle; the bird needs them to be operative when it launches itself into the air for a kill. Midair is a bad place to be if one does not have the necessary attributes. Key executives must believe that what they are driving their organizations to do is on target. They are betting their own careers and the success of their organizations on their convictions.

How do people determine what is "true?" What kinds of experience convince us that we are right? What does being absolutely convinced of something feel like? These are important questions for the strategist (Eisner, 1985).

Most people use a combination of available information and "gut feelings" when they are making decisions. Unfortunately, chief executive officers of organizations also often do this but, in their case, there may be a lot more at stake. Most corporate executives have not studied the issue of conviction. They rely on a very common assumption—which is always wrong—that when a member of the executive team verbally supports a strategy, he or she is convinced that the strategy is the best approach. This assumption is a major factor in the failure of most corporations to implement their strategies.

Despite this pattern, conviction is a very important part of the strategy process. It is part of what allows good leaders to become and stay focused. It is the foundation of the courage they display in making difficult competitive decisions. It is the base on which they form the organizational alignments necessary to make their decisions work. Conviction is the glue that holds executive teams together under difficult circumstances. It implicitly guides their day-to-day actions. Have conviction and you have a compass. Lose it, and you lose your way. It is that simple.

HOW PEOPLE EXPERIENCE CONVICTION

Most people experience conviction in a similar way: they feel it. Individuals may use different routines to convince themselves of something, but the feeling they get from their efforts is the same. Some people report feeling "good." Others say they feel "solid." Still others say they are "comfortable." However it is described, conviction is grounded in a positive feeling. When you are convinced of something, your "gut" knows that you are right.

It also is relevant to point out that people describe at least two forms of conviction (Belenky, Clinchy, Goldberger, & Tarule, 1986). One group describes conviction as "understanding"; the other group calls it "knowledge."

Understanding

Those people who equate conviction with understanding are saying that in order to become convinced of something, they have to develop a familiarity with it. They have to get close to it and intimate with it. In some instances, they suggest that they have to become part of it or have it become part of them. For these people, conviction is synonymous with closeness and familiarity.

Knowledge

Other people equate conviction with knowledge. They say that they have to generate a sense of mastery over the subject at hand in order to become convinced. They have to separate themselves from the issue—get some distance from it—in order to know that they are right. For them, conviction is a matter of knowing, and knowledge involves the ability to distance themselves in order to gain perspective.

FIVE ROUTINES THAT CREATE CONVICTION

Little is known about how people become convinced of something. Some published research and a little anecdotal wisdom describe the steps and procedures used. What is available suggests that people use at least five different "routines" to produce the internal experience of conviction for themselves (Lazear, 1991). These are as follows (Belenky et al., 1986):

- Authoritative validation
- Experiential immersion
- Adversarial debate
- Collegial dialogue
- Trail blazing

Authoritative Validation

People who use this routine become convinced when someone whom they respect as an authority agrees with them that something is necessary or correct. These people, to become convinced, need to listen to the voice of a respected other. In a sense, they are "received knowers."

People who use this routine typically believe that truth and reality are external and objective to them. They see truth and reality as concrete and fixed. Knowledge of "what is" exists and is to be discovered. It is not constructed or enacted. People who become convinced of something through authoritative validation do not believe in "situational" ethics; they need to "know" before they act.

Consequently, they must gain knowledge from the "right source" in order to become convinced. They look outward for the truth. The validating process typically happens at the end of some extensive preparatory work. At this point, conviction comes as a punctuation mark—a period provided by an external expert who reinforces what the person already has come to believe.

Experiential Immersion

People who use this routine become convinced through direct experience. They need to get their hands dirty, to become deeply and personally involved in the issue. They learn by doing; they become convinced by immersion. For them, conviction comes only from personal experience.

This routine, in contrast to the previous one, is an internal, intrapsychic experience. No one else is allowed into the experience. External sources are discounted and invalidated. To become convinced of something, these people have to prove it to themselves. They must have inner knowing. If you ask such people how they know something, they say, "I don't know how, I just know."

Experiential knowers typically believe that truth and reality are neither absolute nor external. For them, truth is a matter of personal opinion; it is subjective. Their opinions are related to nothing in particular; they are personal issues. Truth is absolute only for the individual. Such people do not believe that they have to accept what others—even "experts"—say. Because they see their convictions as only their opinions, they usually are silent about a particular issue. The more convinced they are that they are right, the more silent they become.

Adversarial Debate

This routine is simultaneously an internal and an external process. Although the adversarial debate often looks real and serious, the fact is that the person who becomes convinced through adversarial debate is just using the external debate as a mechanism to become convinced that he or she is right in adopting the position that he or she is debating. The literature calls this routine the "doubting game" (Elbow, 1973). As a routine, it is grounded in rational rules and procedures. Regardless of the emotion displayed, distance is key and objectivity is called for. For the individual who uses this routine, the point is to subtract the emotion from the issue at hand and to step back and rigorously criticize the position that is about to be adopted. The assumption is that if the position about to be adopted can stand up to vigorous criticism, it will suffice in practice.

Adversarial debate requires that one have the ability to use oneself as an instrument of knowledge. For some, winning the debate is the punctuation mark that people who use this process need in order to become convinced. It is as if they are saying to themselves, "If I can persuade others of my point of view, then I must be right."

Other people who use this procedure are doing something quite different. They are using the energy that is created while debating to ignite their internal passions. Quite literally, they are "psyching themselves up."

Still others are using the debate to compare their points of view with other perspectives. It is as if one of the stops that they have to make along their route to personal conviction is to look at the issue from multiple perspectives. Such people often have several debates with different people, or the same debate repeatedly with the same person but using different arguments.

Collegial Dialogue

This routine of collegial dialogue has the same generic dynamics as the "doubting game." As a conviction routine, it is interactive; the participants are fully engaged in the conversation. Like the adversarial types, the people who use this routine are using the dialogue as a means of convincing themselves. The difference is that they are playing the "believing game" to generate conviction.

This routine, in its deep, procedural structure, is vastly different from the "doubting game." The "doubting game" is conflictual, adversarial, and distant. The "believing game" is just the opposite; it is intimate, empathic, and cooperative (Belenky et al., 1986).

In the believing game, discovering the logic behind the others' ideas is the issue. This requires the ability to use oneself as an instrument of understanding. The people in this dialogue function as helpers, not as opponents. The job of the other persons is to help the talkers to uncover their experiences and then to examine them. In this process, one learns through empathy.

People who use this approach believe that authority and conviction rest in and grow from shared experience. "If we are wrong, we are wrong together. If we are right, we will be right together." Thus, the conversations that form the heart of this routine grow from personal connection. Private conversations cement personal connection, and this connection provides the conviction necessary for action.

Trail Blazing

People who use this routine as a mechanism for conviction have one central belief as the centerpiece of their philosophy. Truth and reality are social concepts. Both concepts are constructed and enacted by people in the process of living. Truth and reality are not static, objective, or external. They are created in the doing of something. Truth and reality are things that you and the others with whom you interact look back on. Therefore, conviction does not have as much to do with what they are about to do as it does with what they have just done. In this routine, conviction—although still a "gut feeling"—is more a sense of satisfaction than of rightness.

Although collegial dialogue generates feelings of comfort, trail blazing creates feelings of accomplishment. As a result, trail blazers spend little time looking for or relying on answers of any sort. Experts are of use to them and are used. But, as one trail blazer said, "A good expert is somebody whose answers reflect the complexity I know the situation holds." Trail blazers use experts to stretch their own perspectives regarding possibilities. They do not look to experts for answers.

Trail blazers see actions as steps based on large elements of faith. They take leaps of faith. Implementation steps, large or small, are taken by them in order to see what will happen. They look back, and their conviction results from a survey of the results.

These people continually nurture their conviction by a survey of the work they have in progress. They need conviction, not in regard to what they are about to do, but in regard to the results they have already achieved and the process in which they are already engaged.

PRACTICAL STEPS

People use the five routines to convince themselves of something. The available research says nothing about what teams that need to conduct a common enterprise can do together to generate the common conviction they need.

Regardless, the issue of strategic conviction is important. Conviction is what allows good leaders to become and stay focused and to display courage. Given this, there are several things senior executives—and the teams of which they are a part—can do to be sure that the conviction on which their success rests is present. These things produce conviction in a remarkably clear and reliable way.

1. The senior executives involved in forming and managing a corporation's business strategy can benefit from familiarizing themselves with the five routines and identifying their own. It is relatively easy for an individual to identify the style that he or she uses to gain conviction. This does not take long; it merely involves remembering the last time the individual knew that he or she was right when there was a crucial decision to be made. Such memories almost always reflect one of the routines described in this article.

2. The second step is for the individual to spend thirty minutes discussing the conclusions reached as a result of Step 1 with someone who knows the individual well. This should generate support for or disconfirming evidence in relation to the individual's apparent routine. Honest dialogue about one's past behaviors is an invaluable tool for gaining clarity about one's preferred means of gaining conviction.

3. After each individual has completed Steps 1 and 2, the executive team can discuss the subject. Two hours spent reviewing the five routines and the ones the members have identified as their own should provide significant insights.

   Some of the questions to be answered during these two hours are as follows:

   ■ How do the individual team members convince themselves of something?

   ■ What support, if any, is necessary for each team member?

   ■ If anyone uses trail blazing, does he or she have enough experience to judge the organization's strategic track record?

   Answering these questions helps considerably: at a minimum, it creates tolerance of one another's strategic ambivalence. More importantly, it legitimizes the most cogent of all strategic questions: "Is anyone not absolutely convinced that the strategy we are about to pursue is the right one?"

4. Together, executive team members should work hard to generate understanding and empathy among themselves about the possible differences that exist among them. Serious conflicts break out in relation to the differences in routines. Everyone must be convinced if there is to be alignment of goals. So, if everyone involved

needs to get ready in a different way, everyone should be given—in a formal way—the necessary time to prepare. This kind of tolerance is very important.

5. Finally, the executive team should recognize and emphasize the need for joint conviction. In practical terms, it should provide the necessary time and energy within its strategy-formation process to ascertain whether or not everyone on the team is convinced that the strategy in hand is the one on which to bet the business and the members' careers.

CONCLUSION

Strategic conviction is like a radium atom. It has a "half-life"—a time span during which it is at full strength and a specific point in time when its power deteriorates. Strategic conviction evaporates over time. Circumstances change, the executive loses touch with his or her original feelings, or a competitor does something to change the competitive environment (Light & Butterworth, 1992).

One client, after being told about strategic conviction's half-life, yelled at the author, "You've got to be kidding; you mean I've got to go through this exercise more than once?!" This outburst came just after his company's chief competitor had introduced a remarkable new product line and usurped his company's competitive advantage. The response to him was, "Of course; how could you or your staff remain certain in the face of changes like these? You have no choice but to look at your strategy again, to see if you are still convinced that it is strong enough to carry the company."

Strategic conviction does not stay firm or solid; it ebbs and flows, changing with one's perception of the world. It is remarkably responsive to changes in external conditions.

Because strategic conviction is a "gut" feeling, most people are not aware of changes or shifts in their outlooks. They are aware of their intuitive sense on the day that a strategy is finalized. But months, weeks, or even days later, under the press of day-to-day events, the feeling of confidence and well-being will disappear, leaving only traces of the original confidence.

This is why executive strategy has to be reviewed again and again. Each time it is reviewed, the conviction routines of those responsible for creating the strategy need to be reviewed. Experience shows that this is the only way an executive team can keep its intuitive feelings of conviction abreast of the environmental realities in which the organization's strategy is being implemented.

References

Belenky, M.F., Clinchy, B.M., Goldberger, N.R., & Tarule, J.M. (1986). *Women's way of knowing: The development of self, voice and mind.* New York: Basic Books.

Eisner, E. (Ed.). (1985). *Learning and teaching the ways of knowing.* Chicago: NSSE.

Elbow, P. (1973). *Writing without teachers.* London: Oxford University Press.

Lazear, D. (1991). *Seven ways of knowing: Teaching for multiple intelligences.* Palatine, IL: Skylight Publishing.

Light, P., & Butterworth, G. (1992). *Context and cognition: Ways of learning and knowing.* Hillsdale, NJ: Erlbaum.

Dave Nicoll, Ph.D., is an independent business consultant and the president of Merlin & Nicoll, Inc., in Los Angeles. He specializes in strategy formation and implementation assistance, process improvement (EI, TQM, reengineering) consulting, and organizational learning support. He has served as a Marine Corps officer in Vietnam, as a diplomat with the United Nations, and as the director of strategy formation for Kaiser Permanente in Southern California.

CONTRIBUTORS

B. Kim Barnes
President, Barnes and Conti Associates, Inc.
Managing Partner, The Influence Alliance
940 Dwight Way, Suite 15
Berkeley, CA 94710
(510) 644-0911
fax: (510) 644-2101
e-mail: kimbar@aol.com
www.barnesconti.com

Beverly Byrum-Robinson, Ph.D.
Professor, Department of Communication
Wright State University
Dayton, OH 45435
(513) 873-2710
e-mail: BRobinson@desire.wright.edu

Heather J. Campbell
Outdoor Education Instructor/Counselor
Battle Creek Public Schools Outdoor Education Center
10160 Bedford Road
Dowling, MI 49050
(616) 721-8161

Heidi Ann Campbell
Facilitator/Counselor
Eagle Village Inc.
4507 170th Avenue
Hersey, MI 49639
(616) 832-2234
fax: (616) 832-1729 or
(616) 832-2470

Meredith Cash
Training Specialist
South Dakota Bureau of Personnel
419 S. Fort
Pierre, SD 57501
(605) 773-3148
e-mail: meredithc@bop.state.sd.us

Robert K. Conyne, Ph.D.
Professor of Counseling
Human Services Division, Counseling Program
University of Cincinnati
Teachers College 526g
Cincinnati, OH 45221-0002
(513) 556-3344
fax: (513) 556-2483

Kevin R. Daley
President and CEO
Communispond, Inc.
300 Park Avenue, 22nd Floor
New York, NY 10022
(212) 486-2300
fax: (212) 486-2680

Gilbert Joseph Duran
Information Management Assistant
School of Business
University of the Incarnate Word
4301 Broadway
San Antonio, TX 78209

Cynthia A. Franklin
Consultant
Enterprise Management Ltd.
9812 Falls Road
Potomac, MD 20854
(301) 365-1800
fax: (301) 365-1804
e-mail: caldrichf@aol.com

Roger Gaetani
Director of Training
Sunrise, Inc.
1145 Sunrise Greetings Court
Bloomington, IN 47404
  (812) 336-9900
  fax: (812) 336-8712
  e-mail: rgaetani@interart.com

Erna E. Gomar
University of the Incarnate Word
4301 Broadway
San Antonio, TX 78209
  (210) 829-6034
  e-mail: egomar@the-college.iwctx.
  edu

Robert Hargrove
President
Transformational Learning
39 Harvard Street
Brookline, MA 02146
  (617) 739-3300
  fax: (617) 738-9149

B.J. Hennig
Manufacturing Training Specialist
The Iams Company
7250 Poe Avenue
Dayton, OH 45420
  (513) 264-7348
  fax: (513) 299-4387
  e-mail: BJIAMS@aol.com

Steven B. Hollwarth
Vice President
Service & Administrative Institute
3101 Sawgrass Village
Ponte Vedra Beach, FL 32082
  (904) 273-9840
  fax: (904) 273-9906

Cher Holton, Ph.D., C.S.P.
The Holton Consulting Group, Inc.
4704 Little Falls Drive, Suite 300
Raleigh, NC 27609
  (919) 783-7088
  fax: (919) 781-2218
  e-mail: Dr Cher@aol.com

Robert Inguagiato
132 Sinclair Street S.W.
Port Charlotte, FL 33952
  (941) 766-7019

Bonnie Jameson
1024 Underhills Road
Oakland, CA 94610
  (510) 832-2597
  fax: (510) 832-2597

William Frank Jones, Ph.D.
Foundation Professor
Department of Philosophy and
  Religion
Case 268
Eastern Kentucky University
Richmond, KY 40475-3140
  (606) 622-1400
  fax: (606) 622-1020
  e-mail: PHIJONES@ACS.eku.edu

H.B. Karp, Ph.D.
Personal Growth Systems
4217 Hawksley Drive
Chesapeake, VA 23321
  (757) 483-9327
  fax: same as above
  e-mail: PGSHank@aol.com

Kevin M. Kelleghan
President
The Business Writing, Training and
  Consulting Corporation
504 Fairview Boulevard
Rockford, IL 61107
  (815) 399-4826
  fax: (815) 963-6965

Janet Mills, Ph.D.
Professor of Public Administration
  and Communication
Boise State University
1910 University Drive
Boise, ID 83725
  (208) 385-3778
  fax: (208) 385-4370
  e-mail: jmills@sspafac.IDBUS.edu

David Nicoll, Ph.D.
President
Merlin & Nicoll, Inc.
2013 S. Selby Avenue
Los Angeles, CA 90025
  (310) 474-1577
  fax: (310) 475-7620
  e-mail: dnicoll@merlinnicoll.com

Michael O'Brien, Ed.D.
President
O'Brien Learning Systems
949 Woodcreek Drive
Milford, OH 45150
  (513) 831-8042
  fax: (513) 831-8045

Lynn S. Rapin, Ph.D.
Consulting Psychologist
4022 Clifton Ridge Drive
Cincinnati, OH 45220
  (513) 861-5220
  fax: (513) 861-5220

Gaylord Reagan, Ph.D.
Reagan Consulting
5306 North 105th Plaza, #9
Omaha, NE 68134
  (402) 431-0279
  fax: same as above, call first
  e-mail: 75753.2230@CompuServe.
    com

Irwin M. Rubin, Ph.D.
President
Temenos, Inc., and Temenos
  Foundation
37 Kawananakoa Place
Honolulu, HI 96817
  (808) 528-2433
  fax: (808) 528-2434

Karen L. Rudick, Ph.D.
Assistant Professor
Department of Speech
  Communication
Eastern Kentucky University
Campbell 306
Richmond, KY 40475-3140
  (606) 622-1317/1315

John Sample, Ph.D.
Principal
Sample & Associates
2922 Shamrock South
Tallahassee, FL 32308
  (904) 668-1067
  fax: same as above
  e-mail: sample@gnn.com

Morley Segal, Ph.D.
Professor, Public Administration
School of Public Affairs
The American University
Washington, DC 20016
  (202) 686-1234

Larry Shook
South 4327 Perry
Spokane, WA 99203
  (509) 747-8776

Michael Stanleigh
President
Business Improvement Architects
85 Scarsdale Road, Suite 302
Don Mills, Ontario M3B 2R2
Canada
  (416) 444-4108
  fax: (416) 447-6867

Marianne Stiles, C.P.A.
Comstock Enterprises
222 E. Fair Oaks Place
San Antonio, TX 78209
  (210) 829-5157

Christina A. Vele
384 Treeline Park Boulevard, Apt. 1124
San Antonio, TX 78209
  (210) 828-2876

Judith F. Vogt, Ph.D.
Professor of Organizational Studies
University of the Incarnate Word
4301 Broadway
San Antonio, TX 78230
  (210) 492-1578, (210) 283-5004
  fax: (210) 829-3169
  e-mail: vogt@the-college.iwctx.educ

Mindy L. Zasloff
Organizational Change Consultant
28728 Plainfield Drive
Rancho Palos Verdes, CA 90275-3151
  (310) 544-4250
  fax: (310) 544-0864
  e-mail: mindy4250@aol.com

Contents of the Companion Volume, the 1997 Annual: Volume 2, Consulting

*See Experiential Learning Activities Categories, p. 5, for an explanation of the numbering system.

Inventories, Questionnaires, and Surveys

Presentation and Discussion Resources